# Praise for
# *A Woman's Place*

"Astute and unapologetic, *A Woman's Place* is an ultimately hopeful dispatch from the resistance in the Trump era. Cheung shows us how young feminists have—and will continue to—carry on the fight for justice."

—MAYA DUSENBERY, former editor of Feministing.com and author of *Doing Harm*

"How do young women negotiate the truth that, under a late-capitalist patriarchy, the labels 'victim' and 'oppressor' almost always coexist within the same person? Such is the central meditation of Kylie Cheung's *A Woman's Place,* a clear-eyed chronicle of the feminist movement's fourth wave.

The Gen-Z daughter of Asian-American immigrant parents in California suburbia, Cheung offers sharp analysis of how our overlapping identities inform the experience of this political moment and all it entails: the fight to save Roe v. Wade, post-#MeToo backlash, and the interconnected struggles of marginalized populations. Through it all, she shows that traversing a path forward still matters, despite the jarring back-and-forths between small victories and defeats. In *A Woman's Place,* Cheung reveals herself as one of today's most exciting new voices for a generation of emerging feminist thinkers."

—KELLI MARÍA KORDUCKI, books editor at Forge by Medium and author of *Hard to Do*

"Kylie Cheung is one of the most talented feminist writers of her generation. Cheung educates her readers on the erased histories and nuanced intricacies of today's feminist issues in an approachable way, truly ensuring feminism is for everyone. *A Woman's Place* is a thoughtful memoir of a young feminist exploring the systemic misogyny, racism, xenophobia, and classism surrounding her and taking the reader on a journey toward understanding intersectionality, challenging white supremacy, and fighting for a vision of a feminist future grounded in reproductive justice."

—RENEE BRACEY SHERMAN, reproductive justice activist and founder of We Testify

"Cheung's book captures the journey of a feminist awakening in a particular, and particularly fraught, moment in time. Her clear-eyed writing is both introspective and outward looking. With impassioned, intelligent young thinkers like her leading the next iteration of the feminist movement, we are in capable hands."

—LINDSAY MILLER, news and culture director at PopSugar

"With every new 'wave' of feminism, comes the inherent criticism that some are doing it wrong. Every generation of feminists has faced accusations of being 'too radical, too angry, too sensitive, too loud, too feminine, not feminine enough,' and the old standby of being 'hysterical' about freedoms that so many believe we no longer need to fight for. In this informative, personal account of how feminism shaped her generation, Kylie Cheung shows how this ever-evolving political ideology is as necessary as ever, and that in many ways, the fight has only just begun."

—HEATHER WOOD RUDULPH, managing editor of *Dame* magazine

"Journalist Cheung debuts with a sharp and reflective examination of the state of fourth-wave feminism . . . [She] skillfully communicates the urgency of these issues, and demands respect for her Gen-Z cohorts from an older generation of feminists. This galvanizing call to arms will resonate with young activists."

—*PUBLISHERS WEEKLY*

# A WOMAN'S PLACE

# A WOMAN'S PLACE

## Inside the FIGHT for a Feminist Future

### Kylie Cheung

North Atlantic Books
Berkeley, California

Published by                                  Cover design by Jasmine Hromjak
North Atlantic Books                          Book design by Happenstance Type-O-Rama
Berkeley, California

Printed in the United States of America

*A Woman's Place: Inside the Fight for a Feminist Future* is sponsored and published by the Society for the Study of Native Arts and Sciences (dba North Atlantic Books), an educational nonprofit based in Berkeley, California, that collaborates with partners to develop cross-cultural perspectives, nurture holistic views of art, science, the humanities, and healing, and seed personal and global transformation by publishing work on the relationship of body, spirit, and nature.

North Atlantic Books' publications are available through most bookstores. For further information, visit our website at www.northatlanticbooks.com or call 800-733-3000.

Library of Congress Cataloging-in-Publication Data

Names: Cheung, Kylie, 1998- author.
Title: A woman's place : inside the fight for a feminist future / Kylie
   Cheung.
Description: Berkeley : North Atlantic Books, 2020. | Includes
   bibliographical references and index. | Summary: "A fearless primer to
   the feminism we need now: tactics for advancing reproductive justice,
   promoting intersectionality, and pushing back against misogyny,
   gaslighting, and patriarchal systems of oppression"—Provided by
   publisher.
Identifiers: LCCN 2020003938 (print) | LCCN 2020003939 (ebook) | ISBN
   9781623174842 (trade paperback) | ISBN 9781623174859 (ebook)
Subjects: LCSH: Feminism. | Women's rights. | Sex discrimination. | Sex
   role. | Equality before the law.
Classification: LCC HQ1155 .C445 2020  (print) | LCC HQ1155 (ebook) | DDC
   305.42—dc23
LC record available at https://lccn.loc.gov/2020003938
LC ebook record available at https://lccn.loc.gov/2020003939

1  2  3  4  5  6  7  8  9  KPC  25  24  23  22  21  20

This book includes recycled material and material from well-managed forests. North Atlantic Books is committed to the protection of our environment. We print on recycled paper whenever possible and partner with printers who strive to use environmentally responsible practices.

For the endlessly dedicated, endlessly
courageous abortion providers and
reproductive health-clinic staff across
the country and around the world—
I know how thankless your work is;
I wrote this book to try to begin
to thank you.

# CONTENTS

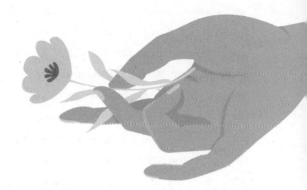

# 1

# Seventh Wave

Often, I've found the most common error in mainstream narratives about feminism is the notion that this fight can somehow be won or lost by one, grand societal event, be that the years-long struggle for universal women's suffrage or the election of Donald Trump, the federal legalization of abortion rights through *Roe v. Wade* or the confirmation of Brett Kavanaugh to the Supreme Court in 2018.

To be certain, there are everyday wins and losses, big and small. But no single outcome will ever end this fight that we shoulder as women, the fight of and for our lives: to be autonomous, credible, respected, human.

Feminism embodies the broad assertion that all people across lines of gender, race, ethnicity, orientation, class, and ability deserve equal status and the same fundamental rights, self-determination, and access to resources. It is not a race toward one gain or another, but a steady, determined evolution taking place on the individual and societal levels, with progress on either of these levels never made in isolation but through constant interaction and synergy.

That said, feminism is hardly something I gave much thought to throughout my childhood and early teenage years cloaked in the privilege and ignorance of youth in an affluent, upper-middle-class suburb. Then, suddenly, I was sixteen and needed it as a matter of survival, safety, and means of understanding the cruelty and rigidity that had come to govern my life. And in all the years since, through personal gains and losses and colossal changes in the world, the need for it in my life has never lessened.

I was born and raised in Fremont, California, a quiet, relatively homogeneous Asian American suburb near the outskirts of San Francisco. My nuclear family consisted of my two immigrant parents—my father from Hong Kong, my mother from the Philippines—and my two older sisters. For the first eighteen years of my life, Fremont served as a stiflingly ordinary backdrop for my stiflingly ordinary coming of age. For me, those were years fraught with commonalities most girls would admit to experiencing while growing up if they felt safe enough to be honest: bitter fights with parents, social anxiety, nervous trips to a local Planned Parenthood, sexual violence by someone trusted, a high school culture of normalized sexual harassment, and carefree trips to the mall.

Of course, I lived some life before descending into teen angst. Throughout my childhood, my family often spent summers in Asia, and I looked forward to them to will myself through fall, winter, and spring in Fremont. Some of my earliest memories outside Bay Area suburbia include strolling through night markets in dense, summer air; traveling by way of ferry and train; and, between lavish meals of dim sum and sightseeing embellished by privilege, encountering homelessness and human suffering that often weighed on me, if for no other reason than for how helpless these encounters made me feel.

At home in Fremont, I grew up during years of desolation and revolution, hope and change. During the final months of my eighteen-year stint in the Bay Area before moving to Los Angeles for college, I'd felt nothing but hope for my country. Often as it disappointed me, often as discoveries about its past and present have repulsed me in their cruelty and absurdity, I'd felt hope. More than hope, I'd felt certainty—that we were moving in the right direction, that our next president would be our first woman president. But you know the rest. (Deserving woman loses to entitled man; marginalized people everywhere are reduced to collateral damage; and so on and so forth.)

The 2016 presidential election took place during the first semester of my first year of college. I went home to Fremont a couple weeks later for my Thanksgiving holiday, and I was at once shocked by the feeling of normalcy. During my final years in Fremont, the apolitical nature of my community became clear to me as I began to self-identify and become politically active as a feminist. In contrast, political activism among residents of the predominantly upper-middle-class, Asian American suburb I called home often seemed limited to issues like opposing affirmative action or virtually any zoning policies that would accord homeless people recognition as human beings.

Yet, I'd never encountered this dysfunction so clearly as I did in those few days that I was home. I was struck with the realization that the choice to *not* be political—which my community seemed to have made—is, in itself, inherently political. Existence is political; the ability to opt out of uncomfortable conversations and situations, to refuse to learn about or acknowledge oppression and systemic, identity-based persecution, is political. Specifically, being apolitical is about privilege. It concerns power and social capital, which millions in this country simply don't have. Choosing to be silent about injustices isn't a neutral, victimless act—it is, rather, an oppressive act of consent to the abuse of others. Marginalized people talk about their lives, their realities, their experiences, their needs, not out of feelings of self-importance, nor as a means to disrupt the lives of those around them, but as a mechanism for survival.

To unequivocally declare that you are a feminist is often about survival as much as it is about empowerment; many women and marginalized people do not have the choice to disengage or sit out this fight. For many men, the ability to pontificate about whether feminism includes them or is defined by explicit "man-hating," or to feel offended by what they perceive as broad generalizations about their character—all while women die from lack of access repro-ductive health care or are murdered by abusive partners—reflects a chasm between privilege and oppression across gendered lines.

Self-identification as a feminist is powerful, because, for better or worse, the word "feminist" conjures up powerful images that summon powerful reactions. For the growing demographic of young women who proudly identify themselves as feminists, these images and reactions carry the power to dramatically mold their everyday experiences, perceptions of self, and, certainly, their rela-tionships with others in a patriarchal society.

Nearly anyone but perhaps a wealthy, Christian, straight, cis-gender, white man could assure you through his or her own expe-riences that the personal is the political. LGBTQ people, people of color, people with disabilities, immigrants, and women of all ages share the experience of being otherized and politicized on the basis of immutable facets of their identity. Yet, in contrast, to identify oneself as a feminist is ultimately a choice, which more often than not draws backlash, sexist assumptions, condescension, and even threats and danger. So, why choose to do so?

———————

The first time I thought seriously about the waves of the feminist movement was during my senior year of high school. I'd learned about them earlier, in my eleventh grade AP US history class: The first wave, in the 1920s, centered around suffrage and property rights; the second, from the 1960s through the 1980s, around reproductive rights, sexual violence, and labor rights; and the third, from the 1990s through the 2010s, around diversity and intersectionality. Feminism, as my history classes revealed, has continually changed and evolved for the better, adapting to address a more diverse array of needs with each generation, and, certainly, to correct the problematic, noninclusive mistakes of previous generations. But we hadn't discussed feminism's current fourth wave much, nor had I done much of any thinking about it until the following year.

Fresh off the US history class that had fundamentally transformed my understanding of everything around me, during the summer of my junior year I began to write professionally about national news and politics, with a focus on women's-rights issues, as an intern at a growing online women's-interest magazine. That summer was marked by the advent of the presidential-election campaign, an onslaught of tragic mass shootings, and a bizarre and deeply dangerous Planned Parenthood scandal manufactured by anti-choice activists, among other culturally impactful events.

The more I've tried to forget that summer's events, rich in both trauma and inescapable life lessons, the more I remember, and the more I realize the power in embracing my past. Certainly, my past and all its vibrant colors and gray areas has shaped much of my writing work and my deep passion for the issues I've focused on.

Feminism as a social theory, rather than a movement for fair public policy and electoral outcomes, had first appealed to me as early as my middle school years, when I developed a voracious appetite for history books about queens and bold, pioneering women in general. I was drawn to the idea that women did not have to fit so neatly into artificially imposed binaries, that we could be sexual and smart, sexual and kind, kind and ambitious. To be multiple things at once is to be human; to suggest that women cannot be that way is to strike against the very heart of our humanity. Still, I didn't fully consider how this related to public policy and national politics until that summer.

Returning to school in the fall as a high school senior, for the first time in my life, the heat of political passion coursed through my veins. Politics felt like real life, not obscure, and it *was* my life. I was giddy for any opportunity to converse about the issues of the day with anyone. Incidentally, so were some of the young men in my history, government, and economics classes, ready with their skepticism about the gender wage gap, their insistence about the injustice and racism of affirmative action, their frustration with the phenomenon of the "social-justice warrior."

The term "social-justice warrior" is nuanced; at its core, it chastises those who care "too much" (whatever that even means) about purportedly unimportant subject matter (criteria for "important subject matter," of course, often being defined by privileged men). And it carries gendered implications, considering the majority of people who work for social-justice issues are young women. But the term also carries the connotation that young women don't actually care about the issues and merely posture as social activists to aspire to some sort of imagined individual benefit, as if young women aren't routinely harassed off the internet for expressing an opinion about anything.

Perhaps posturing activists are out there, those who say the right things and diligently play the part of concerned, caring citizens to reap benefits—there are many, actually. But it seems there are far more white men exploiting the cultural phenomenon of the "low-bar Jesus"—the inherently low moral standards men must meet to be celebrated and praised—than there are young women posturing as activists, as they often have real stakes in some of the most daunting social-justice issues of our day.

I knew that with every comment I offered at my school, voicing my concerns about women's rights, civil rights, and racial justice, with every article I shared on my social-media accounts about the wage gap or sexual violence or how 90 percent of US counties lack an abortion provider,[1] "social-justice warrior" was precisely how I was labeled. Nonetheless, I knew my only option was to accept this persona or be silent—and it was not a difficult choice to make.

Years later, I distinctly remembered the afternoon I went home from school and performed a cursory search of the varying waves of feminism. My curiosity had been piqued when one of my male peers told me after class that we, feminists, had so desperately run out of things to be angry about in the real world, that we'd manufactured our own crises as part of what he called "seventh-wave feminism."

To set the record straight, 2012 marked the advent of fourth-wave of feminism, and much of my memories and formative experiences have been shaped by growing up in the thick of it. The fourth wave emerged to modernize the conversation around sexual violence and rape culture, to address the gaps and blind spots of feminisms that are not intersectional, and to speak about the new, pervasive, and constantly expanding forms misogyny has taken in the modern era.

That exchange took place years ago, and his was hardly the cruelest or most insensitive comment I've received over the course of years of writing about feminism on the internet. But I was and remain struck by the realization our conversation instilled in me, that privilege and oppression are not a dichotomy.

Rather, privilege and oppression are often simultaneous experiences; in plenty of scenarios, those who oppress are often oppressed themselves. He and I were both the children of Asian American immigrants in white America. We lived in an upper-middle-class suburb with an SAT tutoring center posted on nearly every corner, raised by parents who were not just capable of, but also insistent on, providing access to these and any other resources to support our going to college.

I think often about my own privilege as a cisgender, able-bodied person, born to parents who had had the profound fortune in life to achieve economic security, who have taken care of me and my equally healthy sisters so that we could go to school each day without worrying for our family's economic future or our own future educational prospects. While I've never intended to oppress others in any way, the social position into which I was born ensures that I benefit from the oppression of other marginalized groups. Yet, this doesn't change the reality that I've also regularly experienced oppression as a woman of color, in ways that range from frustrating to devastating.

Almost no one is fully victim or oppressor in the patriarchy; beyond politics, not even straight, cisgender, wealthy white men fully benefit from the patriarchy, if you really think about it. Male privilege requires full conformity to patriarchal standards for noninclusive, heterosexual, white constructions of masculinity. Meeting these standards requires sacrifices that often deprive men of full, meaningful relationships and, certainly, good health, if they're socialized to perceive opening up and seeking help as weaknesses.

Before going further, I must admit that the experiences I'm able to speak about are vastly limited. But certainly, I can speak about the experiences of sexism and misogyny and everyday racism and the unique forms these prejudices take when directed at young women—and I'm more than happy to do so.

When my male classmate told me that I and other young feminists had, by sheer force of will to be angry for the fun of it, invented a seventh wave of feminism, I laughed. What other response was there? The fact that we are making history as we speak, that all around us, women and girls are putting in the blood, sweat, and tears to usher in a new world order, is often lost on those who cherry-pick their favorite pieces of our male-written human history, lost on those who benefit from an unjust world and feel threatened by the idea of a just one.

At the core of this snide remark was the suggestion that today's young women-led feminism has taken things too far. It's an objectively false narrative that exhausts and frustrates women, but it's hardly a surprising one in the context of history. Privilege breeds feelings of entitlement, and specifically, feelings of entitlement to privilege. And when one feels entitled to privilege, the idea of equality seems like a grand, existential threat. Perhaps, in some ways, it is—a grand, existential threat to an unequal and oppressive way of life, to a bygone era of exclusivity and monopolistic distributions of social and political capital.

Comments like my classmate's aren't made in isolation; this is the reality of how many men and privileged people perceive feminism. History is written by men, the way most modern media narratives are; newspapers and news stations and media companies are predominantly headed by male executives, male producers, male editors—no shortage of whom have been exposed for abusing or exploiting women employees or covering it up, and no shortage of whom have simultaneously directed sexist media coverage. Women live in a culture of men telling our story, men explaining our lives to us, men telling us that problems we struggle with every day are either not real or hysterically exaggerated. We live in a persistent and dangerous culture of gaslighting.

It's always been like this, and you can either trust me or enroll in an introductory history class. But especially in the aftermath of the 2016 presidential election, the pervasiveness of male-led narratives about a national tragedy for women felt like a new era of gaslighting—or if not a new era, then certainly a new level of shamelessness. Beyond a news cycle that constantly lambasted the Democratic nominee, Hillary Clinton, for supposedly failing to talk about economic issues, we've since watched the male-dominated media industry focus on male narratives and perspectives about anti-women violence exposed about a year later by the #MeToo movement. Some might say media has failed to learn its lesson about the dangers of sexist coverage; others might say it has functioned as it was supposed to in a patriarchal society.

The realities that women—and predominantly low-income women of color—are dying at steadily increasing rates due to the horrifying laws around abortion in this country;[2] that young black men are nine to sixteen times more likely than any other group to be fatally shot by the police;[3] that black and brown bodies are routinely incarcerated, cheated, and plundered within the criminal justice system; that LGBTQ people remain legally disenfranchised and discriminated against and disproportionately targeted by homicides and assaults; and that millions of women and people of color live in abject poverty in "coastal, liberal, elitist" cities are fundamental, existential human-rights issues. When we shrug these issues off as "identity politics," as we've so often seen in male-dominated political media, we label them as fringe, niche, and dismissible, compared to more "serious" political discourse concerning men and white people.

Of course, this is all just more gaslighting. The narrative of identity politics pretends that women, people of color, and LGBTQ people are not the mainstream, that anyone but the rural, white male working class is not the mainstream. It ignores that women comprise 51 percent of the population, people of color are set to outpace white people in the national population,[4] and, already, LGBTQ people have become an increasingly formidable voting bloc.

Perhaps each of these groups would disproportionately benefit from the sweeping economic reforms often proposed by the male progressives who are some of the most vocal critics of identity politics. Women are 35 percent more likely than men to live in poverty,[5] and job and pay discrimination have yielded the economic disenfranchisement of marginalized groups for generations. But our struggles and our oppression do not exist in a vacuum. Identity-based oppression would persist and continue to divide our experiences from those of low-income and middle-class white men, even in the actualized, democratic-socialist society white male leftists dream of. Pretending these fundamental divisions and differences don't exist for the sake of a manufactured, politically expedient narrative of "unity" helps no one.

Power and social capital are inextricably bound to narrative construction. Perhaps many progressive and left-wing male thinkers work in good faith for a gender-neutral, race-neutral, broadly identity-neutral democratic-socialist economic system that requires robust unity to be achieved. Their goals are often vastly different from those of bad-faith, right-wing actors whose attempts to erase women and marginalized people's oppression are an attack on our rights and safety. But no matter the intention, identity-neutral rhetoric and policies can be harmful if they erase existing identity-based oppression from mass consciousness.

The irony of backlash against identity politics is that, if anything, these issues aren't discussed anywhere near enough. In recent years, marginalized people have faced the greatest threat to their existence in the modern history of this country as racist, misogynistic, xenophobic, bigoted, and abusive voices have been given larger platforms within institutions, including at the level of the presidency in 2016. Trumpism is the product of more than one election; foundational bigotry has lain just beneath the surface at every corner of society, plaguing and endangering the lives of marginalized people for generations.

Of all people, we, marginalized people, knew what was coming after that election. Nonetheless, we were indirectly blamed for giving rise to the Trump presidency, the most potent, modern symbol of racism and sexism, because we had had the gall to occupy political spaces, speak up about what we had faced, and demand that politicians recognize us.

We are currently fighting to survive in the fourth wave of feminism; today's patriarchal institutions and their broad, toxic culture of gaslighting and narrative-hijacking are the inheritance of young women and feminists. And in this context, we see our fight clearly for what it is: once again, the fight of our lives, for our lives—to be autonomous, credible, respected, human.

Many young women are not feminists, choosing not to recognize gender and identity-based oppression. Many people of color, LGBTQ people, and other members of marginalized groups voted for Donald Trump, and women in states like Alabama and Georgia voted for lawmakers who went on to pass laws banning abortion. Some survivors of sexual assault do not believe other survivors. No one's experience is universal or normative, and no one's lack of personal experience with oppression invalidates others' experiences with it.

Historically, many women avoided political awareness or involvement to be safe in a country that accorded wives virtually no protections from domestic violence prior to the 1994 Violence Against Women Act. Immigrants and people of color avoided social-justice activism in order to draw minimal attention to themselves and survive in a climate bent on otherizing and criminalizing them. Even as women, people of color, and other marginalized individuals have emerged as some of the most vocal and dedicated activists and leaders today, the aforementioned restraints persist in holding many people back from publicly identifying as feminists or engaging feminist advocacy.

As much as it frustrates me, I understand why some young women reject feminism or don't get involved in feminism publicly. Young women make stiff social sacrifices to identify as feminists, and benefits—albeit temporary and conditional—to patriarchal complicity, to being a "cool girl," abound. In the patriarchy, "cool girls" ✕ give men cover for their misogyny by being perpetually unoffended by casual slurs, and they therefore enjoy male approval. They have nothing to say about identity-based issues.

Many women may directly benefit from the white, capitalist patriarchy in a variety of ways. Association with powerful white men has had no shortage of socioeconomic perks. Siding with racist partners, or proactively helping them carry out their agendas through voting behaviors or anti-feminist activism, puts white women in a position to maximize their white privilege. Women of color who engage in anti-feminist work alongside anti-feminist male partners can reap similar rewards by maximizing their access to what privileges their partners have.

But feminism is not about the empowerment of one single woman or one single class of women; it is about the rights, safety, autonomy, and greatest benefit to all women, across lines of race, sexuality, class, and ability.

The beliefs—or lack of them—of "cool girls" and rabidly anti-feminist young women do not affect the reality they choose to ignore: In the decades since *Roe v. Wade* in 1973, more than one-third of all restrictions on abortion access were enacted from 2011 to 2018 alone.[6] For millions of American women, the right to safe, legal abortion has become all but theoretical; throughout the 2010s, 90 percent of counties lacked an abortion provider, and seven states had just one,[7] forcing thousands of women to travel great distances to access abortion care and shoulder tremendous costs, inconvenience, and, at times, danger.

These wide-ranging barriers to access have led to a public health crisis: The United States has the highest maternal mortality rate in the industrialized world, which has only continued to rise[8] and is significantly higher in states with more restrictions on abortion access, and for women of color.[9] Black women are 243 percent more likely than white women to die of pregnancy or birth-related causes,[10] highlighting the intersectional nature of who is often disproportionately affected by oppressive laws around reproductive health.

Each restrictive anti-abortion law—and the anti-abortion movement, broadly—is rooted in false science and deep misogyny, a yearning to control and punish the bodies of women and pregnant people, to sweepingly dehumanize and disenfranchise women as a unit. And of course, this yearning manifests in laws regulating not just pregnancy but also gender identity and expression, which give companies, employers, and landlords free rein to disenfran-chise LGBTQ people.

Who is viewed as human and a citizen is always a launching point in trying to understand someone's biases and prejudices. It simply can't be stated enough that a fetus is not a person, but preg-nant people—and, of course, the born children often neglected or harmed by anti-choice lawmakers' economic policies—are. You cannot bestow personhood upon a fetus without taking it from the pregnant woman. Regardless of whether every single woman sees the abortion debate this way or speaks up about reproductive rights, the deep urgency around this issue stands.

And it's not just the oppressive culture around reproductive rights. One in five women has experienced sexual assault, and an estimated 65 to 85 percent of sexual assaults are unreported.[11] The term "violence against women" is, in many ways, dangerously gender-neutral; after all, violence against women is not some nat-ural, untraceable phenomenon, something that just happens to so many women. It is caused by choices of abusive men who know their power and what they can get away with in a sexist society. When we fail to acknowledge the consequences of a culture of toxic masculinity, lack of accountability, male privilege, and mainstream misrepresentations of gender violence, we enable this violence to persist.

Men are more likely to experience sexual violence themselves than to be falsely accused of it.[12] Women and survivors of sexual violence are forced to exist within a persistent culture of victim-blaming and prosecution of survivors, to come to terms with the rarity of the reporting of sexual violence yielding justice. Every year, unsaid numbers of women—and disproportionately women of color and transgender and nonbinary individuals—are killed by a domestic partner, or killed for telling a man "no" or offending violent men's sensibilities.[13] Partisan conflict among legislators about whether to fund resources for survivors and whether firearms belong in the hands of abusers creates a climate in which gendered violence is not only possible but also virtually encouraged.

In its quest to expose a pervasive culture of sexual violence and demand justice, the #MeToo movement does not require the unanimous support of all women to be valid and necessary.

Not every woman will tell you she has experienced pregnancy discrimination or prejudice and misogyny in the workplace. Not every woman will tell you that full, legal access to reproductive rights is absolutely requisite for women to exist and participate in public life. Not every woman will tell you that sexism is real. But every woman has experienced sexism, nonetheless.

The #YesAllWomen hashtag, conceived in the beginning of fourth-wave feminism, served as a resounding, powerful rebuttal to the #NotAllMen hashtag, which was a response by young men to perceived attacks on their character in the wake of a devastating campus mass shooting targeting young women in 2014. Often, I think of #YesAllWomen as an all-encompassing response to anyone who tries to make their experience with feminism universal and normative. Not all men are violent toward women; not all men perpetuate misogyny. But certainly all women have experienced sexual violence or fear of it, and certainly all women have experienced misogyny.

Contrary to self-victimizing male critiques of feminism, no woman has ever really blamed all men for sexism and misogyny. Even flippant, off-the-cuff commentary like "I hate all men" or "Men are the worst" by women—lines young women and feminists so often find themselves unjustly in hot water for—can hardly be equated with men saying the same about women. To do so ignores the fundamental power dynamics of gender and society. The same words and actions applied to different groups of people can hold very different meanings and implications.

✗ The men offended by women saying "I hate men" are the men who *should* be offended, the men whom the expression "I hate men" is about. Generalized criticisms of men refer to the institution of masculinity that strips women and femininity of respect and social capital. Anyone who understands this is not offended by "I hate men" because they know the expression is not about individuals. "I hate men" is about men who rank themselves and their feelings over listening to the very real issues women raise.

That said, a particularly condescending straw-man argument posits that women consider all men to be misogynists and rapists. We know this isn't true; you'll find that few women need the realities of misogyny and sexual violence explained to us so simplistically. Yet, we also know that most men, regardless of whether they would ever use it, have the ability to hurt and rape. That ability, ✗ even in the most hypothetical and abstract of terms, is social capital, which most men have and most women do not.

---

Why choose to be a feminist?

Many young women have gone far and above identifying themselves as feminists. Young women have become one of the most potent—and reliably Democratic and progressive—political forces in the country. Fifty-five percent of voters in the landmark 2018 midterm elections, which saw unprecedented numbers of progressive women elected to public office, were women.[14]

For decades, young women have volunteered outside women's health clinics to safely escort patients inside. They were the lead organizers and protesters on college campuses fighting for sweeping

Title IX reforms and justice for survivors as early as the 1960s and '70s. They've always stood at the forefront of the fight for justice; no one should be surprised by the sight of young women at the forefront today.

Women, and especially young women, are the backbone of political and social-justice organizing efforts. They are running for—and winning—elected office, and they are on the front lines, unafraid and sharing their ideas for a litany of deeply progressive reforms to anyone who will listen. And even in the face of so much skepticism and condescension, young feminists have shown no fear in embracing the controversial, proudly fighting for rights in the realms of reproductive justice, economic equity, sexual violence, and civil rights that have long been deemed too radical, blazing their own trail forward.

Every aspect of feminist self-identification is exhausting, at times even debilitatingly so. The role of being "brand ambassadors" of the feminist movement is placed on our shoulders, requiring us to always take time and energy out of our already stressful lives to explain feminism and complex identity issues to those around us.

Feminism can sometimes feel like cognitive dissonance, simultaneously demanding deep skepticism and unbounded optimism. The feminist movement requires us to see the world for what it is and has always been, for all its needless suffering and bullying and devastation; it requires us to be rational and pragmatic and wary of institutions.

But the love and solidarity upon which the movement was built invites us to audaciously envision the world as it could be, if only everyone did their part. Amid a mounting, transnational dialogue of walls and barriers, of exclusivity and exploitation, often I find myself thinking of feminism as reinventing society from the ground up to respect and serve the needs of all people.

The ability to care—instinctively and reflexively, regardless of whether something affects the person directly—is strength. We draw strength from the knowledge that this fight is one we can only lose by quitting. We are in this fight not because it is easy, but because it is worth it.

I didn't choose to be a feminist—most women don't. I didn't choose to be a feminist the way I didn't choose to experience sexual assault as a young woman. I didn't choose to be a feminist the way I didn't choose to experience an early-stage miscarriage, also as a young woman. I didn't choose to be a feminist the way I didn't choose to experience severe sickness and complications from my birth control. I didn't choose to be a feminist the way I have never chosen to be routinely sexually harassed for the way I dress, for my sexual and bodily decisions, for fetishized mythology around my racial identity, for my writing and very public opinions about feminism.

But for better or for worse, these have been the realities of my life. Lived experience makes all the difference, and any gaps in experience, I like to think, could easily be filled by a little thing called empathy. This is, ultimately, a guiding and defining trait of most young women, and everyone, across age, gender, or any other identity, should follow their example.

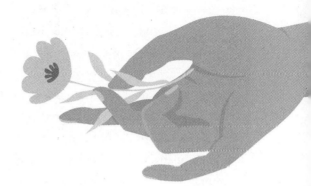

# 2

# The (Young, Female) Writer's Life

I've always been an avid writer and storyteller, and a lover of books too, often regardless of whether or not I'd even read them. To hold a book in my hands and wonder about the infinite thought processes, conversations, and experiences that informed its creation has somehow always been enough.

Growing up, my love for reading, writing, and books steered me to consider a number of potential academic and professional tracks; there were times I saw myself becoming a historical romance novelist, a professor of British history, and even a researcher traveling Europe studying sixteenth century dynastic politics. Across all of these imagined careers, I envisioned a life of learning and writing about what I learned, publishing and sharing original ideas and perspectives with the world around me.

Truth to be told, these earlier aspirations were all in part shaped by my failure to see the value of my own lived experiences. I thought the lives of people—namely, women—before me, often hailing from western European societies during the Renaissance period, were infinitely more interesting than my own life; sometimes, when the stresses of being a teenage girl became particularly difficult to manage, stories of kings and queens and wily courtesans from faraway lands were the escapism I needed.

It wasn't until I began writing about news and politics for a national women's magazine as a young woman that I began to realize my formative experiences with misogyny carried value, including rich potential to inform my work in a meaningful way.

Personal challenges I'd faced to safely access reproductive health care guided my passion to produce work that shined a light on the infinitely human side of the fight for reproductive rights. When I wrote about the endless cases of reproductive health clinics being harassed, threatened, or targeted by protesters and state laws, I wrote from the vantage point of someone who had been harassed outside of my local clinic; I wrote as someone who had purchased a pregnancy test at a drugstore as a teenage girl while a cashier looked on, offering crude attempts at jokes.

When I wrote about efforts by the then-fledgling #FreeTheNipple movement, or political activism to change local laws prohibiting female public toplessness, I wrote as someone who had regularly experienced sexual harassment from my high school peers for my decision to not wear a bra, among other needlessly controversial fashion choices. And when I wrote about the dangers of noninclusive, anti-sex health education in public schools, I wrote as someone who had grown up experiencing unhealthy sexual relationships, sexual violence, and persistent sexual harassment and slut-shaming.

There is something deeply, viscerally empowering about having the ability to see society from the lens of your own unique, identity-based experiences. Often today, we hear from politicians and white media men who decry "identity politics," a framework of understanding how identity shapes the living standards and politics of marginalized groups, as trivial, divisive, and somehow not relevant to mainstream political discourse. Yet, the color and dimension that identity-based experiences contribute to our lives are anything but trivial, gifting us with a vision of the world that is nuanced, compassionate, and inclusive.

In the years prior to writing this book, I've steadily written essays, columns, and reported features about feminism and politics for national progressive publications and have cherished every opportunity to project my voice into the world. I've engaged in activist work to help elect diverse candidates, support reproductive justice, and advocate for the rights of survivors and had the privilege of working for some of my favorite women's-rights and reproductive-justice advocacy organizations. And through it all, lived experience has added a critical dimension to my writing and activist work, impressing on me the importance of lifting the voices and stories of people with similar experiences with oppression, and certainly, the importance of trusting and valuing my own.

But in addition to my lived experiences, my identity as a young woman of color in itself has also necessarily shaped my work. I've always theorized my editorial writing skills and zeal for constructing arguments with relevant evidence to support each point are inherently bound to my gender, and the skepticism and dismissiveness that femininity unfailingly attracts across all contexts. However men identify across the political spectrum, however progressive and feminist they may purport to be, when women speak to them about our ideas as women, we will always come from a place of lacking credibility and a higher burden of proof for our claims.

The hyperscrutiny my opinions and arguments attract, whether in my writing or everyday conversations with men, has trained me to be a stronger writer and advocate, with statistics, studies, examples, and current events always at the ready, because I know my voice and perspective alone will never be enough—not in the way men's are. As young women, we're accustomed to being required to back up everything we say, and this reality has only become more prevalent as social media has come to encourage more and more young women to vocally embrace feminism.

Our values automatically draw cynicism within a patriarchal culture that suggests in so many words that we women inherently lack minds of our own and certainly lack for the cognitive ability to develop our own opinions. When we express support for feminist values, we are viewed as simply reproducing popular, "mainstream" talking points in a self-serving attempt to be morally righteous—in other words, that we're "social-justice warriors"—or to gain access to whatever imagined benefit in the public there is to being a young woman who voices support for feminist political viewpoints.

Women's inherent lack of credibility is more than an everyday annoyance; it can also impede on our ability to participate and exist in public life. Our lack of credibility consistently impacts our health care outcomes, because we are systematically denied credibility regarding even our own bodily experiences. Notions of women as more likely to exaggerate, or be hypersensitive and "hysterical," prevent our pain from being taken seriously, yielding everyday neglect and misdiagnoses.

Today, thirty-nine million Americans regularly experience migraines, and women are biologically more vulnerable:[1] as of 2018,

18 percent of adult American women regularly report experiencing migraines. Yet, despite how migraines can hurt women's ability to work, go to school, and generally participate in public life, this common experience remains widely unaddressed. There is still no real, long-term cure for migraines, nor any apparent sense of urgency to develop one. In 2019, a Danish study found female patients are often diagnosed several years later than male patients for the same diseases,[2] at least in part due to gender biases skewing whose pain and complaints about pain are actually taken seriously.

The idea that women's concerns are dismissible or trivial or even fundamentally dishonest has become especially harmful in recent years. In 2018, when conspiratorial, conservative forces successfully established a conservative Supreme Court majority positioned to dismantle *Roe v. Wade*, still, 72 percent of voters in a Pew Research survey said they didn't believe abortion rights were in danger.[3] And in the early months of 2019, when the passage of all-out abortion bans in states like Georgia, Alabama, Missouri, Louisiana, and others became a near weekly occurrence, still, about 75 percent of respondents to another Pew survey at the time insisted abortion would still be legal in thirty years.[4] Stubborn, conscious refusal to listen to women's voices for generations has culminated in dangerous complacency around women's rights, all but giving clearance to the horrific and draconian anti-women political landscape of the Trump era.

Lack of credibility across gendered lines is foundational to the oppression of women and girls, foundational to the masking of existential attacks on our lives and our rights—from reproductive rights to civil rights to protections from sexual violence—by dismissing our concerns as hysteria. The systemic denial of women's credibility has been key to the maintenance of a culture of sexual violence that unfailingly gives men cover. Yet, it's also a driving

force in what's made many of us into exceedingly talented politicians, activists, organizers, and writers: We are prepared to put in
the work to convince members of a society that is primed to disbe-
lieve us that we deserve their trust. We are capable of overcoming
vast hurdles to raise our voices above thousands telling us to be
silent, and speak our truth. No one creates spaces for women and
our voices—so with our voices, we have learned to create spaces for
ourselves and each other.

Of course, having these skills is a sort of grim consolation prize
for being subjected to the societal realities that have forced us to
develop these skills in the first place. But as the saying goes, when
life gives you lemons, change the world—or something like that.

In recent years, my work as a young, female writer on the internet
has given me not just a front-row seat to the ongoing, conservative,
white-male-led debate around free speech but also a direct, deeply
personal stake in it.

I was a teenager when the notorious 2014 Gamergate scandal,
which involved extensive, graphic and horrific harassment of several prominent women in tech and media, plagued the internet.
These women's experiences sparked a critical conversation about
the prevalence of rape and death threats and other gendered harassment lodged against women online, endangering and all but negat-
ing their ability to communicate and interact freely on the internet.
About a year after Gamergate, I got a firsthand taste of it when
I started publishing writing and feminist commentary in online
magazines.

I learned quickly that if you're a young woman and your writing
or opinions are remotely visible, they naturally draw comments and

feedback, solicited or not. And typically, the response to your work is less about the specific content of your work and more about your appearance and identity-based perceptions of your character and credibility. Even as a teenager and a minor, I recall men and trolls on the internet finding my private social media profiles to send me bizarre messages, interspersed with both angry responses to my writing and commentary about my appearance and photos.

I started publishing writing at a young age, and as I'm writing this, I suppose I would still be considered young. This means that for years, I've watched my femininity and youth interact to draw an onslaught of backlash, condescension, and harassment. I've been fortunate enough to evade the rape and death threats that have defined the experiences of so many female journalists and writers, and especially female or LGBTQ writers of color. Unsaid numbers of diverse women writers and journalists are pushed out of a field that relies on their voice and perspective, because of these attacks.

Of course, to say that I am "fortunate" to write about gender, politics, and my life without being subjected to threats of violence has a bitter taste to it. Such attacks are singularly meant to remove diverse writers and activists like me from public spaces and discourse, to make it clear that we do not deserve to take up space and have a voice because of who we are. And yet, I'm here anyway, so surely I'm one of the lucky ones, aren't I?

I am lucky to be here at all, participating in the dialogue; receiving the harassing emails and gross commentary I attract by nature of my identity is simply the price of entry that I pay. I forced myself to grow accustomed to unsettling, fetishizing emails and private messages, emails featuring graphic photos of bloodied fetuses, emails from random men determined to explain abortion rights and the pay gap and other issues I'd spent years researching or been directly affected by. It's a price that all women writers and activists, all women who express opinions in public spaces and especially on the internet, are forced to pay.

Still, we who are every day the victims of hate speech, sexual harassment, and, in many cases, threats of violence that could at any moment escalate into physical, real-world violence are the ones who so often have free speech condescendingly explained to us. We, whose free-speech rights are shuttered by the unabridged, violent speech that targets us on the basis of identity, are told that we are not the ones being marginalized, that, instead, advocacy on behalf of our right to exist marginalizes our oppressors.

The modern, mainstream free-speech debate is centered around the college campus as a mythic, liberal echo chamber, a conservative fantasy that any female, LGBTQ or minority college student could quite easily assure you does not exist. It is predicated on the pretense that the First Amendment guarantees the right to resources and a platform and, further, the right to resources and a platform to spew bigotry, when all it guarantees is freedom from censorship by the state.

As a former college student, I could attest to how the obsession with whether universities should allow controversial—shorthand for white supremacist, misogynist, or otherwise bigoted—speakers to come to campus marginalizes many vastly more important issues of campus speech. Milo Yiannopoulos and Richard Spencer and Ben Shapiro and all the other self-identified "provocateurs" whose brands center around self-victimization deliberately obscure real, everyday oppression and censorship of marginalized people, whenever they try to portray whining about being protested as a crusade for First Amendment protections. And when we listen and argue about and give oxygen to their whining, we help advance their agenda of erasing real, substantive free-speech issues that target marginalized people.

Targeted harassment of people on the basis of race, gender identity, orientation, and religion remains rampant, on and off college
campuses, and has been on the rise across the country, notably
beginning after the 2016 election. In nine US metropolitan areas,
hate crimes targeting immigrants, people of color, and Muslim
people rose by almost 25 percent between 2015 and 2016 alone,
according to research published by the Center for the Study of
Hate and Extremism.[5]

Modern boldness of white supremacy draws on a long, rich
history of government-empowered bigotry, often through the
exploitation of ambiguous laws around hate speech. Racist violence
and harassment have been common in American history, from
frequent racist rallies permitted in Marquette Park by the city of
Chicago due to First Amendment protections, taking place in the
1960s and well into the 1980s; to frequent, oft-overlooked fire-
bombing and targeting of black homes and churches throughout
the 1950s and 1960s.

The history of identity-based hatred and organized attacks in
America is as important as ever, as we reckon with the reality that
modern-day bigoted speech and behaviors are by no means out-
of-left-field, that this is the history and these are the foundations
upon which America was built. And when we fail to draw lines
around violent behaviors and ideologies, as modern, conservative
provocateurs demand, this is the direction—backward—in which
we are pulled.

Ultimately, such acts of hatred expose the power dynamics
inherent to conservatives' beloved "marketplace of ideas," where
all ideas, from revolutionary eco-socialist, feminist liberation to
white supremacy, can supposedly compete on an equal level for
support among the masses. But in a patriarchal landscape where
credibility is gendered male, where white men maintain hegemony

over platforms, resources, authority, and social capital as birthright, this idealized marketplace simply does not exist. Hate speech is not free speech, and the solution to hate speech isn't more speech—not when identity skews who is listened to and who has access to platforms and resources to be heard. Rather, hate speech is objectively more likely to be effectively addressed through strong and thorough content-moderation practices and aggressive rejection of bigotry on campuses, in workplaces, in media, and in politics.

According to a survey by the children's charity Plan International UK from 2017, half of all girls in the United Kingdom report having experienced harassment on the internet.[6] In 2013, the International Women's Media Foundation reported 46 percent of women journalists have reported experiencing sexual harassment, including rape threats, simply for doing their job.[7] A few years later in 2017, Vox shared a feature telling the stories of female journalists who left their industry after being overwhelmed by the gendered harassment they faced. Women of color and members of the LGBTQ community face targeted backlash to their writing and social-media activity that is even more severe.

There is no such thing as equal footing in a marketplace of ideas that gleefully creates space for white men to spew violent, bigoted ideologies. In contrast, when women and minorities are directly targeted by internet theories about whether rape is even real, or whether ethnic cleansing is a noble, beneficial pursuit, it's simply impossible to expect that they can respond to these inherently violent ideologies and share their ideas publicly with the same feelings of safety and detachment as white-male thinkers.

Additionally, the immense role of the internet and social media in today's dialogue around free speech can't be emphasized enough: this is now where the bulk of speech happens. And unequal access to the internet due to targeted, identity-based harassment, is not

accidental, but an extension of the real-life white, cis-hetero patriarchy, as well as notions of whose voice and existence carry value
and credibility and whose do not.

Hate speech and harassment on social media and the internet
are the product of real life, identity-based divisions, and, as such,
they carry real-world threats and implications. Just ask women's
health clinics and abortion providers, who often report upticks in
targeted violence or threats of violence when anti-choice politicians
and activists escalate their morbid rhetoric about abortion on social
platforms, according to research annually published by the Feminist Majority Foundation.[8]

The frustrating reality is that all of the energy we routinely pour
into debating whether racist, sexist white men are being oppressed
through being denied guaranteed platforms on college campuses is
energy we could invest into keeping marginalized people safe and
uplifting their voices. And yet, through it all, I believe in the power
of having a sense of humor: Recurring, right-wing outrage about
their ideas being "censored" on social media, just because their
reach is limited by the fact that their ideas are inherently unpopular
in a modern, evolving society, is funny. Right-wing narratives about
how they are discriminated against, solely because they face social
consequences for their conscious choice to espouse hateful views,
are funny.

We can laugh at these delusions of grandeur simultaneously as
we condemn and act against the discriminatory, hateful, and silencing treatment of marginalized people on the internet and in public
life. We will have to multitask—our sanity and our safety depend
on it.

Often, I think of the term "political correctness" and its insinuation that respect for marginalized people is taken too far, or simply
asking too much. The term exists to validate the people who believe

"inconvenient" terminology or limited language options are some-how equally as oppressive as systemic, violent racism and misogyny.

I go to great lengths to avoid using and dignifying the term, which really ought to just be substituted with the words "basic respect for different people and lifestyles." Yet, I often see political correctness manifest in other ways—particularly in the condescension, dismissal, and blatant, misogynist rage that female expressions and opinions and political participation unfailingly attract. Political correctness is marketed as frustration with what can no longer be said in today's soft, coddled liberal utopia. But I understand it more as frustration, bitterness, and, yes, hypersensitivity in response to what now, today, *can* be said—by women and marginalized people.

Groups that have traditionally been expected to accept oppression and bigotry as inherent to existence, without a word of complaint or option for recourse, have become increasingly empowered to respond to their oppression, to speak up about how these bigoted comments make them feel about their experiences and demands for a just society. So often we hear about the importance of preserving free speech in the context of people with privilege no longer being able to say and propose awful, dehumanizing ideas, or tell cruel and bigoted jokes, or harass and abuse women, all without facing social and professional consequences. Yet, so rarely do we hear praise of a broad, mounting cultural shift toward inclusivity, thoughtfulness, respect, and safety.

After all, we often hear of liberal-leaning people of color living in coastal parts of the country being told they "live in bubbles" if they do not know everything about the lives of rural Trump voters (whose votes, for what it's worth, led to an administration that has denied many marginalized people full recognition of their humanity). But how often are rural Trump voters told they live in bubbles if they fail to empathize with, or know about the lives of, coastal people of color?

Needless to say, there is work to be done. But the progress we've seen in recent years, spearheaded by young women who risk it all to speak up and demand better treatment, is undeniable. It's also progress that oppressive male figures would like to ignore and deny, whether they're brushing us off as insincere social-justice warriors or "paid crisis actors" when we gather at protests. It's easier for powerful men to pretend that we, young women, lack for our own minds, our own opinions, our own growing political power, so they dismiss us as disingenuous dolls and caricatures. It's easier this way, because it's less scary. For them, it's comfortable to think of women as too weak-willed and simple to challenge their power—it's comfortable, and it's safe.

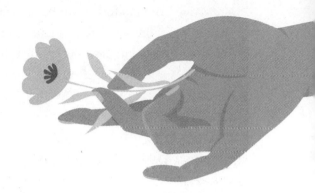

# 3

# The Right to Bear Anger

I spent most of the day in bed when Dr. Christine Blasey Ford and Brett Kavanaugh testified before the US Senate. Everyone everywhere was talking about it, and I knew that listening and being prompted to express opinions about what had just happened would exhaust me. I was exhausted.

The University of Southern California hardly has a reputation for being politically engaged. Yet, despite how the setting of this monumental cultural event was Capitol Hill, something about that day simply transcended politics. It seemed to pervade every sphere of human conversation, and it prompted every woman everywhere to defend the credibility of Dr. Ford as if we were defending our own. And that morning, I just knew I wouldn't be able to do so without my temper flaring up—only to then be brushed off for "overreacting," or God forbid, for being "crazy."

In a culture obsessed with gaslighting any woman who dares to point out problems with how she or other women are treated, aren't all of us who speak up and refuse to ignore injustice just "crazy"? In either case, that day simply wasn't a safe one for known, opinionated women to be out and about.

I believe Dr. Christine Blasey Ford, as I believe Kavanaugh's other accuser, Deborah Ramirez, and before them, Anita Hill, who testified before the Senate in 1991 that then-Supreme Court Justice nominee Clarence Thomas had exploited his power to sexually harass her. I believe each of these women, who had nothing to gain and everything to lose—including potentially their lives and loved ones—from coming forward. One in five American women has experienced sexual assault, according to the National Sexual Violence Resource Center, and that may be only as far as we know, considering an estimated 65 to 85 percent of sexual assaults are unreported.[1]

Low reporting rates are the byproduct of a culture of misogyny, violence, and compelled silence that is meant to keep us women and survivors in our place. We know what happens when we come forward: intimidation and harassment from law enforcement, skepticism and cynicism from those around us, and social ostracism and punishment from the mutual friends we may share with our attacker, who is, more often than not, someone we know and trust.

Before allegations against Kavanaugh became public, and even before Kavanaugh was nominated to join the court, the announcement of Justice Anthony Kennedy's retirement was a tragedy for American women, in itself. Despite Kennedy's mixed record on the court, he had consistently used his vote to uphold the precedent of *Roe v. Wade*. In contrast, President Trump and the Republican Party had explicitly stated their intention of stacking the judicial system with anti-choice actors to hack away or override *Roe* altogether, making it abundantly clear what Kennedy's retirement opened the door for.

American women knew whoever Trump nominated would be entrusted with the destruction of our rights, our autonomy, our access to public life in this country. That it would ultimately be Kavanaugh, a man with a record of violating and degrading women's bodies that allegedly spanned decades, added another dimension of cruelty to this reality.

So many of us saw ourselves in Dr. Ford, as we saw our attackers and oppressors and their complicit, male allies in Kavanaugh, President Trump, and their Republican cohort. We watched the hearings and thought of our lives and the worlds we had lived in when we were teenagers, as Dr. Ford and Kavanaugh had been at the time of the alleged assault. And we marveled at how much had changed and how much had stayed the same through all the time that had passed.

Republican politicians' responses to, as well as media coverage of, the abuse allegations against Kavanaugh comprised a master class in why the overwhelming majority of women and survivors do not come forward. Many of us make this choice not because the assault lacked trauma or impact, not because we're unconcerned with the women our assailants will likely go on to attack, but to protect ourselves and loved ones—and certainly, to dodge the humiliation and cruelty of having our own experiences and traumas explained to us by men.

Conversations like this can be especially agonizing and difficult with people we love and want more than anything to be able to trust. I'll never forget having to listen to my father's barrage of insensitive, politicized conspiracy theories tying Dr. Ford with

Democratic Party leadership and writing everything off as a farce. He didn't offer any consideration to the possibility of Kavanaugh's guilt, nor the implications this gruesome episode in political history would have on survivors like me, his daughter. And I blamed a rape culture and militant right-wing media for deluding so many men like him to a point of callous, venomous cruelty. The views my father held weren't isolated; rather, they seemed commonplace among men who are taught by right-wing media narratives to identify with accused abusers, to be adversarial and doubtful toward women, or risk someday becoming accused men, themselves.

Like my father, politicians accused Dr. Ford of lying, or as Senator Susan Collins suggested, not lying about being assaulted, but somehow mistakenly identifying Kavanaugh—as if women can't even be trusted to know the face of their rapist. Senator Orrin Hatch echoed that Dr. Ford, whom he referred to as "this woman," was simply "mixed up," while Senators Lindsey Graham and Dean Heller openly admitted that their minds were made up prior to hearing Ford's testimony. A media personality on Fox News notably commented that even if the events Ford described had transpired as she said, it was just the dismissible "horseplay" of teenage boys being teenage boys. Dr. Ford said she had been assaulted; she, in turn, was told she had not been, but also, maybe, that she had been, just not by Kavanaugh, but also, that even if the assault had happened, and Kavanaugh had been the assailant, it really didn't matter, anyway.

One in six men has experienced some form of sexual abuse;[2] men are quite literally more likely to experience, than to be falsely accused of, sexual assault, and substantially so. But given the opportunity, our institutions opt every time to ignore this truth, and instead advance the narrative that is more salient in marginalizing, dehumanizing, and demonizing women.

With the eyes of the world on her, and certainly, with the knowledge that the events of that morning would reverberate across generations, what Dr. Ford was subjected to was infuriating; she had every right to be outraged and give voice to that outrage. But it was not her testimony before the Senate that shocked the nation with its vivid expressions of fury—it was Kavanaugh's.

Kavanaugh's testimony comprised thunderous outbursts of anger, inappropriate references to partisan conspiracy theories, and pronounced disrespect for the Democratic women who questioned him. His rage appeared to stem from shock, disbelief, and, certainly, self-pity that, outrageously enough, women's voices were being taken somewhat seriously—that a woman could be the reason he, a white man from a wealthy family, might not get what he wanted.

Photos of Kavanaugh's face contorted in unrestrained anger quickly went viral on social media and drove a critical conversation about the role of identity in shaping how anger is perceived. A key question is posed by this dialogue: who is allowed to be angry, to express intense emotion, and still be taken seriously, even sympathized with? As the Senate hearings of Dr. Ford and Kavanaugh illustrated, white men are; women are not.

Of course, I say white men, specifically, because expressions of anger often aren't an option for men of color seeking rights and respect. Stereotypes of black and brown men as bestial, dangerous, and predatory would never permit them to behave like Kavanaugh did in a public place, let alone before the US Senate and the eyes of the nation.

White, patriarchal institutions strive to see the worst and detect violence and destructiveness and inhumanity in every breath men and boys of color take; this can often lead to deadly consequences, as seen in recurring episodes of extreme, racist police brutality and extrajudicial killings targeting black men and boys. The false rape charges against the notorious Central Park Five group, the lynching of the black child Emmett Till for allegedly whistling at a white woman, and, more recently, the police killings of twelve-year-old Tamir Rice and eighteen-year-old Michael Brown all stand as unsettling indicators of societal perceptions of black male existence as inherently dangerous and predatorial. It's difficult to imagine any of the aforementioned men behaving in a manner so expressively, colorfully, aggressively angry as Kavanaugh had, and surviving, let alone being appointed to public prestigious office. In contrast, white men are able to behave like Kavanaugh with no consequences because anger, threatening others, and causing those around them—especially women—to feel unsafe are seen as their birthright.

Kavanaugh's anger that a woman had the gall to challenge his word as a white man served as a broad reflection of the institution of white male entitlement. Men like him are allowed to be angry, because they are allowed to expect the world for themselves; that is, when they expect the world and everything they want without challenge, opposition, and accountability for their own behaviors, their anger arises as a natural, expected response when that isn't what happens.

President Trump responded to vocal, viscerally angry reactions of women who protested Kavanaugh's nomination by repeatedly referring to these women and survivors as "paid actors." By this point, I had been navigating the Trump era for some three years and loathed to dignify his ignorant and cruel words with my emotions. But I was helpless in the face of my own rage and despair: I seethed, I wept; I had been among these protesters, called to the streets by my experiences and empathy for others. The president's words, echoed by many of his supporters and leading Republican politicians, felt like a twist of the knife—the assertion by the most powerful man in the country that all of this was farce, that we, female protesters, lacked minds of our own, that our physical bodies and presence at these sites of political unrest were merely constructed and bankrolled by rich, liberal men seeking to get a rise out of Trump.

It's a notion that is inherently gendered, tied to the patriarchal idea that we women exist solely to perform for men, that our political activities and belief systems are entirely shaped and commanded by men in our lives, rather than our real experiences, our emotions, our rage. A leading argument against according women voting rights throughout American history was that suffrage would hardly change the political fabric of our nation, because women would just vote in line with their husbands—so what was the point?

President Trump's claim was as cruel as it was normal: the hyper-scrutiny to which the convictions of women, and especially young women, are subjected is, ultimately, common. Do women really care? Do we think, at all? We are so fundamentally lacking in the credibility and respect that white men are born with, that whether or not we are even capable of real, sincere rage has been reduced to a political question.

The sympathy Kavanaugh's rage-fueled performance received from Republican leadership and across the Republican Party reminded me of broad cultural sympathy for Trump voters and supporters: all the humanizing, gentle *New York Times* profiles; all the prime-time interviews; all of the attentive efforts to understand, as if these were not the people whose votes created inhumane immigration policies of family separation, created the white supremacist Charlottesville rally, created Kavanaugh and the existential threat he poses to women's human rights. The overarching narrative was that these men and women were the Real Americans, the ones whose rage and experiences and voices mattered, as opposed to the unsaid numbers of women, people of color, LGBTQ people, and urban Americans who live in poverty, the majority of whom voted for Hillary Clinton. These Real Americans had the clearance to be angry, to lash out and create unspeakable devastation for everyone else—and still deserve broad cultural sympathy.

Media fixation on white men, and lack of consideration into the lives and stories of literally anyone else, is written into the fabric of history. It shouldn't surprise us today—not when the pages of US history books fawn over the quaint, plucky stories of white colonists and settlers, with only passing references to the Native Americans they subjected to genocide, and tales of the strange, foreign countries the US military "liberated" and "democratized," lacking any truths about the regions we destabilized, the people and children we slaughtered.

In the aftermath of her 2016 loss to Donald Trump, Clinton was called upon by leading Democrats (including her primary rival, Bernie Sanders, whom she had bested) and Republicans alike to step aside and exit public life. Her public statements and speeches drew constant outrage, her criticisms of the atrocities and injustices of the Trump administration dismissed as "petty." Arguably more than any of us, Clinton of all people had the right to be angry and express anger with the state of American politics. But she didn't.

Expressions of anger only strip women of what little credibility we have, permitting men to dismiss us as too emotional, too sensitive, too unstable to be taken seriously; whatever we say in an angry tone goes unheard, the ravings of madwomen. Instead, Clinton retired quietly from politics for some time, popping up now and then to criticize the Trump administration's human-rights abuses, only for critics across the aisle to tell her to be silent, tell her that her time had passed and her bitterness and soreness hurt the Democratic party. Notably, the same commentary has yet to be lodged at former, unsuccessful, male presidential candidates who remain politically active.

Nonetheless, that Clinton had won the popular vote (and been the first woman to do so in US history); won the Democratic primary over Sanders, who faced no such similar demands for his silence despite having lost to her; and dedicated more than four decades of her life to public service and civil-rights advocacy made no difference in the court of public opinion. Still, she was asked to be silent and step aside for the next Democratic star, and certainly, in light of the ceaseless criticisms of the Democratic Party's reliance on "identity politics" for supporting her, a woman, "next Democratic star" was all but code word for charismatic white man.

The classic, mainstream explanation of what had empowered Trump to win the election is "economic anxiety," despite how the poorest demographic of Americans (black women) voted for Clinton at a rate of 94 percent; 53 percent of voters earning less than $30,000 per year voted for Clinton, compared to 41 percent for Trump; and 52 percent of voters who regarded the economy as their top concern voted for Clinton, compared to 42 percent for Trump.[3] Data journalists found Clinton spent more time speaking about her economic platform, which included wide-ranging and unifying economic proposals for affordable, accessible health care, housing, education, and job growth, than any other issue.[4]

Support for Trump was never about the economy, but white male frustration not unlike Kavanaugh's. That's because white male identity in America is intrinsically rooted in domination. And when this domination is challenged by strides toward equity, justice, inclusion, or, certainly, the accountability that Dr. Ford sought to deliver with her courageous testimony, white male rage is allowed, because it is expected.

The privileges that not only permit but ultimately empower white male expressions of rage have always dictated and set the standards of American politics. Almost a decade before Kavanaugh's testimony, one Rep. Joe Wilson of South Carolina in 2009 famously interrupted President Obama's speech before Congress about health-care reform to yell, "You lie!" The outburst is the sole memorable incident of Wilson's tenure in Congress and elucidates sharp racial divides in what behaviors male politicians and men in general feel entitled to perform, especially when juxtaposed with President Obama's eight years of quiet, reserved dignity.

Through eight years, Obama suffered endless strings of personal, racist attacks as America's first black president, but never once did his temper flare, never once did he punch down. Perhaps this is because that's just the sort of man he is—and perhaps, because he knew doing so would only further strip him of what credibility and respect he had, understanding how black men who express anger and rage are received. The simple truth is he could never do what Wilson had done to him and expect to peaceably stay in office.

White-male birthright to credibility and hegemony has accustomed men like Kavanaugh to power, such that equality and accountability feel like oppression and necessitate rage and backlash on their end. Their rage is a defense mechanism they believe can save them from societal progress that is slowly, steadily burying their way of life.

Gendered credibility is also a defining factor in which issues are taken seriously. Despite how we women comprise a narrow majority of the US population, issues pertaining to our rights and living standards are marginalized as tangential, fringe "women's issues," as if we are somehow separated from mainstream political discourse.

Surely, it is not a problem to recognize how certain issues disproportionately impact women's lives and, as such, are "women's issues." The problem instead lies in how we are led to understand these "women's issues" as somehow lesser, how we treat women's anger and passion and stakes in these issues as less relevant to politics than those that are falsely seen as nonwomen's issues. Women's anger is not taken seriously; the need for movements like Emma Watson's well-meaning HeForShe campaign, or Vice President Joe Biden's It's On Us campaign calling on men to actively fight violence against women, speak about how our movements, activism, livelihood, and, certainly, our anger are all but dismissed in the absence of male mouthpieces.

Many rural, white-male Trump voters may have lacked Kavanaugh's economic privilege and social capital, but at the very least, they grew up promised domination over women, people of color, and marginalized people. In the face of this promise, our success in America where they have struggled similarly feels like oppression, and similarly necessitates their rage and backlash. And we, women and marginalized people, are always, unfailingly the collateral damage of this white male rage and backlash.

A week after the Senate testimonies, Brett Kavanaugh was ultimately confirmed to the Supreme Court by the narrowest Senate vote in US history. His confirmation around the one-year anniversary of the #MeToo movement for justice for survivors purposefully sent a message to women and survivors that this world has not yet changed so much, that it remains ruthlessly governed by white men at the expense of everyone else. His confirmation reflected the trend, the direction we had been moving in for the past decade, delineated by the appointments and voting records of the likes of Justices Antonin Scalia, Samuel Alito, Clarence Thomas—all of whom have voted and argued in ways detrimental to women's human rights. Kavanaugh's confirmation felt like an accumulation of all of this—the nail in the coffin for women's rights in a country with nearly half of its states frothing at the mouth to ban abortion, hand-in-hand with the spectacle of Kavanaugh's confirmation hearings, which had served to put the credibility of all-American women and survivors on trial.

Republican politicians' enthusiastic approval of Kavanaugh asserted to women that, put simply, we do not matter; our lives, our experiences, our safety, our traumas do not matter. What matters to them is the affirmation of male hegemony, the power to dismantle women's most fundamental freedoms, the maintenance of white men's birthright to treat women however they want without consequences. All of this is of higher priority than our rights, dignity, and existence as women and survivors.

---

Sometimes, I think back to the day of Dr. Ford and Kavanaugh's testimonies and wonder why I chose to stay in bed. Was it really exhaustion or deliberate, calculated restraint? I vacillated between feeling heartbroken and demoralized, and irrevocably, implacably furious. But I am not Brett Kavanaugh; I do not have the privilege of being able to simultaneously express rage and be taken seriously, listened to, sympathized with.

Perhaps this might read strangely, coming from the author of a book of unrestrained, unfiltered rage directed at the oppressive, white, cis-hetero patriarchy, but I hold back my anger and emotions often, if not daily. And part of this, certainly, is about seeking respect in a patriarchal society—but the other part is the reality that emotional energy is not cheap, that engaging unproductive, hurtful conversations with people who come from a place of bad faith isn't worth the toll, the exhaustion, the heartache. Many people, and often people with malicious intentions, will take young women's self-identification as feminists as a direct invocation for debate and an invitation for aggressive, contrarian thought—this has certainly been my experience, whether it's men in my everyday life, or men in my emails and social media inboxes spewing their hatred, thirsting for an embittered, typical "feminazi" response. Their views and entitlement are maddening, frustrating, outrageous, even—but, I've found, simply not worth the labor that would come with taking the bait.

Tropes about militant, angry, man-hating young feminists have followed me around my entire life, the way they follow every young woman who vocally and publicly advocates for social justice. I knew if I left my apartment that day and engaged with the outside world, gave my rage and emotion half a chance to boil over, nothing I said would have been taken seriously, and I would feel even worse.

Women are taught early about the consequences of expressions of anger: We're called crazy or too emotional to be trusted, or we're simply dismissed altogether, and it's over. We don't get another chance. The manner in which we conduct ourselves is often the deciding factor in whether we have any prayer of a chance to be heard or believed.

And most dangerous of all, as we encountered in Dr. Ford's case, expressions of emotion by women rob us of fundamental, life-saving credibility.

When our words come from a place of emotion, we are immediately dismissed or discredited for being too hysterical to be objective or taken seriously. Yet, in contrast, when men like Kavanaugh or Trump speak from a place of emotion, they're regarded as real, authentic, and somehow even more believable.

It's hard to imagine Hillary Clinton swearing or shouting or violently gesticulating on the 2016 presidential campaign trail the way her rivals Bernie Sanders and Donald Trump did on a regular basis. Sanders and Trump, in their own ways, were recognized as uniquely genuine, candid and authentic, because they "told it like it is." In contrast, something tells me that if mainstream media took issue with Clinton not smiling widely enough at campaign stops, they might just as well take issue with her embracing the same angry and emotional expressiveness of her male candidates— expressiveness that allowed them to be perceived as honest and real.

It's no coincidence that lack of authenticity and trustworthiness were the most prevalent, bipartisan complaints lodged against Clinton, which certainly had to do with conceptions of powerful politicians as exclusively white and male, and anyone else as therefore inherently less credible. The pronounced double standards in how expressions of emotion are perceived across gendered lines carry profound political consequences.

The paradigm of an identity-based right to bear anger is a hard pill for women like me to swallow. Yet, it's one our oppressors expect us to swallow without a word of complaint, regardless.

In the summer of 2018, the Trump administration rolled out a family-separation program meant to deter illegal southern border crossings by kidnapping an average of forty-five children and babies from migrant parents[5] per day for several months. And not only were children and babies being kidnapped by the state, with no plans or means to ever reunite families, but they were also locked away in cages, or filed into inhumane outdoor camps subject to extreme weather conditions. The administration embraced a litany of other deeply cruel policies against migrants crossing the border, including denying asylum to women fleeing domestic violence and rape, often with young children in tow.

Migrants crossing the border to seek asylum—a notably very legal pursuit—were fleeing from, rather than perpetuating, violence. Many sought to save their children's lives from instability and violence extending directly from generations of US imperialism, intervention, and sabotage in Latin America. Put simply, the US government had made a policy of punishing brown people for trying to survive and protect their children from circumstances the United States had created.

It seems natural, then, to expect such abject cruelty and inhumanity to be met with rage and energized protest by decent Americans, lest we passively allow it to be normalized. Yet, when Trump administration officials were vehemently protested in public for their active choice to participate in this violently oppressive policy, protesters were met with bipartisan criticism and chastising, often from politicians and mainstream media alike. Representations of these protests by media or politicians were often void of any meaningful context into why they were happening, and soon, the purported, great evil of disturbing Homeland Security Secretary Kirstjen Nielson's dinner at a Mexican restaurant was somehow treated with more concern than the administration's policy of stealing and locking migrant babies in cages.

After experiencing a public disruption herself, Press Secretary Sarah Huckabee Sanders and her supporters went so far as to equate her experience with a civil-rights violation, as if her participation in the Trump administration and all its human rights atrocities, by extension, isn't a conscious and proactive choice. The victimization Trump administration officials gleefully cloaked themselves in reminded me of a typical response to accusations of racism or sexism—that is, a defensiveness and sense that those called racist or sexist have been wronged, rather than the actual victims of those individuals' racism and sexism. There is a persistent cultural tendency to be more angered and outraged by the words "racist" and "sexist," or being called those things, than with the actual acts of racism and sexism being committed. In a similar vein, there is an equally persistent cultural tendency to be more angered and outraged by methods of protest against bigotry and human-rights abuses than with the acts of bigotry and human-rights abuses themselves.

Protesters were primarily accused of incivility, rowdiness, and unpleasantness, despite how their only options in the face of this administration's racist terrors were to either speak up or look away and be quiet. The vast majority of Americans watching family separation unfold were not lawmakers, nor did they posses institutional power to change policy; the only power they had was protest. And if anything is uncivil—other than stealing and putting children in cages, that is—it's the choice to be quiet in the face of such abjectly cruel human rights abuses. In the context of a government regime separating families fleeing violence and certain death, the only thing "incivility" should refer to is the oppressive regime.

One particular criticism of the "incivility" of anti-Trump protesters from this time has stayed with me. A *Washington Post* editorial board denounced the protesters by suggesting that they look to purportedly peaceful anti-choice protesters, who, in this contrived fantasy world, evade disturbing the personal lives of women and abortion providers:

> *Those who are insisting that we are in a special moment justifying incivility should think for a moment how many Americans might find their own special moment. How hard is it to imagine, for example, people who strongly believe that abortion is murder deciding that judges or other officials who protect abortion rights should not be able to live peaceably with their families?*

At the time of the article's publication, George Tiller, the last late abortion provider in the state of Kansas, had not yet been dead of assassination by an anti-abortion activist for ten years. Violence, threats of violence, arson, and even attempted and completed murders of abortion providers are at a near all-time high in this country, ever since an anti-abortion group released fabricated and illegally obtained videos of Planned Parenthood doctors discussing "selling baby parts" a few short years prior to the *Post*'s editorial, in 2015. In fact, violence and harassment on the weekends, during which most clinics offer abortion services, are so routine that most clinics across the country recruit and train special volunteers called clinic escorts just to help patients safely enter the facilities.

Giving and receiving abortion care is inherently, fundamentally personal; protest of abortion care, even during "business hours," is in violation of the very moral code the "incivility" police claimed to hold sacred, and for a far viler reason. The act of receiving or administering a health-care service is in no way equivalent to separating families and locking up children as punishment for trying to survive. But it was complicit Republican lawmakers—often the same ones who evade their constituents' criticisms by never hosting town halls and are therefore only accessible via protests, in the first place—and not health-care providers who received the *Post*'s sympathy.

Certainly, violence has arisen among anti-Trump protesters, although it's often in protest of racism, unlike Trump supporters who routinely commit violence in the *name* of racism. And certainly, anti-Trump protests are loud and passionate and disturb the peace. But it's critical that we question the widespread expectation of docility, good behavior, and traditional respectability from communities who are routinely, systemically subjected to state-sanctioned trauma and oppression. There is a cruel, twisted sort of victim-blaming in demanding fully respectful conduct from groups that are so deeply oppressed by our institutions, or punishing and blaming them for the very cruelty to which they are subjected by the power systems in place.

Such is the nature of respectability politics—that we shame and criticize marginalized groups that are fighting for survival, if they fight in a way that disturbs or brings any measure of discomfort to powerful people. From the Black Lives Matter movement and its protest of horrific, racist policing and institutional violence, to the anti-fascist movement, better known as Antifa, to the pro-Palestine Boycott, Divestment, and Sanctions (BDS) movement, groups whose methods of protest stoke discomfort in privileged groups that benefit from existing power structures are unilaterally portrayed as radical and violent. And all of this is in no small part due to powerful people's ownership of the platforms and media companies that tell these stories to the public.

History is paved with a wide breadth of examples of this: the Black Power movement that called for radical, disruptive anti-racism activism; the suffragettes, who differed from suffragists taught in history class through their militancy and boldness, and often faced intervention and policing from law enforcement; the activists of the 1960s who made all of feminism's 1970s gains—abortion rights, Title IX, fair-pay legislation—possible. The afore-mentioned groups are often listed as footnotes in history textbooks, if listed at all, rather than noted and glorified at length like their quiet, comely, and often less productive counterparts.

Specific to Black Lives Matter, protests by mourning and justi-fiably outraged people of color who have experienced tremendous loss in their communities at the hands of the state are regularly portrayed as riots in the media and by law enforcement. In 2018, police went so far as to arrest Stevante Clark, the brother of an unarmed black man who was killed by police in his own grand-mother's backyard for the crime of holding an iPhone while black.

Stevante was arrested for using "threatening language" directed at police officers in the wake of his brother's death. Certainly, the right to bear anger isn't universally accessible to men across lines of race; rather, it is exclusively accessible to white men.

If critics of "uncivil" anti-Trump protesters are genuinely concerned about violence, rowdiness, and incivility and not simply annoyed that minority groups have the audacity to protest and demand better treatment, one would think they'd share in outrage at state-led violence and abuse, at police violence and appointments of alleged sexual abusers to the Supreme Court. One would think they'd be concerned with jarring rates of anti-abortion violence, or the reality that young black men are between nine and sixteen times more likely than any other group to be killed by police.[6] Certainly, one would think they would take issue with babies in cages.

Our collective obsession with the presentation and temperament of those who protest abuses of power exposes the power dynamics that govern who gets to be angry and emotional and still demand respect. And this obsession serves a distinct purpose within the white patriarchy: to devalue legitimate complaints and protests by marginalized people through excessively policing and nit-picking their methods. The right to bear anger is quintessential to white, male identity in America—all in the same breath that anger, passion, and emotion are disqualifying for members of marginalized groups who seek to participate in public life.

And yet, in recent years, I've watched the reclamation of women's anger become an increasingly salient topic in feminist discourse. The prevailing narrative around the empowerment that belies women's rage tends to be that angry women become motivated to run for office, and angry women—backed by countless angry women voters—win. We saw it first in 1992, the first Year of the Woman that saw the greatest number of women elected to

Congress following the Anita Hill hearings, and again in 2018, shortly after the confirmation of Brett Kavanaugh, and we'll likely continue to see it in the years to come.

However, the reclamation of women's rage isn't just an electrifying tool in electoral politics, or a trend in the voting behaviors of women. Rather, it necessarily starts on the ground, in communities of real, everyday women; it starts with each of us recognizing the validity and proportionality of our feelings and our frustrations and our anger, each of us finding the power to say how we feel without caring whether we'll be seen as crazy.

The anger of women is not like the anger of men; it is inherently political, inherently bound to social justice and hierarchy and gender power dynamics. It is a feat of defiance, an insistence that yes, we, too, can demand more, demand better; we can say this is not fair, this is not good enough, and we won't accept things the way they are.

Our anger is our assertion that we, like men, have a say in things. And no matter the ultimate outcome, the expression of our anger is transformative in itself.

# 4

# Love, Sex, and Juicy Peaches

When I was seventeen, I liked a boy who didn't like me. He was funny and light and didn't seem to care about anything, and I guess that's what I thought I needed at that age.

To say the least, I was disappointed my feelings weren't reciprocated. But I wasn't devastated. At the time I was much in the honeymoon phase of my relationship with feminism, so if there was one thing I knew, it was that male perceptions, approval, and general feelings toward me had no bearing on my identity and worth.

That said, I was still sad—being a feminist doesn't mean you aren't a human being subject to the full range of human emotions. It doesn't mean you have the supernatural ability to bend your emotions to align with your rational understandings of a situation.

That's just not how being a human works. His rejection also caused me to feel bad about myself, and that surprised me. I thought I knew better than to allow for male opinions to impact my perceptions of self, and I was disappointed that apparently, I really didn't.

What ultimately helped me feel better wasn't some transformative, uplifting feminist epiphany. And in all the years since, while my feminist values have helped me to cope with many of my most disappointing romantic losses and heartaches, I've coped with plenty more losses and heartaches the way anyone else would: wine, casual sexual relationships, rebounds, and more wine. (I can't stress enough how much being a feminist doesn't mean somehow transcending basic human needs—hence, wine.) Anyway, a friend of mine comforted me by explaining to me that not everyone likes peaches. I didn't understand the relevance at first, so she elaborated: "You could be the juiciest peach. But not everyone likes peaches."

It's not about you. It's not about them. It's not about how objectively wonderful you are. It's about different people wanting different things.

Hearing the analogy of the peach made me feel better at the time, but it's not as if this one wise, little metaphor made me henceforth immune to getting hurt, to internalizing feelings of not being good enough for someone. It's such an awful feeling, insufficiency, and what makes it worse is being consciously aware that you shouldn't feel it, knowing that just by existing you are enough—more than enough—and that another person's feelings or lack of them for you have no bearing whatsoever on just how enough you are.

Core to feminism is the unwavering recognition that beauty standards are a tool of the patriarchy, that everyone is beautiful, everyone is valuable, everyone is deserving of love, and in the context of heterosexual romance and attraction, attracting male desire isn't the ultimate prize in life. It isn't really much of a prize at all.

But that said, there are still plenty of young women who identify as feminists, are still forced to question everything about themselves in the face of rejection, and feel even worse because of their awareness that this is all just internalized misogyny at work.

Of course, it's not just rejection that's made me question myself in matters of love and sex. When you present yourself as a feminist, as opinionated and independent and strong, plenty of men take this as a green light to mistreat you. They'll sell it as a compliment: "You're strong," they'll say, so you don't need this, you don't need that, and you certainly don't need a supportive partner who's there for you.

To know rationally that you are above something but nonetheless feel as if you aren't is crushing. It's such a twisted, wicked cognitive dissonance—loathing misogyny but not being immune to practicing it on yourself; loathing to see other women feel bad in the face of male rejection, wishing for them to see how beautiful and worthy of love they are, all while you've felt the same way in countless, similar situations.

Often, this is the way I've perceived love, rejection, and the deeply nuanced experience of all of it as a young woman and a feminist. We know better, but we feel things, too; we know better, but sometimes knowing better makes things even harder.

———

Often when I think about male-constructed confusion and panic around consent, what it is, and whether and how to ask for it, I think about the details of a 2018 news report alleging comedian Aziz Ansari had repeatedly tried to coerce a date into having sex. By no means had Ansari been accused of rape or explicitly criminal behavior, as plenty of men wholly missing the point were so quick to condescendingly point out. But, on top of the fact that legality doesn't inherently equate to morality, the story was about so, so much more than that.

According to the report, Ansari's date reluctantly gave him oral sex several times after going home with him, but repeatedly offered verbal and nonverbal cues that she was not interested in sex and wanted to leave; nevertheless, Ansari persisted. Declining sex is never an invitation to be convinced to have sex, and there's simply no excuse for a grown man not to know this. Ansari's apparent ignorance, as well as his defenders' ignorance, show an alarming gap in knowledge about the fundamentals of consent—that it is freely and explicitly given on a case-by-case basis, can be withdrawn at any time, and ought to be reciprocal and enthusiastic.

At the time of this writing, among the twenty-four states (and the District Columbia) that require sexual-health education in public schools, just eight states require teaching about affirmative consent.[1] Across lines of sexual orientation and gender identity, the ability to know how to ask for consent and ensure that your partner feels comfortable could help broadly dismantle the global crisis of rape and sexual violence. At the very least, on an individual basis, it could help individuals feel safer and—a real concept, here—enjoy sex more.

While everyone across lines of gender identity and sexual orientation is endangered by a culture that trivializes and devalues consent, certain groups are more impacted and threatened by the risk of sexual violence than others. LGBTQ women are between 9 and 26 percent more likely than straight women to experience sexual violence, while LGBTQ men are more than twice as likely as straight men, according to research by the Human Rights Campaign.[2] Native American and black women and girls are more likely than any other groups to experience sexual violence.[3]

And when we fail to educate young people about consent, we feed a greater culture of male entitlement to women's bodies by teaching young men that sex is not something they have to ask for but can just feel entitled to. On top of suggesting that women's sexual desires— or lack of desires—don't even matter enough to inquire about, and likely diminishing women's enjoyment of sex as a result, women are also placed in abject danger by this culture of silent ignorance.

It should go without saying that broad cultural (and often male) ignorance about consent is inextricably bound to the devaluation of female sexual pleasure and desire. In the context of heterosexual sexuality, if men feel entitled to women's bodies and entitled to sex from women, it's highly unlikely they feel obligated to please or consider the needs and desires of their female partners too—which would in part explain the persistence of the gender orgasm gap. According to research published by the Natural Survey of Sexual Health and Behaviors in 2015, 91 percent of men said they experienced orgasm during their last sexual encounter, compared with 64 percent of women.[4]

To be sure, we've seen many critical strides toward inclusivity and equality in love and sex in recent years. In TV and film, we've seen greater representation of LGBTQ love stories; on the internet and in both women's and men's magazines, we've seen greater attention paid to how to improve women's sexual experiences. Yet, ultimately, the ongoing gender orgasm gap makes it clear the straight male experience remains upheld as a sacred priority.

It's not just that the male sexual experience is prioritized—the degradation of female sexuality, of the idea of female sexual pleasure itself, remains rampant in our politics and culture. In 2012, conservative political commentator and alleged human being Rush Limbaugh responded to feminist activist and lawyer Sandra Fluke's advocacy for birth-control coverage by calling her a prostitute. Fluke had cited her experiences in law school with female peers who paid exorbitant amounts of money to access safe, effective birth control, and another peer who was hospitalized due to a pregnancy that could have been prevented through birth-control access. Fluke notably never spoke once about any barriers to birth control access that she had faced in her own life.

"What does it say about the college co-ed [Sandra] Fluke, who goes before a congressional committee and essentially says that she must be paid to have sex, what does that make her?" Limbaugh said to his listeners. "It makes her a slut, right? It makes her a prostitute. She wants to be paid to have sex. She's having so much sex she can't afford the contraception. She wants you and me and the taxpayers to pay her to have sex."

Of course, for all Limbaugh's chastising of Fluke for supposedly having such an obscene amount of intercourse, he had nothing to say about the men who therefore must have been having sex with her.

Perhaps Limbaugh's comments were extreme, to say the least, but they're hardly out of touch with mainstream perceptions of birth-control costs, and misogyny-laced opposition to taxpayer funding for essential health care for women. Slut-shaming has always had a way of dressing itself as fiscal conservatism. Yet, it's quite difficult to pretend concerns about birth-control coverage are budgetary and unrelated to misogynist loathing of female sexuality, when universal cost-free access to IUDs (the most expensive and reliable form of hormonal birth control) would actually save the United States $12 billion in public health costs annually.[5]

I've been told it's far-fetched to associate the gender orgasm gap with broader themes in rape culture, but is it, really?

On the surface, who is more likely to experience orgasm may not seem like a political issue. Yet, who is accorded the clearance and privilege to enjoy something as commonplace yet profoundly, uniquely powerful as sex is perhaps the most revealing indicator of where social capital resides. Women are more than passive objects on a sexual marketplace for male consumers; their experience—and certainly, the quality of their experience—matters as much as their male partners'. For many people, sexual enjoyment is a natural and important part of life, despite the discomfort and skittishness that continue to govern the topic, and positive experiences with sex can be critical to achieving health and happiness for men and women alike. In contrast, when we ignore the wants, desires, comfort, and general experience of women during sex, not only are we advancing frustrating sexual inequality, but we also may be placing women in abject danger.

The devaluation of the female experience certainly curtails female sexual pleasure, but more than that, it can also curtail women's sexual autonomy and safety. As a result of societal emphasis on arbitrary expressions of consent amid hysterical, straight-male narratives about being "falsely accused," ensuring that women not just have consented but also are actually enjoying sex and fully reciprocating male sexual pleasure becomes secondary.

Speaking of rape culture and women's safety in heterosexual sexual encounters, a 2002 study revealed many sexually active college-age men self-report practicing behaviors that legally constitute rape and sexual assault, and continue to practice these behaviors on a regular basis as they evade accountability and confrontation.[6] The study found 120 out of 1,882 surveyed men self-reported acts meeting the legal definition of rape or attempted rape, and these same 120 men were collectively responsible for 1,225 acts of sexual violence, reflecting an alarming trend of repeat sexual offenders. For all the frequent, outraged invocations of #NotAllMen to counter critiques of rape culture, when actually exposed for the predatory behaviors they originally sought to deny, many men are quick to pivot to the age-old "boys will be boys" mantra in an attempt to normalize violence.

In many ways, these research findings are inextricably bound to the broad devaluation of the female experience in heterosexual sexual encounters: Even when women are violated and feel violated, they are socialized to not see the value of their experience, and therefore, not understand what happened as assault. In many cases, even women who do recognize their experience as assault ultimately think better of speaking up, or internally question whether they are even right to feel violated.

The marginalization of women's experience during sex ultimately permits harmful and abusive sexual behaviors from male partners. When we women are taught to internalize that only men's experience and enjoyment of sex matters, conversely, we're taught that our experience—including even our feelings of safety and comfort—do not.

That's not at all to say the burden of preventing assaults should depend on women being decisive and assertive, or that women should shoulder even an ounce of blame for the sexually predatory behaviors of men. Rather, it's past time we recognize the consequences of telling women their experience in sex and enjoyment of it is secondary to men's.

And if life, indeed, imitates art, real-world devaluation of female pleasure and safety should hardly come as a surprise: In mainstream cinema and television, and in most heterosexual pornography, female pleasure is tangential if it appears at all.

We already know about the gender orgasm gap, but in media, there also exists a gender oral-sex gap (which at least in part could help explain the former). In film, women are substantially more likely to be performing oral sex—and predominantly on men—than receiving it. In contrast, films that depict women receiving oral sex are disproportionately more likely than films depicting men receiving oral sex to receive NC-17 ratings, which could all but serve as a death sentence for viewership.

Female sexual pleasure or the female perspective in sexual encounters, in general, is just as difficult to come by. Often, I think of depictions of sex and sexual violence in the HBO series *Game of Thrones* as a stark example of this. Where naked female bodies are often used as props and sex objects, and rape and violence against women are excessively used as narrative devices in a twisted, reductive attempt to make female storylines more "interesting," sexual encounters prioritizing the female experience are a rarity. In the same season that multiple lead female characters were subjected to rape and sexual abuse, one episode in which Queen Daenerys Targaryen initiated a sexual encounter that centered around her desires as a woman cut out almost immediately after she asked her male partner to remove his clothes.

I also think of the *Fifty Shades* erotica trilogy, which repeatedly saw its male lead deliberately withhold orgasm from his female partner as a "sexy" form of punishment when she angered him.

And before all of this, Elana Levine's 2007 book, *Wallowing in Sex: The New Sexual Culture of 1970s American Television*, explores the rise of hypersexualized imagery in film and television in the 1970s. This is often associated positively and fondly with the increasingly feminist politics of the 1970s, which were the same decade that abortion and birth control for unmarried women became legal on the federal level, the same decade sexual violence and issues of campus sexual assault finally became culturally relevant. Yet, as Levine contends, the objectifying rather than empowering sexual imagery of women on screens seemed less about applauding the work of feminist activists and more about serving "as an antidote to concerns about the destabilizing effects of the women's movement," she wrote. In other words, depictions of sexuality in media have a long history of positioning women as objects, and catering to male ideals, perspectives, and desires.

In light of how tangential female sexual pleasure and safety are in media depictions of male-female sexual encounters, it should hardly come as a surprise that in 2016, Pornhub revealed the second most-viewed category among female audiences was gay porn. Surveyed women who consume gay porn have cited its general themes of sexual egalitarianism as attractive and enjoyable, where heterosexual porn frequently casts the female sexual experience as tangential and centers instead around male pleasure.

It matters whose experience is upheld as the priority in media representations of sex, which inform the sexual habits of media consumers en masse. Suffice to say, if schools offer sexual-health education programs at all, these programs seldom include lessons about how to engage in mutually pleasurable sexual encounters, meaning most people learn what they know from what they see and consume in media.

The erasure and censorship of female sexual pleasure in media mirror the cultural reality that female sexuality remains deeply taboo. If barriers to access female birth control aren't indicative enough of how uncomfortable society is with women engaging in casual sex, then, at the very least, we can look to studies of contrasting adolescent attitudes about sex across gendered lines. Shocking to no one, where young men are celebrated for sexual activity, young women are often ostracized or socially punished for the same behaviors; the marginalization of female sexuality starts early.

Certainly, people like Rush Limbaugh are saying the quiet part loud in their comparisons of women who engage in sex for pleasure rather than pregnancy as "sluts" and "prostitutes." But their views about women and sex are hardly relics of the past. We continue to exist within a persistent culture of institutionalized slut-shaming, which informs the policies of our lawmakers, the sex education we receive in schools, and the dangerously dismissive treatment of women in everyday sexual encounters.

And yet, women aren't just punished for having sex: they're punished for not having it too. More often than not, the Venn diagram of people who disdain female sexuality but also blame the actions of violent men on the women who don't indulge these men is a perfect circle.

Mass shooters are nearly all men, predominantly with records of domestic abuse, violence against women, or documented anger and resentment toward women who reject them. We often hear the term "violence against women" as if it's something that just naturally happens, rather than active decisions made predominantly by men to hurt women. And contrary to the relatively few media narratives that actually recognize gender constructs as playing a distinct role in mass violence, men are not biologically disposed to be violent; rather, they are socialized to view domination, violence and the ability to commit violence as intrinsically bound to male status, credibility, and identity.

In far too many cases, women are reduced to collateral damage within a culture of glorified hypermasculinity. Every year, more than fifty thousand women are killed by domestic violence and, in particular, by former or current male romantic partners.[7] In other words, a leading cause of early death among women is quite literally being killed for telling men "no."

In the aftermath of a 2018 attack in Toronto that saw a man who appeared to identify with the hateful, anti-women "incel" (involuntary celibate) movement bulldoze a crowd with his truck, conservative thinkers published articles suggesting the "redistribution" of sex, implying inherent male entitlement to sex and women's bodies.

Other op-eds published in mainstream outlets like the *New York Times* even argued for government-funded sex robots. (I wonder what they'd think of government-funded birth control?).

The underlying message of such arguments is that mass, male violence can be indirectly blamed on women not having sex with them. Certainly, such was the line of thinking employed by Elliot Rodger, the young man and original incel who killed seven people in a 2014 shooting at UC Santa Barbara because women didn't date or sleep with him. In some cases, Rodger had been rejected, but in most cases, those around him say he hadn't even approached women at all, yet felt entitled to sex and affection from them without any effort on his part.

Of course, if mass gun violence by male domestic abusers should be blamed on anyone, other than, of course, the men who make the independent decision to harm others, it should be blamed on Republican lawmakers who have stalled common sense gun-control efforts for decades. We should absolutely understand government failure to implement reformed gun laws that protect women as a fundamental issue pertaining to money in politics, due to the power of the gun lobby. But we should also understand this failure in the context of its misogynistic consequences: in the absence of laws that keep guns out of domestic abusers' hands, women die— often for rejecting men.

If domestic abusers lacked legal access to firearms, not all but certainly many of the mass shootings in recent years could have been prevented—and so, too, could many of the murders of women in abusive relationships. Failure to take life-saving action on gun control is misogyny, and the ultimate embodiment of societal devaluation of women's bodies, free will, and, yes, women's sexuality.

In 2018, Walmart announced it would no longer sell *Cosmopolitan* magazines at checkout stands, citing the #MeToo movement as it rejected the magazine's sexualized content. Of course, that's the way of slut-shaming, to take benign and often patronizing action in order to survive in 2019.

*Cosmopolitan* is, historically, one of the first publications to recognize and celebrate female sexuality and sexual autonomy, through offering advice and education about sexual health, the female orgasm, and female sexual pleasure, as well as women's perspectives on how to lead balanced lives, in general. Certainly, much of the magazine's earlier content has not stood the test of time, as is the case with nearly all feminist publications. Previous issues have idealized thinness and other regressive ideals for women, or focused on teaching women how to sexually please men, rather than vice-versa. Yet, nonetheless, in contrast with Walmart's citation of #MeToo to criticize the magazine, the modern *Cosmo* has often offered a healthy framework to carry out the #MeToo movement's vision: It offers career advice to help more women find their place in power, where they are substantially less likely than men to exploit and abuse subordinates. And it offers women-centered sex and relationship advice to give women necessary authority over their bodies and how they are treated.

*Cosmopolitan* recognizes sexuality and intimacy as a contentious and deeply important battleground for women's liberation. The magazine recognizes women as fundamentally worthy of the same clearance men have always had to live nuanced lives of sex, ambition, professional success, friendship, and fun. It recognizes the many-sidedness and intrinsic value of the female experience in sex as in public life.

Walmart's co-opting of feminist language to erase and stigmatize *Cosmo* shows enduring puritanical attitudes about women and sex, and the persistence of a culture of slut-shaming and marginalizing female sexuality. Perhaps, all things considered, *Cosmo* is just a magazine, and Walmart is just a store, and there are greater, more important frontiers for the ongoing war for gender equality and women's liberation. But gender equality is political, which therefore mandates that it is also deeply, fundamentally personal. The liberation of women must take place from the skin in to take place from the skin out; it must take place on Capitol Hill and in workplaces, as it must take place in households and, certainly, in bedrooms.

---

In the way many, often more dated, romantic comedies so often do, *Think Like a Man*, based off comedian and entrepreneur Steve Harvey's even more dated dating guide for women, relied on some of the most pernicious assumptions of gender essentialism. That is, certainly in the context of heterosexual relationships, men are predisposed to want certain things, and women are predisposed to want other, very different things, and we can somehow "crack the code" of dating through generalized stereotyping about what each gender wants by nature.

Through these essentialist generalizations, we encounter a number of everyday gender tropes about love and sex, including but not limited to men thirsting after promiscuity and meaningless sexual encounters, and women being perpetually on the hunt to ensnare poor, unwitting men into relationships. In addition to being reductive, condescending, and often inaccurate, generalizations like this enforce heteronormativity and the erasure of LGBTQ identity from necessary, nuanced dialogue about what healthy love and sex mean for people who do not conform to the rigid narrative standards of the cisgender, heterosexual patriarchy.

Stereotypes of sex and relationships often run along racial lines. The bodies of women of color, for example, are often fetishized, such that black and Latinx women tend to be hypersexualized and scrutinized for their sexual decisions, while Asian women are reductively understood in mainstream Western culture as exotic, submissive sex objects.

Historically, notions of nonwhite women as inherently more likely to be sexual and promiscuous have helped inform US immigration laws, creating heightened scrutiny around the parentage of children whom US male citizens father abroad with noncitizen women in nonwhite countries, as well as additional barriers for these children to be recognized as US citizens. In 2001, the Supreme Court ruled in favor of sections of the Immigration and Nationality Act of 1952, codified in the United States Code, in *Nguyen v. Immigration and Naturalization Service*, and permitted higher standards and more stringent timelines for women in foreign, nonwhite countries to prove the father of their child had been an American citizen rather than some other foreign man. The Immigration and Nationality Act itself and its explicit provisions regarding fatherhood and procreating with foreign, nonwhite women ultimately seem less about establishing a code for responsible citizenship and more about protecting white American men from being swindled by deceitful, promiscuous foreign women.

Men of color are also subjected to categorically racist understandings of their sexuality, with Asian men often stereotyped as sexless, docile, and boring, while black and Latinx men are stereotyped as being predisposed to sexually predatory behaviors. Meanwhile, white-male privilege and perceptions of white men as inherently more respectable and credible consistently advantage or absolve white men accused of sexual violence. In contrast, there is a long, extensive history of white women successfully falsely accusing black and brown men of rape and sexual violence, contributing to dehumanizing tropes of black and brown men as bestial, sexualized, and dangerous creatures.

From the presidential campaign trail to the White House, Donald Trump and his supporters have played a decisive role in advancing racist narratives centered around imagined differentials in male violence and sexuality across racial lines.

The president, himself accused by almost two dozen women of sexual misconduct, has consistently used his platform and influence to defend white men in his administration alleged to have commit acts of sexual violence, and simultaneously attack their accusers. Among the allegedly abusive white men who served his presidential campaign or administration are Corey Lewandowski, Trump's former campaign manager; Steve Bannon, Trump's former White House chief adviser; Rob Porter, a former White House secretary; David Sorensen, a former White House speechwriter; and Andy Puzder, a former labor secretary nominee. Yet, despite these unprecedented numbers of men involved in Trump's campaign or administration publicly outed as abusers, xenophobic and racist policies meant to shut out nonwhite people from entering the country are nearly always justified through invocations of imagined, bestial brown rapists crossing the border to plunder white women and girls.

Of course, identity-based essentialism in love and sex isn't always so nakedly political. We also encounter it in condescending everyday gender tropes:

- Women will only feel fully satisfied with their lives upon getting married and experiencing pregnancy and birthing and raising children.

- Unlike men, they can't "have it all" and will have to cheerfully make sacrifices in their careers and social lives to be adequate mothers and housewives.

- These sacrifices are more than worth it in order to fulfill their existential purpose as women.

And we young women often shoulder the brunt of this. Whenever we express doubt about wanting to marry or have children, our often carefully considered answers are dismissed by the common response "Don't worry, you'll change your mind in a few years."

Women remain generalized as warm, dutiful nurturers, happy to make any sacrifice necessary for their husband or children; if not, they're reviled as selfish and cruel. The enforced binary around who is naturally predisposed to domesticity has deep political and economic implications, contributing to professional environments unfavorable to supporting female labor, despite a growing trend of female breadwinners in heterosexual-parented households. According to data from 2018, an estimated 40 percent of women are the primary earners in their households,[8] but the wage gap has persisted at roughly the same rate. Despite their breadwinner status, women remain professionally penalized, either due to suspicions that they'll eventually have children, or due to the fact that they already have children. Many employers and supervisors assume childbearing responsibilities fall solely on the mother, and this single-gender burden will entirely prohibit women with children from being functional employees.

In contrast, male employees, too, could have children at any time, or could already be fathers; but the assumption is that there is some woman, somewhere, carrying this burden for them, that having children necessarily turns a woman's world upside down without causing so much as a ripple in a man's. Many women are increasingly breaking the patriarchal tradition of staying home and focusing on the family, and despite how families are increasingly relying on women to be breadwinners, women remain punished by gendered expectations in the workplace all the same.

Despite the persistent stigma around working motherhood, many American mothers, and certainly, single mothers, simply lack the privilege of being able to stay at home—not with this country's archaic policies around family leave. Single mothers especially shoulder the brunt of cultural disapproval, with Republican politicians like former Louisiana Governor Bobby Jindal and Vice President Mike Pence happy to blame any given crisis, from mass shootings to poverty, on "incomplete" families.

In either case, speaking of skewed, gendered understandings of who is responsible for child care and domestic duties, plenty of tropes in turn govern our notions of what straight men want in dating and mating. Look no further than mainstream sitcoms like CBS's *How I Met Your Mother* or the 1990s classic *Friends*. The trope of the playboy with the secret heart of gold is all but timeless. Of course, before said playboy eventually meets the woman willing to invest the tireless emotional energy to change him, it should speak volumes that we, audience members, are supposed to laugh off and easily forgive all of his sexist behavior before meeting her; it should speak volumes that storylines involving men hurting, misleading, using, and arguably even abusing women are often meant to embody comedic plot points, all while the female characters hurt by these men are reduced to props for male character development.

But ultimately, that's just how low societal expectations and standards for straight men are. We're so thoroughly conditioned to understand all men as inherently relationship-averse that young, straight women merely seeking casual sex are forced to walk on eggshells, lest we come off as trying to trick men into entering committed relationships that we, as women, so naturally, desperately

rely on for fulfillment. Of course, women aren't the only ones neg-
atively impacted by this type of stereotyping: men who do seek
long-term, emotionally fulfilling relationships are often categorically understood as less masculine, or even less attractive for having
fewer sexual partners.

Our often intuitively low standards for men feed what a gender
studies professor of mine so aptly called the "low-bar Jesus" effect.
When men do the bare minimum, or perform tasks and behaviors
traditionally assigned to women, they're often celebrated disproportionately. In the case of my gender studies professor, she recalled
PTA mothers at her child's school seeming to worship the fathers of
their children for taking on a proactive parental role traditionally
associated with mothers. When she would occasionally encounter
these PTA mothers at important school events, some would refer to
my professor as a "unicorn," saying they hadn't been sure whether
she was actually real, they so rarely saw her. Certainly, they didn't
refer to all the fathers they rarely—if ever—saw as "unicorns"; they
just accepted it as normal that fathers were less involved in their
children's lives.

When men do basic things like make remotely feminist or
progressive comments, ask their dates questions about their lives,
express receptiveness to commitment, or share in some child care
and domestic responsibilities, we're so unaccustomed to this, so
accustomed to shrugging off or dismissing awful behaviors as "boys
being boys" or "men being men," that it becomes easy for a vaguely
decent man to come off as, well, Jesus. I'm not saying there are
quick fixes to this—just that hopefully someday, we can all collectively think twice before falling immediately for the next man or
person who replies to our texts within five minutes.

Our collective low societal standards for good men and male partners have made a number of everyday, unexceptional behaviors by men oddly endearing, and this certainly includes the ongoing love affair between women on the internet and photos of men spotted purchasing tampons and menstrual hygiene products for their partners at their local drugstore. And despite my reluctance to celebrate small, everyday actions of men, even I can appreciate a man who's comfortable being seen in public with menstrual products.

The stigmatization of menstruation can often pose a silent, unsaid strain on heterosexual relationships, as broad cultural discomfort and disgust with periods mean few cisgender men think to educate themselves about menstruation's physical and often emotional impact on women. Instead, when men do refer to or acknowledge female partners' periods, it's often in a derogatory, insensitive, and stigmatizing manner that often leads to women being unsupported in their experience, or overtly shamed for their hormones and emotions.

Menstruation and the attitudes and ignorance that surround it are perhaps the most apt example of the personal as the political. From discriminatory content-moderation bans that prohibit period imagery and representation on most social media platforms, to the ongoing struggles of male politicians to so much as say the word "period," stigma around menstruation carries a steep price—and it's a price that unsurprisingly women, often without the emotional support of their male partners, are the ones paying.

Having a period is challenging in itself, but external conditions such as affordability and access to menstrual products only make things worse. And we have disproportionately male lawmakers, who comprise 75 percent of state legislatures, to thank for that.

There is a long, extensive history of male politicians on nearly every level of government being unable to talk or hear about periods, while simultaneously using their power to uphold state-level "luxury" taxation of menstrual hygiene products that are essential to women's and girls' survival. In 2012, a female Michigan state lawmaker was silenced from speaking on the House floor for saying the word "vagina." Notably, in 2015, when then-candidate Trump claimed Fox News's Megyn Kelly had been on her period when she asked him adversarial questions while moderating a Republican presidential debate, he said she had "blood coming out of her … wherever," and appeared unable to say the word "vagina," despite once being very forthright in encouraging famous men to "grab" women "by the pussy" in the notorious 2005 *Access Hollywood* tapes.

Nonetheless, despite this discomfort with talking or hearing about women's bodies, male lawmakers in Wisconsin, California, Illinois, Colorado, Utah, and other states have led opposition efforts against bills introduced by female lawmakers to strike the tampon tax, which is a luxury tax imposed on female hygiene products that include pads and tampons in most states. The tampon tax is so prevalent that as late as 2019, only twelve states had successfully repealed it, all while hygiene and health products that have traditionally been gendered male, such as men's razors and Viagra, are not subject to this luxury tax.

It should go without saying that menstruation is neither luxury nor even choice, and access to appropriate hygiene products can dictate women's and girls' health, safety, and ability to participate in public life. The inability to afford hygiene products not only strips people who menstruate of equal dignity but could also amount to so much physical and mental discomfort as to preclude them from going to school or work and to subsequently contribute to gender-achievement gaps as early as elementary school. In extreme cases, lack of access to menstrual products can lead to cervical cancer and infections; this has certainly been the case among many women in developing countries, and in prisons and homeless communities in the United States.

The traditional argument among male lawmakers to reject anti-tampon tax bills is that the tax is so insignificant as to have no bearing on whether someone can afford menstrual hygiene products. But to the contrary, these same lawmakers—including the self-identified pro-choice Democratic Governor Jerry Brown of California—also cite the importance of maintaining the tampon tax to bring in the tremendous revenue that it delivers.

The tampon tax often makes menstrual hygiene products inaccessible to low-income people. This is certainly true in prisons, where incarcerated people earn far below minimum wage, with some earning $0.75 or less per day,[9] and where costs range from $2.63 for twenty-four pads to $4.00 for eight tampons, as of 2019.[10] Across the country, girls miss school because of their periods and lack of access to menstrual hygiene products, and research has shown many American women on SNAP benefits skip meals to pay the "luxury" sales tax on tampons.

The tampon tax and repeated, male-led efforts to maintain the tax comprise a fundamental issue of political representation, and how the disparate legislative authority of male politicians harms women and girls. In Utah, the state's all-male House Revenue and Taxation Committee vetoed a female state representative's proposal to eliminate the tampon tax from even moving out of committee in 2016.

But a deeper problem, even, than male politicians' refusal to acknowledge how profoundly menstruation impacts women's lives, is their discomfort with hearing about it at all. Stigma around menstruation remains so prevalent within patriarchal culture, and not just among male politicians but also among nearly all men, that most can't even engage in basic conversation or stomach hearing about women's genitalia and reproductive systems—all while making these most fundamental decisions about our bodies and lives.

When it comes to menstrual stigma, women, again, are the ones who pay the price—that is, not just in the form of the tampon tax but also in hindrances in our social experiences. Notions and stereotypes of the crazy, unhinged menstruating lady can hold women back in our professional lives, as employers weigh whether a young woman of reproductive age might be "too emotional," and also in our general day-to-day interactions, friendships, and relationships. This stereotype is the product of persistent menstrual stigma and broad unwillingness to dig deeper and learn more about women's experiences with periods beyond reductive, sexist tropes.

Periods are hardly the sexiest topic of discussion for women with male partners. Yet, discussing menstruation might just be the most important and revealing conversation women could possibly have with their male partners—the earlier on, the better—in order to gauge whether a partner is supportive enough to be worth pursuing a relationship with, at all.

---

This essay started on a personal note, then somehow, cycled its way through discussions of porn consumption habits, mass shootings, Jesus Christ, and the politics of menstruation. Which … sounds about right—I've never been great at talking about my own life, and I've always struggled to recognize and unpack the value and lessons and significance of my lived experiences. Yet, those experiences are core to my identity and worldview, and certainly, my conceptions of love and sex as a young woman and a feminist.

That said, my experiences are necessarily shaped and limited by my identity, too, as a young, able-bodied, cisgender woman who has primarily engaged in sexual and romantic relationships with men. I can't state enough the necessity of reading perspectives, meditations, and cultural criticisms written by people with far more diverse and traditionally marginalized experiences. Here, I can really only speak at length about my own relatively narrow range of experiences.

I grew up offering minimal consideration to the role of race in dating and mating, mostly because my community was so homogeneous. I was unprepared for a future in more diverse settings that has so often involved analyzing and disentangling nearly all of my interactions and relationships with non-Asian and especially white men, picking apart their racial dating histories and wondering their intentions, what they liked about me, if they were aware of just how little they would always understand about me and my life as a woman of color. It seemed uncomplicated at first; in the community in which I'd grown up, there were plenty of things I worried about where sexual or romantic relationships were concerned. But because of the racial homogeneity I'd grown so accustomed to, racist fetishization of me as an Asian American woman simply hadn't been one of those concerns.

In other words, as a teenager, I knew little else about love and sex and relationships beyond that I liked boys who were funny and smart and social, and I occasionally suppressed feelings for girls who were pretty and thoughtful and kind. But thoughts about love and racial identity evaded my consciousness until I moved to Los Angeles for college, and the wide-ranging, identity-based diversity that surrounded me quickly became a welcome and essential part of my life.

Not unlike many other young women, I had started college with a weight on my shoulders. My first full sexual encounter a couple years earlier had been an assault. I had been coerced into sexual acts by someone I had trusted, cared about deeply, emotionally relied on. The betrayal stung, especially as I simultaneously grappled with depression and the anxieties typical of any young, female student in an academically competitive high school environment.

I rationalized and justified his treatment of me and continued to see him, forcing myself to brush off what he'd done simply because it was easier that way. It was so much easier that way; nothing at the time seemed more difficult than being without him, however much he had hurt and violated and traumatized me. Besides, it was so much easier, infinitely easier, to be dismissive of my own feelings and trauma, than to look in the mirror and reconcile myself with the feeling of being damaged.

The relationship had been complicated by a number of other factors—namely, that it hadn't been a relationship, that the friendship and affection we'd shared prior to becoming physical with each other vanished almost at once in the aftermath of that first encounter, when neither of us knew how to speak about what had happened. As a result, it didn't take long for me to internalize that my only value to him—and my only value, generally—was sex and the submission of my body; as I write this, it's taken years for me to even begin to shed this mindset.

Despite my willingness to stay with and give in to him, the first time he violated me was not the last. But he took to apologizing and blaming me with cruel, consummate mastery on those occasions in which I was able to express that I felt hurt. Ultimately, as our arrangement dragged on, I never found it in me to end things—that was his choice, and it simultaneously devastated and spared me.

In the fall of 2018, I thought about him for the first time in a while when allegations of sexual assault against Trump's then–Supreme Court nominee Brett Kavanaugh came to light. On September 26, 2018, Dr. Christine Blasey Ford testified before the US Senate that Kavanaugh had assaulted and attempted to rape her when they were teenagers.

Kavanaugh insisted that he had no memory of any such incident ever taking place. And his insistence stuck with me; a small part of me almost believed him. Yet, if this were the reality, then it was even more devastating for the message that it sent: what men subject women to—the lifelong trauma that can stay with a woman forever—can often be so meaningless and forgettable to the male perpetrator that they could forget it ever happened. That is how dismissible the female experience so often is in the eyes of men— that Dr. Ford could be scarred for decades, while Kavanaugh could potentially have no memory of ever even hurting someone.

I struggled to find the strength to watch the hearings, but I read about them. And I wondered if my own Kavanaugh remembered hurting me.

The end of that first physical relationship merely served as a fraught beginning in the construction of my sexual identity. My devoutly Christian mother's discovery of a pregnancy test in a trash bin in my bedroom marked another beginning in itself—the beginning of tough, emotionally laborious conversations about my health, my values, and my identity as a young woman, to an older woman who had lived a completely different life than mine. And when the persistence of day-to-day sexual harassment I experienced eventually demanded the involvement of both of my parents, I found myself forced to engage in less revealing but equally exhausting conversations with my father, a rigid man of tradition and not-quite-forward-looking views on gender.

I felt isolated in my sexuality at this stage in my life; I lacked female friends who shared similar sexual experiences, and my two older sisters seemed to maintain my mother's staunch religious views and rejection of premarital sex. My quest to heal and recover a sense of self after what had happened to me was inevitably a lonely one. Even as other conditions in my life outside the context of my sexuality improved—as I discovered and became active in feminist work, improved my relationships with my parents, and excelled in school—for a long time, my conceptions of my sexuality remained stunted by the physical and mental traumas of that first sexual relationship.

Almost immediately after the breakdown of that first relationship, I continued to engage in emotionless sexual encounters—not out of desire, but because I wanted to know that after what happened to me, I was still capable of having "normal" sex. I went to great lengths to avoid any sort of self-reflection about the impact sexual violence had had on my life, opting instead to bury myself in work and books and casual, thoughtless encounters. It was simply too difficult for me to accept that any part of me had been damaged by what I'd endured, and my refusal to accept this ensured that unresolved traumas stayed unresolved and unexplored for years.

Within two months of starting college, I was surprised to find myself deeply emotionally committed to someone, following what had begun as a casual physical relationship. My feelings for my partner at the time materialized almost out of thin air. I thought about him when I wasn't with him. I wondered what he'd think of ideas I'd encountered in books and articles I read. As the events of my day unfolded, I thought about how I would describe them to him, and when I wasn't with him, more than almost anything, I wanted to be.

Physically, mentally, and emotionally, our relationship marked a deep departure from anything I'd ever experienced before. Often, I found myself feeling wistful and regretful, as the joy I felt with him made me realize all that I had settled for and all that I had subjected myself to before him, because my experiences with sexual violence had made me skeptical that love was possible for me. For the first time, it felt like I was with someone because I wanted him and he wanted me, not just because he knew he could have me, not just because I was too broken to say no. And for the first time, I was compelled to become a more introspective person, as I sought to learn what I could give and what I could feel beyond the confines of my long self-imposed, compensatory sexual behaviors.

Suffice to say, the relationship ultimately didn't work out for reasons that could be the subject of another essay entirely. But it opened my mind to what was possible if I had the courage to be vulnerable and if I had the courage to ask myself questions I'd long avoided asking.

The truth is that I'd spent years punishing and resenting myself because I felt I was to blame for what I experienced when I was sixteen. No single experience is universal, and many, if not most, people who survive sexual violence find means to recover that don't include dating someone. But that was my experience. Rediscovering the ability to feel—to be hurt, to be insecure, to care about someone—marked a milestone after a long period of desensitization. For a little while during and after the relationship, I felt guilt and shame that for all my staunch feminist convictions, I had ultimately needed a relationship with a man to feel better about myself. But I knew it wasn't that simple. I knew I'd wasted enough of my life punishing myself for being human. Once again, I had the choice to either continue punishing myself or accept and embrace healing; this time around, I chose the latter.

That said, this relationship had been unhealthy in its own way, and as I write this, much work remains to be done in determining my needs and preferences in love and sex. But the relationship opened the floodgates. It taught me to trust—not necessarily men, but myself. I was capable of doing all the things I once thought were impossible for me. All I had to do was trust myself and be vulnerable.

And when those floodgates opened, boy, did they open. I've become self-reflective, arguably to a fault; I vacillate between spiraling headfirst into deeply emotional relationships and feeling terrified of them. There is no method nor neatness to what I want at any given time; sometimes that scares me, sometimes that excites me, and sometimes I'm at peace with it. It's all part of being human.

Sometimes I think about the many good men I've interacted with, befriended, or had relationships with, and I'm constantly shocked by how little they—good, nice men—know. I'm constantly shocked by how little even the most well-meaning men understand about gender violence, and I'm constantly shocked by how surprised good men are to learn how terrible many other men are. With some men, it feels right to engage in those difficult conversations, to take a leap of faith and give someone a piece of myself. And with other men, it feels right to walk away.

At times I also think about the perceptions of my character and self that may precede any first meeting with someone. Sexual harassment and hypersexualized notions of me have always felt like a fact of life since I was a teenager, at least partially due to the years I spent embracing promiscuity as a personal means to deal with trauma. Imagined or not, I've always walked around with the feeling that, as a starting point, I am regarded as a sex object. Perhaps in some cases I'm right about this perception of me; plenty of other times, I've happily been proven wrong.

And, of course, being a proud and very public feminist can further obfuscate things. It's all part of the notion referenced at the beginning of this chapter, that strong women can handle themselves and certainly handle neglectful, unsupportive partners, therefore excusing a lack of effort from their partners. To be sure, all women have different needs and priorities, none of which make any woman stronger than another. But the bottom line remains that arbitrary perceptions of feminist women as strong don't somehow make it OK to be a bad partner.

I used to be restrained by fear of these potential characterizations of me, fear of not knowing how anyone really feels about me, or what anyone really thinks of me. But with the passage of time, I've learned that there is power in opening oneself to be surprised, just as there is power in opening oneself to potentially be hurt. As women, we are more than our fears. There is unspeakable power in being vulnerable, taking the occasional leap of faith, and knowing that if we do get hurt, we will ultimately be OK.

# 5

# The War on Girls

I've always considered empathy to be a central, driving force of the feminist movement and understood young women's ceaseless capacity for empathy as a reason so many of us engage in feminism in a litany of personal and political ways in our daily lives. Sitting next to each other on trains, or walking with each other on isolated streets, when we see other young women being subjected to public harassment or stalking; sharing our not-so-cheap menstrual hygiene products with each other whenever the need arises; banding together at rallies and marches for social-justice causes; affirming and speaking up for each other in contentious spaces—the annoyances and struggles and frustrations shouldered by other women around us may have little immediate bearing on our own lives. But we put ourselves in those spaces and offer our time, emotion, and physical presence to other young women like us nonetheless, because we know how it feels and we care.

In a similar vein, today, many young feminists fight as allies for social-justice issues that may not always directly impact us. Of course, "young feminists" is a broad categorization, and many of us are women of color, members of the LGBTQ community, low-income, immigrants, or otherwise marginalized outside the parameters of female identification, and in such cases, our participation in fights along lines of race, LGBTQ identity, or class can carry direct implications for our own lives. But ultimately, young women are the bodies at rallies, or the voices on social media, or the voters at the polls, who are most consistently dedicated to promoting intersectional constructions of social justice in society, not just for ourselves but for others.

As a result, young women are frequently derided for caring too much, and our activism as allies for a wide range of identity-based issues is spun as a performative game we play out of boredom because we, as women and girls, are supposedly no longer oppressed, ourselves. But this notion—that today's young women are the first generation privileged with living in a postgender world—could hardly be further from the truth. Today, a wide range of legislative policies and cultural attitudes interact to permit continued, institutionalized violence on young women's bodies.

We fight for many issues that may not always directly impact us, but to be certain, many, many issues do. And our empathy and caring for others should not be weaponized to erase that reality.

Sexual violence and, specifically, campus sexual assault, comprise one of these many, interconnected issues, such that even if a young woman isn't among the one in five who experiences sexual assault, the threat and fear of violence shapes nearly every aspect of their day-to-day lives. The sheer amount of mental and emotional energy young women must pour into taking any number of precautions to be safe—walking in groups, avoiding public transportation in the evenings, ensuring someone knows where they are at any time of the day—is as much meant to protect against violence as it is to protect against blame for the violence.

As a teenager, I didn't speak of, let alone report, my own experiences with sexual violence to anyone. I'd seen what had happened when I attempted to report a male peer for sexually harassing me online, only to be asked by my school's principal what I had been wearing and what I had done to provoke such treatment. I didn't trust that anything would happen as a result of reporting the violence I'd faced, nor did I trust that it would be worth the distinctly raw, emotional trauma of being either blamed or called a liar. No aspect of this story is particularly unique; the more I've interacted with other women of all ages about their similar experiences, the more I've come to recognize my own story as an everyday, sadly unextraordinary portrait of life and trauma for girls and young women.

Our stories together present a broader problem at the most personal, individual level. And just as much as this problem stems from personal interactions, personal cruelties, personal terrors, it also stems from systemic, institutionalized disregard for the bodies and lives of young women at every level of society.

---

In 1972, Congress formally enacted Title IX as part of the Education Amendments to ensure no one could be excluded or discriminated against on the basis of sex in any education program or activity that received federal funds. Title IX entails a broad range of issues, including equality in resources for athletics programs and coed programs in secondary schools. But today, it's classically associated with campus sexual assault. That's because gender violence on campus is inextricably bound to discrimination and inclusion—exposure to sexual violence, and without accountability, justice, and removal of perpetrators from campuses, poses a substantial if not insurmountable barrier to college attendance for young women, who are disproportionately impacted by sexual violence.

At the core of Title IX is the assertion that women have a right to be on college campuses. And historically, US presidential administrations have played a significant role in either advancing or hindering this agenda. The Obama administration, for example, following previous administrations that had taken a backseat on the issue, played an active role in establishing reformed Title IX policies, such as lowering the standard of proof for survivors and requiring universities to complete investigations of assaults in a timely manner.

But at the end of 2018, the Trump Education Department officially released its long-awaited, proposed Title IX policy changes. The policy proposals came after more than a year of promises by Education Secretary Betsy DeVos to protect the rights of accused men on college campuses, and DeVos certainly did not disappoint the Trump administration's growing base of rape apologists. Notably, formal announcement of the pending changes had been preceded by the Education Department Office of Civil Rights Director Candice Jackson's 2017 declaration that 90 percent of reported assaults "fall into the category of 'we were both drunk'" or "'we broke up, and six months later I found myself under a Title IX investigation because she just decided that our last sleeping together was not quite right'"—a claim that's both provably false and a blatant attempt to trivialize and dismiss the traumatic rapes and assaults experienced by more close to one in four female college students.

The proposed policy changes of the Trump Education Department included increasing the standard of evidence for survivors who report their experiences, as well as substantially narrowing the definition of sexual harassment from "unwelcome conduct of a sexual nature" to "unwelcome conduct on the basis of sex that is so severe, pervasive and objectively offensive that it effectively denies a person equal access to the school's education program or activity." The first proposal could raise already alarmingly high rates of unreported campus sexual assaults, which currently stand at an estimated 90 percent,[1] and the latter could virtually erase or dismiss many if not all of students' traumatic experiences with harassment.

Additionally, DeVos proposed narrowing the scope of universities' ability to investigate sexual misconduct cases to incidents that took place on campus or school-owned property. And in a particularly alarming move to many survivors'-rights advocates, the proposed policy changes also involve permitting rapists and sexual abusers to be in the same room as and cross-examine survivors who accuse them.

The proposed rule changes, some of which went on to be implemented, immediately and justifiably stoked concerns for the safety and rights of young women and survivors on college campuses, as well as concerns about how the rule changes could directly impact survivors' ability to safely attend school and graduate. After all, an estimated 34 percent of survivors of campus sexual assault drop out of school[2] as a result of receiving insufficient care, and, once again, survivors of campus sexual assault are hardly an insignificant population—one in four women college students experience campus sexual assault.

The Trump administration's approach to campus sexual-assault policy certainly marks a departure from the Obama administration, and even from previous conservative administrations that were similarly less-than-concerned about the rights and safety of young women on campuses. That's because DeVos's proposals were uniquely shaped by meetings and conversations with prominent men's-rights groups born of an increasingly misogynistic internet culture, which simply hadn't existed yet during the George W. Bush administration. (The Bush administration's primary contributions to Title IX had been increasing gender segregation among boys and girls in elementary and secondary schools.) Prior to the establishment of Title IX in 1972, if the gender quotas purposed to limit admissions for female students didn't keep women off college campuses, then the prevalence of anti-women violence without accountability certainly did.

Yet, the Trump Education Department's Title IX agenda is tragically not so different from a broader rape culture that has existed for decades and will likely outlast this administration too. And rape culture exists nearly everywhere—in the tens of thousands of backlogged, untested rape kits nationwide; the culture of silence that's ensured campuses will stay a safe space for the perpetrators of the nearly 90 percent of unreported campus sexual assaults; and the university administrations that would rather crack down on alcohol and parties than actual rapists.

Title IX and campus sexual-assault policies do not exclusively affect college students. Rather, K–12 students could be even more vulnerable to the Trump administration's proposed Title IX rule changes. The 74, a non-profit news outlet reporting on public education, revealed a steady increase in reported sexual violence complaints from American K–12 schools sent to the US Department of Education's Office of Civil Rights between 2009 and 2016.[3] One study by the University of Illinois at Urbana-Champaign revealed 43 percent of surveyed middle school students reported having experiencing some form of verbal sexual harassment,[4] while research by Break the Cycle indicated 80 percent of high school guidance counselors said they felt underequipped to handle reports of sexual abuse on campus.[5]

Already vulnerable youth are at the highest risk of being sexually harassed or abused at school: LGBTQ+ youth and youth with disabilities, in particular, experience sexual predation at significantly higher rates than other groups of young people. DeVos's proposed policy changes to impose a narrower definition of what constitutes sexual harassment, in tandem with the Education Department's scaling back of LGBTQ, civil, and disability rights and protections, would carry outsized impact on already marginalized students, who are more likely to experience sexual violence and abuse. And in the case of women and girls of color, this demographic is statistically less likely to be believed when they report experiences with sexual abuse, researchers at Brandeis University found in 2003.[6] The Trump administration's Title IX policy changes drastically diminished many marginalized students' access to support, resources, and care and has likely played a role in forcing many of them to drop out of school as a result.

Even without DeVos's proposed policy changes, sexual violence and inadequate resources for victims already comprise a systemic issue in public and private K–12 schools across the country. In one especially startling case reported by *The Atlantic* in 2017, a female student in Georgia was suspended by her high school after she reported being assaulted on campus. According to her lawyer, the student's educators had asked her such questions as "What were you wearing?" at the time of the attack and "Why didn't you scream louder?"

Another student in Texas was expelled and sent to an alternative high school after telling school officials that she had been raped in the school band room. Cases of victim-blaming questioning and harsh disciplinary action targeting not abusers but survivors reflect just how early rape culture begins. And it's young women and girls whose lives are disproportionately and often permanently impacted by this.

In an ideal world, policies enabling the predation of young
women and girls would hardly be popular or pleasing to the American electorate, yet many survivors'-rights advocates have argued
that these policy changes were implemented by the Trump administration *solely* to appeal to the electorate. And they're probably
right: In many ways, the Trump Education Department's Title IX
policy proposals are just the sort of meat to rile up Trump's predominantly white, male base and certainly rile up Trump, himself.
The president, after all, has been accused of sexual misconduct targeting more than twenty women over the course of decades, and
the appallingly misogynist language he uses to defend himself is
more or less the fabric of his administration's policies, across nearly
all departments. The Education Department is no exception.

It's often said Trump and the horrifying success of his politics
are merely symptomatic of a greater culture of cruelty and violence
festering for generations before his rise. And when it comes to
gender violence, campuses, and a broader, long-spanning war on
young women's bodies, this couldn't be truer. Studies have shown
alarming numbers of surveyed men will voluntarily admit to acts
that constitute rape and sexual assault when those words are omit-
ted from the survey.[7] Despite committing these acts, these men
have faced no accountability and could hide for years, decades,
generations, behind lax federal, state, and campus policies, and a
greater culture that misrepresents and minimizes consent. Through
Title IX changes by the Obama administration and the expanding, increasingly compassionate conversation about sexual assault
that developed as a result, abusers' diminishing feelings of safety led
them to turn to Trump to protect them.

DeVos's proposed and implemented Title IX changes reflect
an ongoing cultural tendency to prioritize the comfort and future
prospects of accused perpetrators (most of whom are young men)

over those of survivors (most of whom are young women), whose ability to receive justice could vastly impact the trajectory of their lives. It's a tendency the Obama administration attempted to counteract, but overhauling an entire culture of normalized, institutionalized violence entails more than eight years of work. If anything, rather than hurt accused men, Title IX policies from the Obama era may have marked a step in the right direction but still came short of establishing full accountability for rapists and abusers, and protecting survivors' rights, safety, and futures on campuses. These shortcomings, which can mostly be attributed to many universities' failure to fully and transparently adhere to Obama-era policies, subjected unsaid numbers of survivors to neglect that ultimately ended their academic careers. The aforementioned 34 percent statistic denoting how many survivors of campus rape are unable to graduate speaks volumes.

Even with reformed, progressive Title IX policies from the Obama era in place, most universities failed to create environments where survivors felt safe and comfortable coming forward. According to the National Sexual Violence Resource Center, more than 90 percent of campus sexual assaults are unreported, compared with the estimated 2 to 10 percent of "false reports" on campus.[8]

And speaking of false reports, it's important that we discuss what, exactly, constitutes a false report. According to research by journalist and author Vanessa Grigoriadis that she breaks down in her 2017 book, *Blurred Lines: Rethinking Sex, Power, and Consent on Campus*, many if not all of these cases involve both the accused and accusing parties acknowledging that an encounter or sexual relationship took place, and merely disagreeing on whether or not one party felt violated. No amount of progressive policy governing the reporting process will ever make it easy or simple to provide tangible evidence of the feeling of being violated, especially when credibility has always been gendered to the disadvantage of female or LGBTQ survivors. The increased evidentiary standards implemented by DeVos could only further endanger college-age survivors.

It can't be stated enough that men, one in six of whom experience some form of sexual abuse in their lifetime, are more likely to be sexually assaulted themselves than falsely accused of committing it. Through its active decision to ignore this reality at the expense of men and women alike and focus instead on an alarmist narrative of a highly infrequent male experience, the Trump administration's Education Department revealed whose experience on campus matters, and conversely, whose does not; who is perceived as belonging on campus and in academic spaces, and who is not.

Low reporting rates among campus sexual assault survivors should not come as a surprise considering the cruelty and institutional abuse most survivors face upon coming forward. There are plenty of documented cases of survivors being punished and intimidated by their schools for reporting their assaults; being pressured to talk to law enforcement, who have a long record of hostility toward survivors and committing sexual violence, themselves; or being subjected to ostracism and social punishment by the mutual friends they may share with their attacker, who is statistically likely to be someone they know personally. Oppressive university and federal policies are not the only mechanism through which young survivors are marginalized on K–12 or college campuses.

In far too many cases, survivors are already forced to face their attackers before lawyers and school administrators and to answer any number of degrading, humiliating, and victim-blaming questions about what they were wearing, how much they had drunk, or their sexual histories. One could only imagine how much worse off reporting rates and general living standards for college-age women became on campuses that adhered to DeVos's policy agenda of normalized rape culture.

---

It's crucial we dispel with the myth that any of this administration's policy proposals or rhetoric are about justice or due process. They are about maintaining and expanding the sacred prioritization of the young, white-male experience on campuses as in society.

Of course, I necessarily distinguish Title IX and Trump Education Department policy as favoring *white* men. Racist stereotypes about bestial, violent, and inherently dangerous black and brown men and boys often marginalize them within white, patriarchal rape culture too. Trump, for all the accusations of sexual misconduct against him and many of his white, male former campaign or White House staff, has the gall to justify racist immigration policies through gross rhetoric that broadly labels all Mexican and Latinx men as rapists. It should go without saying, but race does not biologically make any man predisposed to commit more acts of sexual violence. That said, existing systems of rape culture and white patriarchy are predisposed to dismiss the acts of white men, and sweepingly establish acts committed—or not committed—by black and brown men as representative of all of them.

Let's be clear: this administration is not concerned with due process. The president's rallies—pageants of frustrated, white-male masculinity where thousands of enraged supporters chant, "Lock her up!" about an unindicted female political opponent—throughout the campaign trail and even while in the White House, have made this perfectly clear.

President Trump and his fellow rape apologists in his circle—including his wife, First Lady Melania Trump, and all of her sexist rebuttals of abuse allegations against her husband—have roundly focused the dialogue around sexual violence on mourning the so-called end of "innocence until proven guilty." But for all their criticisms of existing policy and norms, they have yet to offer even one suggestion for how survivors, who were so careless as to not wear body cameras during their assault, or preemptively assemble witnesses, could "prove" the guilt of their attackers.

To her credit, Trump's press secretary Sarah Huckabee Sanders offered one idea for how survivors could prove the veracity of their allegations in 2017. Before a room of journalists questioning President Trump's authority to criticize former Democratic Senator Al Franken, who stood accused of sexual misconduct, Sanders callously dismissed the more than twenty allegations against the president by asserting only cases in which the male perpetrator has confessed (as Franken had) should be investigated and taken seriously. That said, Trump *has* confessed to committing acts constituting sexual assault for all to hear on the notorious "grab 'em by the p-ssy" 2004 *Access Hollywood* tape but has still yet to face any meaningful, substantive accountability.

The Trump administration's proposed Title IX changes reflect a push to protect the sanctity of white, male birthright: the ability of white men to treat women however they wish without consequence. For white-male college students, this presidential administration, which constantly, dishonestly decries Mexican men as bestial rapists, seeks to protect a cherished university experience of casual sexual violence without any damage to young white men's careers, reputations, and general comfort.

When everything is taken into consideration, the racism inherent to rape culture isn't an invention of the Trump administration.

It's an invention of generations of fearmongering, otherization, and dehumanization of nonwhite men, all while absolving unsaid numbers of white-male assailants and ignoring acts of violence on the bodies of women and girls of color, who lack the same credibility and social capital as their white counterparts.

The targeted bigotry of rape culture traces back to the civil rights era of the 1960s and beyond, when dehumanizing, racist tropes about black men imbued with casual white supremacy made black men frequent victims of false charges for violence against white women and girls. Notably, where the notorious Central Park Five, a group of five black men wrongly charged with the gang rape of a white woman in the 1980s, and Scottsboro boys, a group of nine young black men falsely accused of raping two white women, faced sentences including more than a decade in prison time, powerful white men accused of sexual harassment and abuse are repeatedly absolved of responsibility.

The entitlement of white men to commit acts of sexual violence and abuse with little to no accountability, in contrast with the rich history of racist, false accusations against men of color, isn't limited to these select, culturally memorable examples from history. Paying attention to sexual violence has always been inconvenient for people in positions of power—that is, unless the alleged assailant is a man of color, and therefore, his crime (real or imagined) can be used to reinforce and broadly cast a racist worldview onto all other people of color.

The Trump administration's proposed and realized Title IX changes are not about protecting due process. They're about the gendered nature of credibility itself, so that it continues to favor men and disenfranchise the women and marginalized groups who are disproportionately likely to experience sexual violence. Ultimately, due to factors beyond their control, most survivors are simply incapable of providing evidence other than their personal testimony. And so long as white men have a monopoly on privilege and credibility, survivors will continue to live in abject danger. Nowhere is this truer than on campuses, and for no one is this truer than the girls and young women who are disproportionately impacted.

Oppression is experienced at the intersections of our varying identities, across lines of sex, gender, race, ethnicity, class, ability, and age. Anyone who is not an adult, straight, cisgender white man is vulnerable to disadvantage, disenfranchisement, and otherization in some form and to some extent. But arguably no one is more exposed to codified, institutionalized bodily harm than female minors and young women.

A long, persistent history of policies governing girls' access to reproductive health care simultaneously infantilizes them and demands that they take the same responsibility for their actions as adults. As a result, they face increased exposure to forced pregnancy and birth—an imposition to their bodies and still developing minds—all while being less likely to be equipped with the resources, such as knowledge of and access to birth control, to prevent pregnancy in the first place. Across intersections of race, class, and, certainly, citizenship status, girls are even more likely to be denied the agency to access abortion and other health care and are subsequently relegated to a subhuman, second-class-citizen status.

Over and over, we encounter the same paternalistic language used to justify oppressive policies around young women's bodies and reproductive options, including that age inherently precludes them from being able to make the right decisions about their bodies, yet somehow, this decision-making power can be entrusted to predominantly male lawmakers and government actors. We similarly encounter policies and rhetoric around campus sexual assault that marginalize girls' and young women's experiences, deny them credibility about their own bodily experiences, and protect the boys and men who subject them to violence.

Ultimately, this is about more than treating girls and minors as less than adults: It's about treating them as less than human. Humanity necessitates autonomy and basic rights to safety and respect; it necessitates being treated as more than a vessel, an incubator of babies, a physical body of the state. The systemic, state-sanctioned denial of autonomy and abdication of responsibility for what happens to the bodies of girls and young women is nothing short of physical and mental violence, and it's enabled by broad, cultural recognition of young women as "less than"—less than men, less than women, less than boys, and less, even, than human beings.

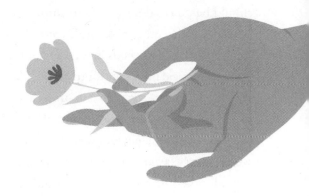

# 6

# Ovary-acting

In 2016, a World Health Organization study of male birth control via hormonal injection became one of the first to go to trial on male human subjects, after extensive testing on male monkeys. (The first female birth control was tested immediately on Puerto Rican women and women with disabilities.) But Stage II of the WHO experiment quickly went awry when the male human subjects began to experience side effects—namely, those prevalent in most common female birth-control methods, such as nausea, depression, mood instability, acne, and changes in libido, among others.

The majority of the study's original 320 male subjects dropped from it soon after, as they were simply incapable—nor expected to be capable—of weathering the same side effects thousands of women around the world experience on a daily basis. Shortly afterward, an independent review panel determined that the study should be canceled for "safety reasons."

Since 2016, other male birth-control tests have proceeded, testing birth-control methods in a variety of forms. Research and development of male birth control traces back as early as 1957, although the development, commercialization, and eventual popularization of female birth-control pills stunted and delayed the process for decades. The prevailing idea was that with female birth control there would simply be no demand for male birth control, as women would shoulder the sole burden of preventing unwanted pregnancy. Certainly, we encounter this in other facets of reproductive health-care norms, such as the ratio of vasectomies to tubal ligation. Despite how tubal ligation for women is vastly more complicated and potentially dangerous than vasectomies, the former occurs significantly more frequently than the latter.[1] And in light of the recent development of symptomless male birth control, researchers continue to struggle with this same challenge: namely, to attract funding or market interest for their product, due to the ongoing assumption that women bear the exclusive responsibility to prevent pregnancy.

Nonetheless, the 2016 study stands out as a pointed example of whose pain, complaints, and recollections of their experiences are taken seriously. Women have complained about side effects throughout the history of our use of birth control, but our complaints have quite obviously come to nothing, as we're still expected to be the ones to take birth control and prevent pregnancy, anyway. That birth control is intrinsically gendered female within the heteronormative patriarchy speaks volumes about who carries the burden and bulk of real or potential consequences for having sex— and conversely, who does not.

Starting birth control pills seemed like the natural step to take when I was a young woman even before I became sexually active, and it was a step I didn't question or put much thought into—even when my mental and physical health began to decline, slowly at first, then quickly, from the pills I took. I was working out-of-state one summer in college without access to insurance, when I had no other choice but to stop taking pills that had made sickness and extreme nausea a daily occurrence.

Thankfully, I found a birth control form that was right for me by the end of the summer. But the realization of what I had put myself through for years, solely because society had deemed pregnancy prevention my responsibility, was eye-opening. It showed me how valueless women's experience and comfort are in the scope of reproductive health care, such that birth-control access is something we are expected to just be grateful for—even when, for some of us, it can come with extreme compromises to our health, and even when pregnancy prevention should be an equitable and shared responsibility between partners. This is a realization that's guided my awareness and understanding of reproductive rights, gender, and the fundamentally great demands we place on women's bodies and lives on a day-to-day basis.

While birth control in its many pioneering forms should always remain available as an affordable—if not cost-free—option for all women, it's no accident that birth control is traditionally assigned to women and not men, while often producing detrimental health side effects like nausea, depression, and effects on libido, among others, as well as steep financial costs and political controversy. Of course, little consideration is given to the potential toll female birth-control side effects can have on women's lives, if we experience these effects. It's simply expected of women to shoulder harmful side effects and health detriments without complaint, because we're "lucky" to have access to birth control, at all.

Of course, it's not just birth control. There are plenty more examples of women's pain or concerns about our health being dismissed due to the gendered, underlying assumption that we are predisposed to exaggeration and hysteria, that we're fragile, overly sensitive creatures by nature, that we complain about everything, and therefore our complaints should be dismissed altogether. The unspoken migraine epidemic among American women similarly reflects the systemic dismissal of our experience within the health-care system, often with dangerous, long-term consequences. And as previously noted in this book, a 2019 Danish study revealed women are often diagnosed years later than men for the same diseases.[2]

Additional research has similarly shown women face a higher, gendered threshold for proving their pain to doctors, from facing longer waiting periods in emergency rooms to increased likelihood of physical conditions being treated and regarded as psychiatric rather than physical. The result is a dangerous disparity in the quality of care received by women and men. This is reflective of who has more innate credibility, and who has the authority to be trusted to know their own needs.

Notions that we women exaggerate our experiences, that our fears and perceptions of the world around us are tainted with a natural, feminine hysteria diminishing our credibility, have specific and damning consequences where our political rights are concerned. Years of dismissing and laughing off the concerns of women and activists finally seemed to come to a head in the first few months of 2019, when more than thirty total or near-total abortion bans were introduced or signed into law in states across the country, most famously in Georgia, Alabama, Louisiana, and Missouri. But this didn't come out of nowhere. The infrastructure and legislative and social culture that ultimately led to these bans took years—and unsaid numbers of women, erased and ignored—to lay.

Since *Roe v. Wade* was decided by the Supreme Court in 1973, American women have technically had the right to safe, legal abortion without undue burden through the point of fetal viability. And the contraception mandate of the Affordable Care Act since 2010 has aimed to bridge gaps in access to birth control that have disproportionately impacted low-income women and women of color. It's been largely successful: in the years since the contraception mandate's implementation, more than fifty-five million American women gained access to copay-free birth control, while the mandate has saved American women $1.4 billion in out-of-pocket costs annually, strengthening both women's health and the economy.

But in many parts of the country, and for many women across lines of racial identity, citizenship, ability, and socioeconomic status, this right has become little more than theory. Within years of the *Roe* decision, states began to enact a wide range of often discriminatory laws restricting abortion, all often specifically targeting low-income girls and women of color. Within three years of *Roe*, the federal government enacted the Hyde Amendment, a law prohibiting federal funding for elective abortion care—an effective abortion ban for low-income women—while more than a dozen states maintained state Constitutions that explicitly ban or terminate the legality of abortion rights pending the reversal of *Roe*. In other words, through a conservative Supreme Court majority, which was solidified in the fall of 2018 when President Trump installed his second anti-choice Justice, the same judicial body that once bestowed human rights upon American women could just as easily take them back.

Yet, in a stark irony considering the significant role contraception access plays in reducing unplanned pregnancy and abortion rates, the administration also repeatedly attacked the contraception mandate on the basis of its perverted definition of religious freedom. In part of a long tradition of conservative hostility toward birth control and anything connoting female sexuality, their definition says that "forcing" employers and insurers to help facilitate women's access to the very health care that permits them to participate in public life is a violation of the First Amendment. In contrast, apparently all but requiring female or LGBTQ employees to conform their private lives and behaviors to the religious views of their employers—and punishing those who don't conform by denying them essential health care or employment—is somehow not a violation.

Notably, the Trump administration's rejection of the mandate wasn't even specific to religion and respecting the Christian values of employers and insurers: it was much broader, giving clearance to any employer or insurer who morally opposes birth control for any reason, whether that be general women-hatred or loathing for any woman who has sex not just to procreate. In this way, President Trump's Health Department built and expanded upon the policies of the conservative, anti-choice administrations that came before it. True, President George W. Bush, like Trump, had vehemently opposed comprehensive sex education and funding for women's health organizations, but not even this administration had opened the door so widely for employers and insurers to discriminate against women for any reason under the sky.

Aside from the "slut" argument against birth control presented earlier in this book, another popular argument for why birth control should not be covered for women is that it's "not even that expensive," according to men who don't realize birth control forms other than the pill exist, or how paying $12 to $50 per month for birth-control pills can make all the difference in a low-income person's life. But depending on insurance coverage and type, birth control can cost anywhere from zero to thousands of dollars, meaning that, as usual, stigma and policies around reproductive health care disproportionately impact and police the lives of certain women—namely low-income women and women of color—more than others.

---

The language of *Roe v. Wade*, that monumental Supreme Court precedent that established abortion rights on the federal level, may be tricky, the way court decisions usually are. But reproductive rights are ultimately simple: they are the constitutional and moral rights to autonomy, safety, and privacy in one's body, and they are and have always been requisite to women, LGBTQ people, and all people's ability to safely and freely participate in public life.

Opponents of abortion and reproductive rights speak often of "personhood," always in reference to fetuses, and never to women and pregnant people. Yet, "personhood" is inextricably bound to fundamental ownership of one's body, and can't be conferred upon unborn fetuses without first snatching it from a pregnant person. Put simply, reproductive rights are fundamentally about whether we view and respect women as human beings, or incubators of the state.

It's impossible to exaggerate the urgency of this issue—whether we women control our bodies, our futures, our destinies. This, our livelihood, cannot be reduced to a matter of abstract theory, debate, or politics. To subject women to watching men (who have consistently comprised some 75 percent of state legislatures and 80 percent of Congress throughout the Obama and Trump eras) pontificate and legislate around the policies that dictate our bodies and lives is not merely dismissive and disrespectful but also an act of abject cruelty.

In 2017, the reproductive-rights online news magazine *Rewire .News* published a report revealing that among the dozens of anti-abortion bills introduced in state legislatures, 71 percent had been introduced by white Republican men. At the heart of this issue lies another of gender representation, and the extensive consequences that extend from a lack of it.

Of course, male control of reproductive rights and the conversation that surrounds this issue isn't limited to legislation. In 2016, a study by Media Matters for America found 60 percent of all comments regarding abortion on cable news were made by men (coincidentally, 64 percent of all comments were inaccurate).[3] Media and narrative control of the conversation around reproductive rights squarely belongs to men, who have historically leveraged this dominance to construct the stigma, shame, and hatred of abortion that have fueled anti-abortion legislation for decades.

This is not, as many "moderate" American politicians routinely suggest, an issue we can safely, humanely compromise or "agree to disagree" on. Such a suggestion, as we have heard from Democratic politicians ranging from Senator Bernie Sanders, when in 2017 he insisted that we move beyond "social issues" like abortion to defend his endorsement of an anti-abortion Democratic mayoral candidate, to House Speaker Nancy Pelosi, who in 2018 insisted compromise with anti-abortion Democrats was key to making progress on "bigger issues," not only excludes from the Democratic Party the one in four women who have abortions but also ignores the power dynamics of "compromise" on abortion rights.

Pelosi's allusion to "bigger issues" seems to imply abortion rights and access are somehow separable from bigger, more serious, more purportedly identity-neutral economic issues. But abortion is an economic issue, as much as it is a human-rights issue. The majority of the one-in-four American women who have abortions[4] are women of color,[5] and 75 percent are low-income; about half (49 percent) live below the federal poverty line.[6] Around three-fifths of women who have abortions are already mothers. Research by the Institute for Women's Policy Research has demonstrated worsened outcomes in living standards for the children of women who seek but are unable to access abortions: those existing children were more likely to live below the federal poverty level for several years later than the existing children of women who were able to receive abortions.[7]

Yet, unsettlingly enough considering the Democratic Party is the only major political party in the United States that identifies as pro-choice, the views of Sanders and Pelosi have hardly been isolated: Democratic National Committee Chairman Tom Perez and Democratic Congressional Campaign Committee Chariman Ben Lujan, who has specifically advocated for continued fundraising for anti-abortion Democrats, have offered similar stances.

Yet, compromise where the politics of abortion access are concerned is as simple as this: Powerful men dictate the laws and cultural narratives around reproductive rights and women's bodies, holding the majority of legislative seats on the state and federal levels. Lawmakers who "agree to disagree" with the women they are elected to serve wield the power to make the final decision about the laws governing those women's bodies; in contrast, women's disagreement with the male, anti-choice lawmakers who create the laws governing their bodies bears virtually no real impact.

And in either case, if you can believe it, politicians who view women's bodies as incubators of the state often aren't particularly interested in engaging conversation with said incubators, or making any real effort to understand the vast range of life experiences that lead women to seek abortion care. Neither I nor any other woman and activist I know who has experienced pregnancy complications or sought abortions has heard sincere or thoughtful responses to our concerns from anti-choice politicians. It can hardly be said that we've agreed to disagree without a conversation even taking place.

Plenty of women may support their anti-abortion, male representatives—but their experience is not universal and does not erase the sheer number of women who suffer indignity, trauma, disenfranchisement, and death in the absence of reproductive rights.

Yet, ultimately, opposition to reproductive rights is not the only modern challenge they face: Apathy is another in itself. Only privileged people who self-identify as "pro-choice"—a term that arguably establishes a dangerous, false binary and implies abortion is an accessible choice for everyone—could dismiss reproductive justice as merely a "social issue," or "identity politics." The right to abortion and convenient access to that right saves women's lives, helps us create our own lives, and broadly grants us the clearance to participate in public life; it is foundational to our existence—and contrary to popular belief, it is far from the settled issue most Americans have believed it to be, ever since the *Roe* decision.

Within our own lifetime, if not within months of my writing this, we could see abortion rights and access dismantled altogether. We could see women jailed for miscarriages alleged to be abortions, we could see pregnant and sexually active women surveilled, we could see the mass imprisonment of women—either through incarceration from violating abortion laws, or entrapment in our own bodies when we are denied health care.

From the day *Roe* was handed down, anti-choice lawmakers and activists have been ceaseless in their fight to scale back its protections and impose disparate barriers on low-income women, people of color, people with disabilities, immigrants, and the LGBTQ community. As a result of their vigorous and ruthlessly effective attacks, advocates for reproductive justice have been forced to fight for and celebrate compromises for decades—all while the right to safe, legal abortion has hung by a thread for years.

The appointment of Brett Kavanaugh, a man who equated IUDs and emergency contraception at his Senate confirmation hearings with "abortion-inducing drugs," to the Supreme Court, as well as the stacking of the judicial system with anti-choice judges in the Trump era, have placed the tattered-but-still-important remains of *Roe* in their most precarious state since before 1973. Yet, 72 percent of surveyed American voters still said they did not believe *Roe* was in danger when they were asked in July 2018, just weeks after the retirement of Justice Anthony Kennedy that would ultimately give way to Kavanaugh.[8] Since the advent of the 2016 presidential campaign, women and allies repeatedly warned about what was at stake at the Supreme Court; our warnings were ignored, and today, even in the face of the greatest threat to our fundamental human rights, our warnings remain ignored, still.

And certainly, candidate and President Trump, Vice President Mike Pence, and the Republican Party at large left nothing to the imagination in their plan to strip women of rights, explicitly and repeatedly stating their goal of ending *Roe* via their judicial nominees. Trump has been identified by anti-abortion activists as the "most pro-life president" in US history, while Pence famously and unequivocally swore the Trump administration would send abortion rights to the "ash heap of history" in 2018. Still, as the July 2018 poll would suggest and Republican leadership's swift insistence that the women protesting Kavanaugh were just "exaggerating," women won't even be believed when we're literally just repeating men's words back to them.

The war on reproductive rights has persisted, and, frankly, only intensified, since 1973. Long before Trump so much as inched toward the White House, anti-choice politicians at the state level spent the Obama era sweeping through state legislatures at alarming rates, gaining more and more ground each election, and using that ground to strip away at all the rights and resources that make abortion and reproductive health access possible—defunding of Planned Parenthood and other women's health organizations, banning insurance coverage of abortion, imposing medically unnecessary regulations on clinics to force them to shut down, and so on.

They paved the way for Trump in the modern era and sought in return from him all they'd wanted from a Republican White House since *Roe*: control of the Supreme Court, and with it, their full, restored power over women's bodies. But even before the arrival of these state lawmakers, without missing a beat since *Roe* was first handed down, anti-abortion activists have worked at every level of government, in every corner of media and society, to demonize and stigmatize abortion, to center it as a salient political rather than human issue, to ensure that even among those who support abortion rights it would be a topic so shameful many would only ever whisper about it behind their hands in ambiguous "pro-choice" platitudes.

The anti-abortion movement experienced a rebirth of epic proportions following the *Roe* decision, developing a stunning, suffocating sense of moral superiority and a victim complex matched with jarring levels of militancy. Over time, the movement would see hundreds of abortion clinics burned; dozens of abortion providers murdered; unsaid numbers of women terrorized, stalked, harassed outside of clinics—and all of this continues to happen, to this day, under the influence of expansive, well-funded groups like Operation Rescue, Susan B. Anthony's List, Live Action, and more, and with the affirmation and support of a broad coalition of anti-abortion elected officials.

Anti-abortion activism has not gone ignored or neglected by feminist activists, who have done what they could through each generation to fight back. They've defended abortion clinics as clinic-escort volunteers; they've formed political organizations and mass voter coalitions to elect pro-choice lawmakers; they've come forward and shared their personal stories with abortion in efforts to destigmatize it. But in the same vein *Roe v. Wade* has served as a narrative victory for the anti-abortion movement, empowering it to present its cause as more urgent than ever before, the decision has served as a narrative loss for feminism, as many potential allies and supporters of abortion rights have since ceased to pay attention or care, regarding abortion rights as a won, resolved battle.

Often, we hear about abortion rights and all that there is to lose from women who lived in pre-*Roe* America, women who have had coat-hanger abortions, or consumed rat poison and laundry detergent, or asked boyfriends to punch them in the stomach, or otherwise endangered themselves to end an unwanted pregnancy. Prior to *Roe*, groups like the Jane Collective in Chicago, among other networks across the country, risked their freedom and safety every day to connect women and girls to abortion, at a time when providing abortions, having abortions, and facilitating abortion access was punishable with prison time. In some parts of the country, and in some circumstances, it still is. We hear these stories because laws that ban, criminalize, or restrict access to abortion often fail to reduce abortion rates, and solely either inconvenience us women or jeopardize our lives, health, and safety, depending on economic status. Abortion bans and criminalization will not end abortion. Only increased birth control access and education have ever impacted abortion rates, and even so, contraception is not a guarantee against unwanted pregnancy. In other words, abortion will always exist—the question is whether it will be safe and legal.

Today, pre-*Roe* stories matter more than ever. They remind us what once was could be again, that what once was still is for many American women—namely women of marginalized identities, and living in rural, staunchly anti-choice regions. They remind us that change and progress have certainly been achieved, but that does not mean oppression has been vanquished; it has merely changed form. Young women have inherited the fight for reproductive justice from their mothers and grandmothers, and where this fight has become lighter in some areas, it has expanded vastly in others. New challenges will always come with a new era.

In 2017, the Population Reference Bureau found American millennial women's living standards had significantly worsened from their mothers'. Despite positive gains in other areas, the maternal mortality rate for millennial women has nearly tripled since the baby-boom generation, from 7.5 deaths per 100,000 live births to 19.2, despite a decreasing global maternal death rate.[9] The study attributed this in no small part to the rapid shuttering of abortion clinics across the country: 90 percent of counties lack abortion providers, and seven states had just one in 2019.[10]

The decline of abortion access in recent years is a result of an influx of anti-abortion laws in the modern era: Since *Roe* in 1973, about 1,200 laws restricting abortion have been enacted in states across the country; 34 percent—more than a third—of these laws were enacted over the course of just seven years, between 2011 and 2018, in the wake of a coordinated wave of Republican gains in state legislatures.[11]

According to research by the Center for Reproductive Rights, across the board, states with more restrictions on abortion access have substantially higher maternal death rates, which paints a similar picture to that of the United States before *Roe*.[12] The America before and the America after the legality of abortion rights are two strikingly different countries for women—the latter of which contains a lot fewer dead women. But the legacy of pre-*Roe* continues to haunt women in states where abortion is more restricted, and arguably the country at large, as it has maintained the highest national maternal death rate in the industrialized world for years.

In the context of splintered abortion access and rising maternal death rates, it's critical to consider the demographics of who has or is more likely to need abortion. Of the one in four women who have abortions, about half live beneath the poverty line, and the majority of women who have abortions are women of color, and black and Latinx women, in particular.[13]

The anti-choice activists and writers who so often decry black women seeking abortion care as "black genocide"—as we've seen everywhere from *Wall Street Journal* editorials to Supreme Court case opinions written by Justice Clarence Thomas—are the same people who support racist, classist policies that prime black women to be more likely to be exposed to unwanted pregnancy, or unable to afford children and child care.

That is, of course, because abortion and reproductive rights are as much an issue of racial justice as economic justice. America's long history of forced sterilizations targeting women of color, as well as discriminatory welfare policies meant to prevent women of color from growing their families, aren't a separate issue from laws targeting their access to birth control and abortion. (The latter is achieved through a range of socioeconomic barriers and so-called race-selective abortion bans.) Together, they comprise a methodical effort to exert state control and ownership over the reproductive decisions of women of color.

As of the most recent available data in 2019, the United States' national maternal death rate of 26.4 deaths per 100,000 live births shrinks to thirteen deaths for white women, and soars to forty-four for black women.[14] And physical danger surrounding reproductive health care is hardly limited to women and pregnant people: In the first half of 2016 alone, 34.2 percent of US abortion providers reported receiving "severe violence or threats of violence," compared with the previous high of 24 percent throughout all of 1995, according to a report by the Feminist Majority Foundation.[15]

The report came just one year after a man claiming to be a "warrior for the babies" shot three people dead at a Planned Parenthood clinic in Colorado. And, certainly, reproductive justice is about more than physical health and safety. Despite pervasive anti-choice propaganda suggesting abortion somehow causes depression and increased risk of suicide, research by the University of California San Francisco shows an ongoing trend of inability to access abortion care having negative impact on women's mental health.

Anti-abortion laws are, at their core, rooted in identity and the wide range of identities that shape women's lives. This includes not only race and gender, not only individual women, but also the people and communities women share their lives with. As previously noted, 59 percent of women who have abortions already have children, and when mothers aren't able to access abortion care they seek, the living standards and economic outcomes for their families are often significantly worsened. In other words, safe, legal, and accessible abortion is critical to the well-being of children too.

Reproductive rights and reproductive justice—which entail full, real-life access to these rights for all—comprise the fight of and for women's lives, and it's a fight that has only grown in scope and danger in recent years for young American women. And we are held back as a nation, as a collective humanity, when women and marginalized people are excluded from living fully autonomous lives and from engaging fully in public life.

I'll never forget what it was like to be a young woman when the Supreme Court gained a solid anti-abortion, conservative majority in 2018, when hundreds of anti-abortion laws were passing each year, when an alarm finally started to sound—after years, decades, generations of women like me voicing our concerns that maybe, just maybe, something was not right. It shouldn't have taken all that it did for news media, "pro-choice" politicians, male allies, and society at large to believe us when we said the War on Women was happening, when we said we were afraid. It shouldn't have taken dozens of men in my life, men sending me emails, men everywhere, telling me that abortion rights were settled by *Roe*, that I ought not to exaggerate and call up a storm over nothing, a few measly, pesky restrictions in some random, far away states—before finally, we were heard.

I knew we had a problem on our hands when I was still a teenager, when I was hollered at and shamed on my way into a women's health clinic near my hometown, when I felt secrecy and guilt upon consuming a misoprostol abortion pill to safely complete an early miscarriage. That experience and those feelings showed me from a young age how deeply wrong the culture around reproductive health care remains in this country. I should have been heard, I should have been believed, regardless of my gender and my age, when I spoke up about that culture, long before the conservative Supreme Court majority and long before the wave of total abortion bans that swept the South in 2019. All things considered, when we fail to listen to women's voices and recollections of their experiences, when we dictate to women the realities of their lives, and when we dismiss their fears rather than believe them, it's not just women we hurt—it's all of society.

The roughly 1,200 state and federal anti-choice laws enacted since 1973 take a variety of forms, some more subtle and contrived than others. But they all follow a general pattern: mandatory waiting periods; targeted regulation of abortion providers, or TRAP laws; judicial bypass; mandatory state-directed abortion "counseling"; bans or restrictions on insurance coverage and public funding for abortion care; bans or restrictions on abortion at later stages in pregnancy; and so on. Many states have some iteration of laws like this, or even all of these laws, and together they interact to ensure abortion is as stigmatized and difficult to access as possible—or inaccessible altogether.

When it comes to unpacking these laws on an individual level, it's difficult to choose a starting point, as explaining one law necessarily leads to unpacking another. Again, they're all interconnected, they all create a landscape of shuttered abortion access, and they all work together to form a reality that women and activists have warned of for years—only for our concerns to be laughed off as "social issues" irrelevant to mainstream, "serious" politics.

In many cases, anti-abortion laws start with mandatory waiting periods that impact abortion access from the moment a pregnant patient attempts to seek care. Mandatory waiting periods, which require a wait of between one and three days from the first consultation at a clinic before having an abortion, simultaneously rely on and exacerbate abortion stigma by suggesting that it is an inherently dangerous, risky, or immoral choice. Waiting periods send the message that we women are inherently incapable of making our own decisions, that we'll fail to take the initiative to think for ourselves unless we're forced by the state to do so. Additionally, based on an individual's travel needs, a waiting period can significantly delay when she is able to have the abortion, or may force her to incur greater costs if their pregnancy is further along.

In a similar vein of paternalism, some thirty-seven states restrict minors' ability to safely access abortion care by requiring some form of parental involvement. Twenty-one states require minors to obtain parental consent to access abortion, and three of these twenty-one states necessitate both parents' consent. Eleven states require parental notification for minors, and one of these states requires that both parents are notified.[16]

Most of these states allow for judicial bypass as a substitute for parental consent or notification, but this "option" comes with its own inconveniences, dangers, and biases. Minors may sometimes have to travel substantial, insurmountable distances to meet with a judge at court, and judges' evaluations of whether a minor is mature enough to have an abortion—as if the ability to become pregnant itself doesn't automatically qualify someone—can be highly subjective, or biased by factors like race, class, and ability.

The judicial-bypass exception begs the question: How can we expect a young person who isn't "mature enough" to have an abortion to somehow be "mature enough" to birth and raise another human being? We can't. Judicial bypass isn't about maturity—it's about producing stigma, punishment, and as many barriers as possible, to police young women's bodies, deny them the health care they need to participate in public life, and prevent them from eventually becoming fully autonomous adults.

Parental consent and notification laws themselves exist to advance these very goals; these laws infantilize young women and girls on a deeper level than treating them as less than adults, and, rather, treat them as less than human. The right to autonomy over one's body, after all, can't be contingent on age, as the right to autonomy is the right to humanity itself.

And when it comes to seeking abortion care, minors often face the same logistical struggles of adult, lower-income women. TRAP laws, or laws that shut down clinics by imposing costly, medically unnecessary standards for clinics to meet, require many women to travel out of state or great distances to access care, and like waiting periods, they tend to specifically target low-income women and mothers. Women who work jobs that do not offer paid time off, as well as women who already have children, shoulder substantial financial burden to travel to have abortions, lose income from missed work, and pay for child care, lodging, and other travel-associated costs. Mandatory waiting periods could require women who travel to have abortions to miss more work and lose even more income, or pay for more lodging and child care.

Notably, TRAP laws are justified by the implication that abortion is dangerous, and therefore abortion clinics must have admitting privileges at a nearby hospital, or clinic hallways must be certain dimensions to fit hospital stretchers. But in reality, abortion results in fewer complications than colonoscopies and many other medical procedures that are equally legal but far less policed than abortion.

To make matters worse, thirty-two states as of this writing impose some restrictions on insurance coverage and public funding of abortion care, in addition to the Hyde Amendment's prohibition of federal taxpayer funding of elective abortion, since 1976. While restrictions on abortion have little-to-no impact on reducing the abortion rate, and simply make the process more inconvenient and dangerous, Hyde has successfully prevented an estimated one in four low-income women from accessing abortion.[17]

In the age of TRAP laws, traveling great distances to access abortion care has become increasingly prevalent. TRAP laws have led to abortion deserts, or regions where women must travel more than one hundred miles to access abortion, across the country; as of 2019, there are more than twenty-seven recognized abortion deserts. The Midwest has been hit particularly hard by the phenomenon of the abortion desert: In Illinois, there is one abortion clinic for every 120,135 women of reproductive age, and one for every 423,590 in Wisconsin.[18] In Texas, between 2013, when TRAP laws were implemented, and 2016, when the Supreme Court recognized TRAP laws as unconstitutional, more than half of the state's original forty-one clinics were forced to shut down.[19] Ninety percent of US counties lack abortion providers, and seven states have just one.

Socioeconomic burdens to reproductive health care are hardly limited to travel costs and restrictions on insurance coverage. The federal and state governments attempt to defund Planned Parenthood and other reproductive health organizations that offer abortion care on a near weekly basis, and just about every state in the union has at some point either proposed or successfully implemented these defunding efforts. Federal funding that organizations like Planned Parenthood receive is legally prohibited from paying for elective abortion services, and abortions comprise a distinct minority of the health care Planned Parenthood provides. To that end, abortion is health care; it should absolutely be covered by federal taxpayer dollars, and it shouldn't matter whether 3 or 90 percent of the services Planned Parenthood provides are abortions.

If this already seems like far too many anti-abortion laws, there are still so many more—there are always more anti-abortion laws, the result of an archaic movement that persists in the modern era through a potent mix of misogyny and skilled, underhanded conniving.

For starters, there are dehumanizing, paternalistic laws that would require women seeking abortion care to obtain the written consent of the fetus's father; in 2017, the writer of one such bill in Oklahoma defended his bill from criticisms by stating of women, "I understand that they feel like that is their body. I feel like it is a separate—what I call them is, is you're a 'host.'" It was certainly an extreme sound bite, but really, he was just saying the quiet part loud: that opposition to abortion rights is fundamentally rooted in the view that women are not human beings, and need male permission to make decisions about their bodies.

But it's not just the right of abortion that's become vastly obstructed by state laws: it's also access to accurate, comprehensive information about abortion care. As of 2019, thirty-four states require women to receive mandatory, state-directed counseling through laws that force doctors and abortion providers to lie to patients, and tell patients about the widely discredited "health consequences" of having abortions, such as increased risk of breast cancer or infertility, or spread other conspiracy theories like "abortion reversal" as fact. Other laws require costly, out-of-pocket ultrasounds, which help fake women's health clinics to rope in disproportionately low-income women by advertising cost-free ultrasounds, only for them to enter and be subjected to anti-choice lies, manipulation, and well-documented harassment and intimidation.

In states like Indiana, laws prohibiting abortion on the basis of the fetus's sex, race, or disabilities have also taken effect and even eluded backlash from pro-choice advocates and evaded mainstream consciousness because of how reasonable they sound on the surface. These laws oversimplify the tremendous nuance that shapes women's decision to have later abortions and construct a false narrative of moral superiority by implying people seek abortions out of sexist, racist, or ableist motives. Certainly, these laws are rooted in racism toward Asian American women in particular, projecting policies and attitudes from Asian countries onto Asian American women's motives to seek abortion care and allowing the state to speculate into the personal considerations that guide their decision to end a pregnancy. The insinuation, as organizations like the National Asian Pacific American Women's Forum have asserted, is that Asian American women are more likely to seek later abortion care based on the gender of the fetus, which can result in Asian American women facing bias and disproportionate challenges to receive life-saving health care.

Bans on abortion at later points in the pregnancy have far and above been the most common anti-abortion laws in recent years. As of 2019, seventeen states ban abortion at or after twenty weeks of pregnancy, while states like Texas, Mississippi, Florida, and others have passed laws banning abortion in the second trimester, or at or after fifteen weeks, only for courts to strike down these laws as unconstitutional.

Contrary to right-wing narratives of abortion as sweepingly taking place in the ninth month, and targeting living, fully formed "babies," 92 percent of abortions take place at or before thirteen weeks of pregnancy, while just 1.2 percent take place at or after twenty-one weeks. This hardly suggests there is no need for safe, legal later abortion.[20] Later abortions most often occur due to extreme health circumstances or fetal abnormalities, because many crucial tests to gauge fetal health can't take place until the fetus is around twenty-weeks old. In plenty of other cases, women are forced to have later abortions because they were delayed from accessing abortion earlier by a litany of other restrictive laws or victimized by the lies of anti-choice, fake women's health clinics until it was nearly too late.

Later abortions are explicitly protected by *Roe v. Wade*, which guarantees the right to elective abortion until the point of fetal viability. Fetal viability is often reached at around twenty-five weeks if the fetus becomes viable at all, but *Roe* necessitates that abortion must be legal past the point of viability in complicated health circumstances, with the permission of doctors. Later abortion has saved unsaid numbers of women's lives, and spared many others the devastation and trauma of being forced to carry to term and give birth, only to watch their baby suffer and die due to severe health conditions. Late abortion access is not only the safe and necessary option, but the humane one too.

Later abortions are also necessarily caused by many other policies, such as fetal-heartbeat bans or other early restrictions, which
are widely supported by the same lawmakers who claim to loathe
them. Even in the absence of anti-choice lawmakers' scrutiny and
demonization of later abortion, fetal-heartbeat bans, which prohibit abortion before most women realize they're pregnant, would
be dangerous and dehumanizing and would carry deeply harmful implications for women's health. But the simultaneous stigma
attached to both early and later abortion reminds us that, despite
how graphic and explicit anti-choice rhetoric denouncing later
abortion is, the stage in pregnancy means little to nothing to an
anti-choice movement that simply wants to ban all abortions.

This is not about unilaterally caring for all fertilized eggs and
more developed fetuses as children and human beings. Anti-choice
politicians rarely if ever cede an opportunity to attack born, living
children through their harmful policies on education, health care,
immigration, gun control, and social welfare. If anti-choice politicians really viewed six-week or twenty-week fetuses as born, living,
low-income children, suffice to say, they would be busy at work
trying to rob those fetuses of health care, food, safe communities,
and quality public education.

Opposition to early and late abortion is wholly rooted in the
anti-choice movement's obsession with controlling and punishing
women's bodies, and the movement achieves its extremist agenda by
relying on salient, emotionally manipulative narratives about babies
and children that, in reality, they either do not care about or actively
hurt through their policies. Their focus on attacking and restricting
later abortion is strategic, as it carries greater narrative power.

Like twenty-week or later abortion bans, many anti-abortion
bills introduced to state legislatures are nakedly, transparently
unconstitutional, even to those who introduce them. But such is

often the anti-choice movement's strategy: to enact as many uncon-stitutional anti-choice bills as possible, hoping they will be chal-lenged in court, and perhaps reach the Supreme Court, where the new conservative majority may either uphold and offer clearance to such restrictive laws or strike down abortion rights altogether. And at the very least, the language in their anti-choice bills could fur-ther advance abortion stigma and pave the way for more restrictive future laws.

As of 2019, more than twenty states have laws that would either immediately outlaw or leave abortion rights in limbo if—or when—*Roe* is reversed. The threat of losing *Roe* at this stage could hardly be overstated: Republican, anti-choice control of the major-ity of state legislatures has produced extremist anti-choice laws at an alarming rate, and as these laws file through the courts, nearly any one could make it to the Supreme Court and either explic-itly end *Roe* or deal an insurmountable blow to abortion access. Yet, whatever the future ultimately holds for abortion rights on the federal level, the reality of nearly half of the United States ready and eager to end abortion rights in an instant is terrifying. In the context of the roughly 1,200 anti-abortion laws enacted since *Roe*, this underlying landscape of anti-abortion hostility, though just beneath the surface, already poses a significant barrier to women's access to health care. In 2019, 43 percent of American women lived in regions deemed hostile to abortion rights by Guttmacher Insti-tute, up from 18 percent in 2010.[21]

State lawmakers have certainly become emboldened by the Trump presidency and its harrowing record of threatening repro-ductive rights, which includes jeopardizing the contraception man-date; proposing laws that would allow doctors to lie to, or withhold information about, reproductive health care from female patients; banning global funding for organizations that offer life-saving education and reproductive health care to women and girls; and propping up abstinence-only programs that provably yield higher rates of unwanted pregnancy among teens.

Extremism has always been core to the anti-choice movement; the idea that the state can force women to be pregnant and give birth against their will is necessarily extreme. But the Trump era has seen to a rise in proposed, all-out bans on abortion, often in the form of fetal-heartbeat bans that would ban or criminalize abortion altogether. A fetal heartbeat is detectable at around six weeks— before most women realize they are pregnant and before many abortion providers are able to offer abortion care. Bills that propose the criminalization of abortion and legal recognition of providing or receiving abortion as murder, punishable with prison time or the death penalty, have also seen a resurgence in the Trump era.

But the anti-choice movement's go-to tool to make its extremism digestible to mainstream audiences is the highly innocuous rape exception, and it's hardly new. Bills that ban abortion or funding for abortion typically include exceptions for those who are impregnated by rape—for example, nearly all of the seventeen states that ban abortion at or after twenty weeks, or restrict insurance coverage of abortions, offer exceptions for rape survivors.

It's estimated that twenty-five thousand pregnancies in the United States are caused by rape each year.[22] However, the rape exception often requires that survivors seeking abortion care disclose and somehow prove their experiences to law enforcement or doctors, forcing many women to relive their trauma and beg to be believed, simply to receive health care that should be their human right.

When we require women to sacrifice their privacy and comfort in exchange for their human right to health care, we deny them power and self-determination in their recovery process, and we strip them of bodily autonomy by making their health care conditional.

Still, an estimated 16 percent of Americans believe abortion should be illegal without any exception, even for rape.[23]

In 2012, during Republican Congressman Todd Akin's race for US Senate, Akin dismissed the possibility of pregnancy by rape by citing religious pseudoscience about how "legitimate rape" rarely results in pregnancy, and therefore, abortion should be illegal without exception. Views like his and the other 16 percent of Americans who believe all abortion should be illegal are appalling—but other Republicans' inclusion of the rape exception in their anti-choice bills does not magically make their bills any less extreme.

In many ways, the rape exception is not to the benefit of women. It suggests the fundamental right to bodily autonomy is contingent on the circumstances in which a woman was impregnated or whether she was able to successfully prove that she was raped to authority figures. Callous invocations of the rape exceptions in anti-abortion bills send the false message that rape is somehow simple to prove, that coming forward is not a deeply personal decision for survivors to make of their own accord.

Unwanted pregnancy with abridged access to the resources one would need to terminate it is, perhaps next to rape, the most fundamental invasion and violation of women's bodies, privacy, and rights there is. It reminds us that consent to sex is not the same as consent to pregnancy, as anti-choice politicians who support abortion bans with the rape exception seem to believe.

There is, after all, a fundamental relationship between reproductive violence and sexual violence, as both involve the denial of autonomy and consent: survivors do not consent to sexual abuse, as women with unwanted pregnancies, faced with barriers to abortion access, do not consent to be pregnant. The rape exception allows for anti-choice lawmakers to manipulate the optics around abortion policy, to make abortion bans and restrictions appear more humane and acceptable, all while advancing harmful narratives about sexual assault.

During pre-*Roe* America, 200,000 to 1.2 million unsafe abortions occurred annually, and predominantly immigrant women and women of color filled hospitals with injuries from unsafe abortions—if they lived.[24] Today, unsafe abortions continue to happen: In the United States in 2015, there were more than seven hundred thousand searches for how perform a self-induced abortion.[25] Also in 2015, it was reported that in the state of Texas, between 100,000 and 240,000 Texas women had attempted to induce their own abortions that year.[26]

That being said, the rise of medication abortion in the first ten weeks of pregnancy has made highly safe, self-managed abortion possible, in a way it wasn't prior to *Roe*. Today, activists are pushing to make abortion pills, which rarely result in complications, available via telemedicine and even as an over-the-counter product. As of 2019, about a third of all abortions in the United States are medication abortions.[27] But despite approval from the Food and Drug Administration, in many states, challenges remain to conveniently and legally access medication abortion.

Additionally, criminalization remains an alarming risk factor associated with self-managed medication abortion. Because the effects of abortion with pills and miscarriage on the body are indistinguishable, the rise of self-managed abortion pill use has come with increased suspicion and even criminal charges against women—especially women of color, who already draw disproportionate suspicion from law enforcement—for the outcomes of their pregnancies. In several documented cases, women have already faced criminal charges, lengthy court trials, and even jailtime for miscarriages and stillbirths suspected to be abortions. In a future without *Roe*, women's sexual behaviors and pregnancies would likely be constantly surveilled on suspicion of self-managed abortion.

Many laws restricting or banning abortion are necessarily challenged in court once they are enacted, and some are upheld, while others are roundly tossed. But in all cases, these challenges require the state to shell out hundreds of thousands of taxpayer dollars in legal fees. These are, of course, taxpayer dollars that could support health care, education, housing and food for born, living children, or otherwise support the needs of low-income mothers and families. Instead, they fund the wealthy, out-of-touch, disproportionately male lawmakers' ongoing crusade on women's bodies, in stark commentary about the actual goals and beliefs of the anti-choice movement.

Historically, wealthy white women who needed abortion care could always afford to safely access it; reproductive justice and the landscape around abortion rights have always been shaped by socioeconomic disparities. These are fraught times for all women and pregnant people, concerning our most fundamental rights. Our advocacy must extend beyond traditional binaries that frame abortion as a viable, accessible choice for all, and rise to a higher standard of inclusivity. The lives of women, women of color, immigrant women, young women, low-income women, and LGBTQ people depend on it.

Attacks on reproductive rights tend to specifically target women and people at the margins. This certainly includes young women and girls, who often lack their own source of income and legal status, among other extensive, identity-based barriers to access reproductive health care. These barriers are the product of laws premised on contradictory, sexist ideas of female minors, who are uniquely, simultaneously viewed as too naive and immature to be entrusted with bodily autonomy but mature enough to shoulder lifelong, life-altering consequences for the bodily decisions of their youth.

The infantilization of young women of reproductive age through previously described parental consent abortion laws is nothing if not ironic. Without receiving the same cover for misdeeds and mis-behaviors that boys do through the cultural tour de force that is "boys will be boys," girls are required to be little adults, almost from birth. Girls have never had the luxury of being able to lash out or act up and evade responsibility. But upon becoming pregnant and seeking out health care, suddenly, they are told they lack the capac-ity for responsibility altogether.

Some anti-choice justifications and lines of thinking about parental-involvement abortion laws frame these laws as consistent with the broader, aforementioned culture of holding girls respon-sible for their decisions and behaviors. For example, these justi-fications frame unwanted pregnancy as the product of a young woman's purported behavioral transgressions, or testament to her lacking responsibility, and frame pregnancy and motherhood as sufficient punishment.

This line of thinking simultaneously hints at the depths of anti-choice hypocrisy and contradiction. It contradicts puritanical obsession with portraying pregnancy and motherhood as a univer-sally blessed and beautiful experience, for starters, instead render-ing pregnancy as a direct punishment for premarital sex. And it similarly contradicts common anti-choice advocacy that all sinners should be "forgiven," and not punished at all. (This advocacy itself comprises a particularly crass attempt at co-opting compassion, all while the anti-choice movement enforces a policy agenda that kills and hurts unsaid numbers of born, living women every day.)

Certainly, it contradicts the anti-choice movement's claims that it cares about babies, children, and families, if anti-choice lawmakers are happy to subject children to being born to young mothers who were "irresponsible" enough to conceive them in the first place and to reduce these children to collateral damage just to punish young women.

The notion that pregnancy is the result of young women's irresponsibility, or a "mistake" for which they must accept consequences, is transparently rooted in misogyny and the obscuring of myriad institutional factors that steer who is more likely to experience unwanted pregnancy. More than half of women who have abortions report that they were using some form of contraception when they conceived.[28] Access to contraception is critical and often dictated by its own set of restrictions—but the possibility of being exposed to unwanted pregnancy will always remain a biological, inevitable reality for sexually active girls and women, or survivors of rape. Unwanted pregnancy and abortion often have nothing to do with who is "responsible" and who is not, but rather, the disparities in access to accurate sexual health education and reliable birth control across socioeconomic and geographic lines—and, certainly, biology.

Unwanted pregnancy and motherhood should never be weaponized as a form of punishment for women but not men's "irresponsible" sexual behavior. The potency and frequency of this narrative reflect the victim-blaming nature of anti-choice politics and its underlying motivation in sex policing and slut-shaming women.

Additionally, parental-involvement laws often place minors in abject danger: some minors may have abusive or rigidly traditional parents who would harm or disown their daughter for getting pregnant, let alone for seeking an abortion. Other minors in states that require the approval or notification of both parents may not have relationships with one or either of their parents.

Teen childbearing should carry no stigma or shame. But we must note its occurrence often as a result of dangerously lacking sexual health education in schools, as well as the disparate barriers minors face to access reproductive health care. Teen childbearing, which disproportionately occurs in states without sexual health education in public schools and with more limited access to family planning resources, is notoriously costly to US taxpayers. According to the US Health and Human Services Department, it can cost "between $9.4 and $28 billion a year through public assistance payments, lost tax revenue, and greater expenditures for public health care, foster care, and criminal justice services."[29] Additionally, teen childbearing can also be highly costly to young mothers, whose ability to access or complete higher education and become fully autonomous members of the workforce can be highly constrained as a result.

One 2018 study published in the *American Journal of Public Health* concluded that those who were denied abortions they had originally sought and who instead gave birth were substantially more likely than those who had received an abortion to experience poverty and less likely to be employed six months after being denied abortions.[30] Specific to teen pregnancy and motherhood, 52 percent of mothers on welfare had their first child in their teens.

Restrictions on minors' access to reproductive health care aren't limited to abortion services. As of 2019, only twenty-six states and the District of Columbia explicitly allow all minors age twelve and older to consent to contraceptive services. Emergency contraception did not become available over-the-counter on the federal level until the summer of 2013, which was notably the same year the Obama administration was forced to give up its ongoing court battle to end the age minimum imposed on emergency contraception. Earlier that year, the Food and Drug Administration lowered the age minimum for emergency contraception from seventeen to fifteen, marking a step in the right direction, but one that still infantilizes, marginalizes, and endangers girls younger than fifteen.

Female minors' reproductive rights are also systematically limited by the vast shortcomings of modern sexual health education in public schools. As previously noted earlier in this book, just twenty-four states and the District of Columbia require public schools to offer sexual health education, and just twenty of these states require medically and factually accurate sexual health education. In many documented cases, sexual health education has been co-opted as a platform to either slut-shame or encourage slut-shaming in public schools: some classrooms have reportedly compared the bodies of girls who have sex to "chewed gum," among other dehumanizing characterizations that simultaneously encourage misogynist bullying and also shame young survivors of sexual violence. In plenty of other cases across the country, sex ed has also been used to push an agenda of homophobia and anti-LGBTQ intolerance as a result of lack of inclusivity.

Central to restrictions on minors' reproductive rights is the predation of girls by patriarchal institutions that regard them as particularly vulnerable and accessible targets. What relatively slim credibility and self-determination adult women gain through becoming adults, girls are utterly lacking. As a starting point, the lack of reciprocity in girls' ability to become impregnated, but not access abortion care, in itself dehumanizes and relegates girls to vessels of the state. Even if their pregnancy is conceived through fully consensual and autonomous sexual decisions, their inability to autonomously end that pregnancy is meant to both rob them of, and punish them for, what little sexual agency they had in order to engage in sex in the first place.

That said, consensual, autonomous sex is not the only means through which girls are impregnated. There are also the persistent, devastating realities of sexual violence and long-term domestic abuse, which often disproportionately affect girls of color, and black and Native American girls in particular, as well as LGBTQ youth. The suggestion that those impregnated by abuse ought just to have been more "responsible" is inextricably bound to victim-blaming and produces a sort of double jeopardy upon the bodies of girls and women of color, who are literally punished for experiencing abuse in the first place.

In the summer of 2018, in the thick of the Trump administration's horrific, racist family-separation policies, the Supreme Court appeared to side with the administration's policy of prohibiting undocumented minors' abortion access. The high court's ruling overrode the DC Circuit Court's ruling from March, which had ordered Trump officials to cease in their repeated attempts to block undocumented minors from getting abortions over the past year.

Internal emails among officials from the Office of Refugee Resettlement have revealed the alarming methods used by Trump administration officials to repeatedly obstruct undocumented teens' access to abortion. These methods included literally holding teenage girls as prisoners and giving them dangerously false information about abortion and pregnancy. In at least one documented case, Trump administration officials even went so far as to attempt to stop a medication abortion that was already underway. (Medication abortion typically requires consumption of two separate pills, with the second taken between six and forty-eight hours after the first.)

Shortly after the ruling, President Trump signed an executive order that (in words) put an end to his original policy of separating migrant families at the border. This policy—the consequences of which would persist long after the executive order—rendered migrant children and minors, who were taken from their parents and locked away in cages or desert tent camps, especially vulnerable to experiencing myriad forms of abuse, including sexual violence. Detailed, extensive investigative journalism has revealed the prevalence of sexual abuse at detainment centers, often committed by border patrol and detainment-center staff themselves.

Violence and sexual abuse committed against migrant women and girls is reportedly so prevalent that one border patrol official in 2018 spoke to the Associated Press about the increasingly common phenomenon of migrant girls as young as twelve being put on birth-control pills "because they know getting violated is part of the journey." It's estimated that six out of every ten women and girls are raped and 80 percent subjected to some form of sexual violence en route to the US border. Upon reaching the border, exposure to sexual violence remains rampant: in 2018, *The Intercept* reported that 1,224 sexual-abuse complaints were filed at immigrant detainment centers between 2010 and 2017, but just forty-three of these complaints led to investigations.

Considering how widespread sexual abuse, both en route to the US border and at shelters and detainment centers, is, pregnancy caused by rape is a particularly grave threat immigrant women and girls face—especially due to the Trump administration's troubling, long-term history of trying to block abortion access for undocumented minors and women without an exception for rape. These attacks are three-fold and intersectional, striking at migrant girls' identities as female, immigrants, and underage, to dehumanize them on several levels.

"Personhood," that ubiquitous word anti-choice politicians use to humanize fetuses, *is* autonomy; to confer it upon fetuses is to necessarily steal it away from us women and reduce our bodies to incubators of the state. When the state has the power to force women to give birth, we are necessarily reduced to second-class citizens. And for immigrant women and girls, these attacks on abortion rights are also about dividing their experiences from those of citizen women and manipulating policy and health care to solidify dangerous, fundamental inequalities in the rights immigrant and citizen women have over their bodies.

Lawyers for then-Attorney General Jeff Sessions, who defended the Trump administration's forced-birth policy in circuit courts and the Supreme Court on numerous occasions, have repeatedly asserted that undocumented minors lack the right to receive an abortion in the US because, as they put it, these girls lack the same fundamental rights that citizens have. It's important to see this argument for what it is: the broad dehumanization of Latinx migrants and noncitizens, through hijacking and weaponizing girls' bodies. And if Sessions's arguments differentiating the human rights of migrants from those of citizens failed to make this assertion clear enough, certainly, President Trump's ongoing rhetorical war on immigrants' humanity should. His comments have included, to be brief, references to immigrants involved in gang-related crimes as "animals," assertions that "they're not human beings," and claims that migrants "infiltrate our country," solely to commit rape and murder.

Policy and rhetoric are often especially interwoven by the Trump administration, and this rhetoric has a very specific policy goal: to equate immigrants to violent animals, attack perceptions of them as human, and, thus, give clearance to policies that treat them as subhuman. In the Trump administration's legal battle to deny migrant girls abortion access, officials have built upon this rhetoric by centering their case around the idea of fundamental differentials in people's human rights based on their immigration status, race, and country of origin.

Throughout history, immigrant women and women of color have always faced disproportionate threats to their reproductive rights. Low-income women and women of color comprised the majority of women in the pre-*Roe* era who sought and were harmed by unsafe, DIY abortions. And today, there remains a long, persistent history of language, economic, or other barriers barring immigrant women and girls' access to contraception and sexual health education. In post-*Roe* America, abortion access remains restricted on different levels for nearly all American women. But this is especially the case for low-income women, migrant women, women of color, and minors, who disproportionately suffer from increased risk of maternal deaths as a result of anti-choice policies.

The policing of migrant girls' access to abortion entails more, even, than the typical policy debates concerning immigration, reproductive rights, and young people's rights. It offers broad insight into who in this country is recognized as human, and the violent, horrific conditions to which those who are not recognized as human can legally be subjected.

---

I often ponder the extent to which abortion opponents truly believe abortion is murder. Could they simply be bent on punishing and controlling women? It's a question I don't think is asked anywhere near enough: are anti-abortion activists' stated motives as authentic and pure as they're made out to be? I ask because, in contrast, women's activism and political leadership are endlessly dissected for any traces of "inauthenticity" and self-serving motives.

More often than not, I've found this is an issue that disproportionately affects young women—young women who are on the front lines at rallies and protests, young women who are proud to share social-justice content on their social-media feeds, only to be brushed off as "paid crisis actors" or performatively "woke" social-justice warriors. The underlying message here is that women are somehow fundamentally incapable of formulating their own opinions and would only speak up about justice for some perceived advantage, be that money or the imagined benefits of publicly engaging in politics as a young woman.

That said, why don't we spend more time questioning the real, genuine intentions and beliefs of a movement that claims to be pro-life, all while either encouraging or failing to condemn anti-choice lawmakers and activists who call for the death penalty for women and abortion providers? In tandem with the rise of Trump, severe violence and threats of violence directed at abortion providers have spiked, and so have proposed bills that would criminalize abortion and potentially make involvement in abortion care punishable by death. In 2018, leading conservative thinker and former *Atlantic* columnist Kevin Williamson unapologetically stated women who have abortions should receive the death penalty by hanging, and around the same time, a Republican candidate for lieutenant governor in Idaho concurred.

Anti-choice leadership has often tried to distance itself from calls for violence against women and abortion providers, instead emphasizing that women should be forgiven if they repent for the deep sin of abortion. Yet, the movement's core message and all its vast hypocrisies and contradictions are the very basis for its inability to effectively condemn its violence. The anti-choice movement states unequivocally that life begins at conception, that a fertilized egg ought to have the same rights as a born, living woman, as well as born, living children, and that a woman's decision to end a pregnancy is equivalent to murder. But if fetuses and born children are the same, and abortion is murder, then shouldn't it logically follow that women who have abortions and abortion providers must face the same consequences as convicted murderers?

Ultimately, when anti-choice politicians, writers, and activists speak about abortion in this way, they are responsible for understanding the potential consequences of such dangerous, violent language. They are equating health care with murder, and their words, for all the potential for violence they carry if they fall upon the ears of extremists, cannot be seen as peaceable.

The Hyde Amendment, a federal law precluding federal taxpayer dollars from paying for elective abortion, is also a point of stark hypocrisy in the anti-choice movement. The law is justified as it purports to protect the consciences of the supposed, many taxpayers who morally reject abortion rights, but incidentally, are often the same people who are unbothered by military spending that routinely, purposefully claims the lives of born, living people and children. Additionally, abortion is hardly unpopular in the United States—more than seven out of ten Americans support abortion, and have since 1973. Women and people who seek abortion care are taxpayers, but unlike men, their access to the health care that their taxes pay for is abridged by Hyde on the basis of gender. Hyde is fundamentally about prioritizing one archaic and discriminatory set of values ahead of the safety and decision-making powers of low-income women and shifting abortion from fundamental human right to socioeconomic privilege.

The anti-choice movement's hypocrisy is apparent in not only its rhetoric about abortion but also its conflicting messaging and policies surrounding motherhood and pregnancy. Anti-choice lawmakers and thinkers alternate between espousing narratives of pregnancy and motherhood as blessings requisite to female joy, blessings that so many deserving women are denied by infertility and other tragedies. Therefore, the movement casts women who seek or have abortions as ungrateful, and somehow responsible for the pain of other women who aren't able to get pregnant or have children. Yet, just as often, anti-choice lawmakers and activists frame pregnancy and motherhood as a matter of punishment and taking responsibility, that women and girls with unwanted pregnancies did the crime, and thus, should serve the time: motherhood.

On top of these conflicting narratives, anti-choice lawmakers ignore how their policies are often a strong contributing factor in steering many women to seek or have abortions. These policies include severely lacking health-care coverage for prenatal and postnatal care and paid family leave, as well as vastly underfunded resources and support for motherhood and families, leading to a broad culture of motherhood regarded as a burden in workplaces and in public life. Conservative, anti-choice lawmakers are often the same people who reject legislation to combat the gender wage gap and pregnancy discrimination, which hurt women workers and mothers. They proactively support policies to make pregnant women's lives more laborious, to make pregnancy and motherhood as difficult and burdensome as possible, and then have the gall to act confused about why women choose to not be pregnant.

Victims of the anti-choice movement's cruelty aren't limited to mothers and pregnant people; they certainly include children, low-income families, immigrant families, and families of color. For several months from 2017 to 2018, the Republican majority in Congress stalled the renewal of the Children's Health Insurance Program, through which more than nine million American children access health care, as a means to pressure Democratic lawmakers to give up on their legislative fight to protect the rights of undocumented children and young people. In the face of mass shootings that routinely, disproportionately target schools and universities, anti-choice lawmakers are often the same people who ceaselessly oppose any meaningful gun-control legislation that would prevent mass shootings at schools—and in general—from occurring at the ghastly rate they do.

The anti-choice movement's silence around often fatal police brutality that disproportionately targets young black men, who are nine to sixteen times more likely than any other group to be killed by police, also speaks for itself. Leading anti-choice politicians, from Texas Senator Ted Cruz to President Trump and Vice President Mike Pence, frequently respond to criticisms of racist police violence by instead standing up for law enforcement against a perceived cultural war on police.

A core criticism of the anti-choice movement is that it cares for children up until they're born and immediately turns a blind eye to the conditions they're subjected to as born, living human beings. These conditions include poverty, death from lack of access to health care, police violence, gun violence, endless war, identity-based discrimination, homophobia, transphobia, racism, misogyny, a criminal justice system that routinely tears apart families of color, and more.

In 2018, leading anti-choice organizations and politicians either failed to condemn or outright encouraged the Trump administration's policy of separating migrant families as a means to discourage illegal border crossings. On top of separating families, at the president's orders, migrant children and babies were also put in cages and subjected to inhumane conditions in border camps or detention centers; for several months, children and babies were separated from their parents at a rate of forty-five kids per day.

It matters that, as a unit, the Republican Party and the anti-choice movement that crowned Trump as *their* president were not able to condemn Trump's most anti-family policies, and it matters that policies and plainly racist narratives they had spent years propagating ultimately yielded family separation.

Far more often than not, migrants who cross the border are fleeing rather than perpetuating violence; many are women trying to escape rape and domestic abuse with their children; many are families fleeing certain death from rampant violence. The violence and instability they flee is inextricably bound to generations of Western imperialism; they are fleeing problems created by the United States, only to be turned away by the United States. Core to the immigration politics of President Trump, America's self-proclaimed "pro-life president," is a racist with abjectly cruel determination to punish people—and certainly women and children—for not being white and for trying to survive.

We know this is not "pro-life." We know this movement is transparently about the punishment and control of women and the devaluation of children and families as collateral damage. Hypocrisy is foundational to the anti-choice movement, yet, for all the questioning of feminist women's convictions and authenticity and the real motives of our politics, media and society continue to regard anti-choice ideology as fundamentally rooted in well-meaning religious and moral convictions.

Reproductive justice issues tend to draw intense, passionate, and emotional reactions from young women and feminists. We see this hypocrisy and cruelty for what it is, as we are its ultimate victims.

———

The aforementioned proposed fetal-heartbeat bans, the uptick in conservative thinkers and lawmakers proposing policies to recognize abortion as murder, and, certainly, suggestions that women who have abortions ought to be hanged, together signal a new era of criminalized abortion and womanhood.

Ultimately, no matter how critically important readily available access to contraception will always be, unwanted pregnancy remains a biological reality. Universal access to contraception will never be a substitute for safe, legal, and fully accessible abortion care. It can't be stated enough that unwanted pregnancy and abortion are not about who is responsible and who isn't. And while we should bear in mind the majority of those who have abortions report using protection, we should also understand the explicit misogyny that underlies our demand for this justification.

Narratives about responsibility and abortion necessarily ignore disparities in access to comprehensive, accurate sexual health education and reliable birth control across socioeconomic and geographic lines. And the bottom line remains that unwanted pregnancy and motherhood should never be weaponized as punishment for "irresponsible" sexual behavior, or simply for having sex.

The trend of calling for abortion to be criminalized is not limited to writing from Kevin Williamson, or Twitter trolls, or deranged, anti-choice gunmen: it's also become an increasingly prevalent demand among state and federal lawmakers.

In 2018 and 2019, lawmakers in Ohio, Florida, Idaho, and other states introduced bills to formally recognize abortion as murder, and in recent years prior, Texas and Oklahoma lawmakers introduced similar legislation. Other bills have similarly focused on the imagined morbid nature of abortion care, by requiring women who have abortions to pay out-of-pocket to bury or cremate their aborted fetus. These laws were briefly enacted in Texas and Indiana before being overthrown in court.

Shortly after fetal burial requirements became the law in Indiana, Vice President Mike Pence, then serving as the state's governor, found himself on the receiving end of a social campaign to educate about menstruation, pregnancy, and abortion, known as the Periods for Pence campaign. Periods for Pence specifically sought to educate about how the fetal burial law could apply to women who had miscarried early in their pregnancy without their knowledge, and thus, it could apply to virtually any sexually active woman who menstruated. The campaign launched hundreds if not thousands of calls to then-Governor Pence's office from Indiana women explaining their periods in vivid detail. The bill seemed to underscore how little most Republican, anti-choice men actually know about the subject matter they so often legislate around to such tremendous consequence for the women affected. Periods for Pence sought to call this ignorance out in an unapologetically explicit manner.

Despite appearing less extreme than bills that would criminalize or categorize abortion as murder, fetal burial requirements bear the same goal of humanizing fetuses, dehumanizing women, and telling us we are murderers for making a health-care decision. And there is, of course, an especially morbid, psychologically abusive element to being charged by the state with responsibility for the remains of a fetus.

Many laws also punish women for having abortion care, taking a wide range of approaches: In Arizona, as of 2018, women are required to justify their decision to have an abortion in a lengthy explanation sent to the state, in a transparent attempt to separate abortion from all other health care and shame those who have it. And in 2016, an Indiana woman named Purvi Patel was released from jail after serving almost a full year for the outcome of her pregnancy. Charges against Patel had been highly contradictory, alleging she had simultaneously committed fetal homicide and neglect of a child, leading many to ask how Patel could have neglected a "child" that had not even been born.

In 2013, Patel had checked into a hospital after losing a pregnancy at about twenty-three or twenty-four weeks, and doctors became suspicious that she had self-induced an abortion. Later, the prosecution argued the fetus had actually been between twenty-five and thirty weeks along by citing the results of a widely discredited "lung-float" test, and proceeded to manipulate laws originally meant to protect pregnant women from violence to charge Patel with fetal homicide, while simultaneously implying she had given birth and neglected her born child.

Patel's story is similar to that of Bei Bei Shuai, another Asian American Indiana woman who was jailed a few years earlier for miscarrying after an attempt to commit suicide by consuming rat poison. And in yet another ominously similar incident 2018, a Walgreens pharmacist refused to give a woman who had miscarried her prescribed medication abortion, seeming to equate miscarriage with abortion. All of these cases expose the stark reality that abortion and miscarriage are often conflated by abortion-rights opponents, creating the potential for the state to penalize women for the outcome of their pregnancy in a society without *Roe*.

In an era of rapidly increasing use of self-managed abortion through medication abortion (which can be and is often purchased online), at least in part due to the shuttering of abortion clinics, this trend of equating abortion and miscarriage is particularly dangerous.

Of course, it can't be overstated that varying versions of Patel and Shuai's experiences occur on a regular basis in states across the country. The racism and biases that made their criminal prosecution for miscarriage and potential self-managed abortion possible also exist in the aforementioned anti-abortion bills that ban abortion on the basis of the fetus's race or gender. These laws are premised on stereotyping of Asian American women as inherently predisposed to have late abortions, simply because of laws prevalent in Asian countries, and on racist distrust of women of color as more willing to commit murder or engage in criminal, "un-American" activity. Ultimately, we see these assumptions shared across race and gender-selective abortion bans, and the disproportionate criminalization of Asian American women for miscarriage and self-managed abortion.

Racialized differentials in how women are treated in the realm of reproductive health care also exist in disparities in maternal death rates, often due to implicit bias from health-care providers who are predisposed to take the pain and concerns of white women more seriously. After all, notions of white, feminine fragility are a fixture in American politics. Consider, for example, Trump's oft-repeated talking point of bestial Mexican rapists coming to pillage and plunder American women and girls—in his eyes "American women and girls" are white American women and girls.

In addition to dehumanizing cultural stereotypes of black women as more masculine and apelike, these notions of fragile white femininity often subconsciously inform the behaviors and tendencies of medical professionals. And while Trumpism has often taken advantage of this cultural phenomenon of selective concern for the safety of white women, juxtaposed with stereotypes of subhuman, criminal people of color, racism in health care, and criminalization as a result, are nothing new.

A world without *Roe v. Wade* and safe, legal abortion would impact more than abortion, extending to all aspects of sexuality, pregnancy, and privacy and autonomy for all. Pregnancies would effectively be policed by the state, and miscarriages looked upon with suspicion as potential self-managed abortions. In so many words, the prosecution of miscarriage—a reality that is already happening—tells us born, living women that we and our rights and freedoms are worth less even than unviable or miscarried fetuses. In the absence of *Roe,* American women could be doubly punished for the pain and trauma of miscarriage through criminalization.

When it comes to reproductive rights, women are being lied to. Fertilized eggs, embryos, and fetuses are not born, living children; abortion is not murder, and contrary to many confused, conservative politicians, Plan B and hormonal birth control are not abortion. Abortion is health care, and a fundamental human right, and there isn't a single good reason that any person's reproductive health-care options should be limited to satiate the ideological preferences of compassionless politicians.

That said, we're not only being lied to, but also being lied to about whether or not we're being lied to.

In the 2018 Supreme Court decision *NIFLA v. Becerra*, the court determined that fake women's health clinics that target disproportionately low-income women of color, spread objectively false lies about abortion and contraception, and fail to disclose that they do not offer any real health care, have the constitutional right to do so. According to the decision, a California law requiring predatory "clinics" to disclose that they are not health-care providers and that health-care options such as abortion and birth control could be obtained elsewhere violated the free-speech rights of fake clinics, and amounted to compelled speech.

The decision upheld the right of fake clinics, which often receive taxpayer funding, to lie to women about their options while posturing as real women's health clinics. In contrast, states with mandatory anti-abortion counseling laws have the power to compel speech from doctors and abortion providers, requiring them to spread lies about potential side effects of abortion, or counsel patients about dangerous, widely discredited conspiracy theories about how medication abortion can be "reversed."

The Supreme Court justices who dissented pointed out how the shifting media landscape advantaged fake women's health clinics at vulnerable women's expense. These clinics are able to take advantage of search engines to advertise their websites, which are rife with misleading language implying that they offer services they do not, and target pregnant women who may be less informed about sexual health and what their options may be.

Fake women's health clinics are able to capitalize on laws that require women to receive ultrasounds before accessing abortion care, and ensnare disproportionately low-income women by advertising free ultrasound services. But because state laws require women seeking abortions to have their ultrasound at the same clinic they have their abortion, "free ultrasounds" from fake clinics ultimately only inconvenience women, who will have to travel elsewhere to seek both an ultrasound and abortion care.

In other words, the internet age in tandem with increasingly restrictive anti-abortion laws have created a landscape in which fake clinics can thrive to the detriment of disproportionately less educated women, low-income women, young women, and women of color. Yet, according to the Supreme Court, we aren't being lied to: anti-choice "clinics" are merely practicing their free speech, despite how this "free speech" could impact the trajectory of many women's lives.

The *NIFLA* decision reflects a similar policy agenda carried out by the Trump administration through its global gag rule on international reproductive-health organizations, as well as its domestic gag rule on American doctors and health-care providers.

The global gag rule withholds funding from organizations that offer reproductive health-care services or advocacy for abortion care around the world. These organizations also offer crucial education about HIV prevention and sexual health for adolescents, rendering many people in developing, majority-nonwhite countries vulnerable to public health crises caused as a result of American politics.

Within a few short years of its implementation, the global gag rule, originally put in place in the Reagan era, has already impacted health and economic outcomes of unsaid numbers of women and girls. In developing countries, girls are more likely to enter child marriages or struggle economically as adults without access to crucial reproductive health education and resources.

In the United States, President Trump and his Health and Human Services Department proposed a domestic iteration of the gag rule on numerous occasions in 2018, before it was finally able to take effect in 2019. The domestic gag rule allows doctors who "morally object" to abortion and contraception to withhold information from their patients and defunds organizations and health-care providers that offer abortion services or referrals. This would effectively shatter the trust that is foundational to doctor-patient relationships and rob women of the right to make fully informed decisions about their bodies and lives. Like *NIFLA*, the domestic gag rule is justified as a means to protect the free-speech rights of Christian, anti-choice doctors and health-care providers and exposes whose "freedom" is prioritized in this country.

That is, doctors and health-care workers who morally reject abortion have the freedom to choose a profession that does not require them to tell patients about their full range of health-care options—because that's precisely what abortion is: a health-care option. In contrast, the domestic gag rule is hardly freedom for women who will have the misfortune of being served by anti-choice, misogynist doctors, for women whose health-care decisions and futures could be limited by what they are or aren't told by a doctor they place full trust in.

Women should be able to trust their doctors and health-care providers—at the very least, they are owed that. But the domestic gag rule fundamentally erodes that trust, and women pay the price.

Both gag rules are fundamentally about putting politics—and, often, the politics of wealthy white men—before American and international women's health, safety, and autonomy. Still, fake women's health clinics and the dangerous, authoritarian gag rules aren't even the only means through which the anti-choice agenda deceives and disproportionately targets young women and girls.

Because only a minority of states require sex ed in public schools to be medically and factually accurate, many programs fail to offer inclusive education that supports the experiences of LGBTQ students, or education about consent and how to access abortion care and contraception. And in direct contradiction with conservative veneration of the "marketplace of ideas," institutions like Planned Parenthood that actually offer accurate, comprehensive education about sexual health are routinely defunded, shut down, and censored on the state and federal levels, while misogynist and plainly inaccurate sex ed is permitted.

Lack of sexual health education in public schools carries dangerous long-term consequences. States that do not require sex ed in public schools have dramatically higher rates of teen pregnancy, as well as higher rates of poverty among women who may be precluded from pursuing higher education or achieving economic instability as a result of unplanned teen pregnancy.

All of this is infuriating. All of this is irrational, dangerous, and unmistakably rooted in misogyny and explicit resentment of women and girls' inclusion in public life. We are being lied to as part of a coordinated strategy to remove us from American life, to keep us in our place—and no matter how many times anti-choice lawmakers say it isn't, *that* is their goal, *that* is the foundation of their movement.

Still, I think of the Quinnipiac poll that found 72 percent of American voters don't think *Roe v. Wade* is in trouble, even with conservative Supreme Court and state legislature majorities. I think of similar polls which have shown liberal American voters who are concerned with the conservative Supreme Court majority are less likely to be concerned about abortion rights than they are about nearly every other issue. I think about Democratic Party leadership's silence and frequent concessions where reproductive rights are concerned, the leaders' inability to even say that word "abortion" aloud, in many cases.

In nearly all spaces, reproductive rights are either actively attacked or passively marginalized, but, still, we are told in so many words that there are more important fights, that "it's not that bad," "it won't come to that," or we're "overreacting." And to those criticisms, amid a culture of gaslighting, deceit, and misogyny, my response is simple: Our health, safety, credibility, and most fundamental rights exist in a state of ceaseless and perpetual jeopardy—it's simply impossible to overreact.

In response to the rapidly shifting, increasingly volatile landscape around abortion and reproductive rights, women and allies aren't overreacting—in many cases, we're just acting. Abortion-rights organizing has been resurgent, as has abortion fundraising, which provides money not just for abortion but also for all logistical support women may need, including travel and lodging if all clinics near them have been shut down. But on top of electoral and community organizing, the last several years have also seen elevated, personal conversation about abortion and women's lived experiences. In 2019, following the prominent wave of abortion bans in the South, actor and activist Busy Philipps launched the hashtag #YouKnowMe to tell her own abortion story and encourage others to do same.

Thousands of stories surfaced in response, all of them powerful and vital to elevating the often highly stigmatized, needlessly covert dialogue around abortion experiences. Yet the demand for the hashtag—not its content—harkened back to a simpler, more

paternalistic time, when men exclusively spoke about issues of violence against women by making references to their daughters and
wives and sisters and mothers. In other words, the fact that we
still *need* social hashtags like #YouKnowMe to both recognize those
who have abortions as human and care about them feels antiquated
and frustrating.

#YouKnowMe almost reminds of #MeToo, the viral, power-
ful hashtag that in 2017 launched the mainstream iteration of the
eponymous movement to expose the prevalence of sexual abuse
and misogyny among powerful men and to demand accountability. Like #MeToo, the movement for abortion storytelling through
#YouKnowMe carried the potential to transform the conversation
around abortion access by raising awareness about how common it
is. Yet, both hashtags expose how dangerous and arguably degrading it is that women who have survived violence or had abortions
are pressured to yield their privacy and safety from sexist hatred,
just to be seen as human.

Abortion storytelling is beautiful, powerful, and important and
a vital weapon against the cloying, persistent abortion stigma that
remains at the heart of nearly all anti-abortion legislation and violence. Yet, the question of why we require women to pour out bot-
tomless emotional energy and potentially risk their lives, just so others
will care about an issue they should already care about, remains.

Those who have only begun paying attention to and caring
about reproductive rights in the face of total abortion bans, and
the anti-abortion Supreme Court majority conservatives have spent
years promising, should have cared a long time ago—and they
should have cared without having to hear the personal stories of
their loved ones.

Ultimately, the reason it took them so long, the reason it took
women in several states losing everything, being threatened with

life in prison if they sought basic reproductive health care, being virtually forced to come forward with their abortion stories in a dehumanizing fight to save their rights, is simple: gaslighting—years and years and years of gaslighting, telling women we had *Roe,* and therefore they should sit down and shut up and be grateful. But abortion bans didn't come out of nowhere. They came first as the innocuous mandatory waiting periods, the regulations on clinics, the second-trimester abortion bans. Women have been warning of the direction we've been moving in; we were ignored. Anyone who was shocked by the events of 2018 and 2019 had to recognize then and there that they were part of the problem—a problem that can only really be solved through listening to women.

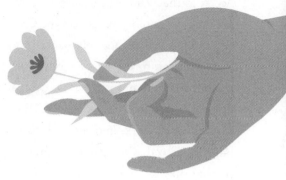

# 7

# We Are the Change We Seek

At the beginning of 2017, California state Senator Connie Leyva and Assemblymember Wendy Carrillo introduced SB 320, a bill that would mandate medication abortion access in public state universities' health centers. Access to the abortion pills would be privately funded (although, for what it's worth, there is hardly any fiscal or moral reason to *not* fund college women's health care with taxpayer dollars) and would also address a crucial gap in female college students' health-care needs. Prior to SB 320's proposal, a UC San Francisco study revealed every month an estimated 519 UC and CSU students already sought medication abortions off campus.[1]

At the time the bill was introduced, the average distance to a medication abortion provider was five miles from California State University campuses and seven miles from University of California campuses. Access to these clinics could necessitate hours of travel time and substantial cost, as most students in the CSU and UC systems don't have cars and face a wide range of financial barriers as college students.

According to the female college students responsible for proposing, writing, and extensively campaigning for SB 320, lack of campus abortion access required students seeking abortion care to miss class, work, and internships or shoulder a steep financial burden, exacerbating gender inequality on campus. In more rural parts of the state, travel to access abortion could be an all-day affair.

Contrary to fearmongering, baseless attacks on SB 320 by California Students for Life and other anti-choice groups, and hence the rising demand for it, the abortion pill is highly safe and results in complications less than 0.25 percent of the time. Feigned, anti-choice "concerns" about students' safety were rooted in anti-choice politicians' incessant need to deny young women control over their bodies and health.

The bill eventually passed both the state Senate and Assembly by a two-to-one margin and was supported by 60 percent of Californian voters—only to be vetoed by Democratic, "pro-choice" Governor Jerry Brown in September 2018. According to Brown, who is notably a white man lacking experience with unwanted pregnancy in college, SB 320 was "unnecessary" because abortion is—in Brown's mind—highly accessible throughout the state, despite how 43 percent of California counties lack an abortion provider.[2]

That word "unnecessary" seemed to serve as code for "too radical," "going too far," "asking for too much"—all the things young feminists who raise their voices and work to push boundaries hear so often. Ultimately, the rejection of SB 320 stung coming from a man who had long claimed to be our ally and support our rights, but it was hardly surprising.

Contrary to Brown's out-of-touch claims that the bill did not reflect real demands, the bill wasn't created by lawmakers sitting in the Capitol and imagining a hypothetical need for abortion access on college campuses. It was created by female college students, who were motivated by their lived experiences with struggling to access abortion and the toll this took on their academic and professional lives and financial situations. Brown's calling SB 320 "unnecessary" and vetoing the bill erases all of this, and necessarily erases young women's lived experiences.

Brown's decision sent a clear message to us young women about just how little our voices and day-to-day lives matter to men in positions of power. And much like his 2016 decision to veto a bill that would have ended the tampon tax and replaced it with a tax on alcohol (notably, drinking is a choice, but menstruation isn't), Brown's vetoing of SB 320 reflects a deep disconnect between powerful men's perceptions and young women's real lives, and how fundamentally disinterested men like him are with actually learning about our experiences and including us in the conversation.

College students' ability to access abortion care, which is obstructed by geographic and financial barriers for many, can decide whether they're able to stay in school or will be forced to drop out and potentially suffer a lifetime of economic struggle as a result. Abortion access for students comes with extensive burdens that highlight a fundamental, gendered inequality on campuses: cisgender male students will never have to worry about facing unwanted pregnancy, being forced to miss obligations like class and work to access prenatal health care, or struggling to pay for their abortions.

Brown's decision to reject SB 320 while continuing to call himself pro-choice is a stark reminder of how the "pro-choice" label must encompass so much more than just the bare minimum of not actively opposing the right to an abortion. Lawmakers have to do more than check off a box for whether or not they theoretically support abortion rights and self-identify as pro-choice. Those words mean nothing if they come from politicians like Brown, who claim to support women while leveraging their power—bestowed upon them *by* women—to do the opposite. We need representatives who share and relate to our experiences, or at the very least, are willing to listen and learn from us. We don't need—nor can we afford—wealthy, out-of-touch male lawmakers like Brown, who take it upon themselves to determine what's "unnecessary" for young women, without listening to our voices or sharing our experiences. At this point, words like Brown's are what we've become used to hearing.

---

Today, we young feminists are given every reason to tone ourselves down, or avoid "controversial" advocacy work when everything we say and do and ask for within the bounds of the patriarchy will always inherently be perceived as radical. But we don't. We never have. Throughout history and certainly today, young women and girls have always emerged as leaders of social-justice movements, because that is the extent of our courage and our power, the depth of our convictions and commitment to equality—not just for ourselves, but for everyone.

Young black women were the founders of the dynamic and unabashedly powerful Black Lives Matter movement in 2013; it was young black women who emerged with the courage to state a truth so simple, yet still so tragically revolutionary. Despite media narratives that often frame racist police brutality as limited to attacks on heterosexual, able-bodied black men, the movement's leaders and core base of young, black women have always been vocal about the disparate targeting and violent treatment of black women. From Sandra Bland's 2015 death by way of a routine traffic stop to the dozens of black women a white, Oklahoma police officer raped and sexually assaulted over the course of years, black women are often even more vulnerable to state violence due to the lesser attention, media coverage, and sympathy their experiences receive.

And from Emma Gonzalez, Jaclyn Corin, and Lauren Hogg, of the March for Our Lives movement for gun control, to the youth-led *Juliana v. United States* lawsuit taking the United States to task for advancing climate change, to alumni of the formerly active, youth-feminist blog Feministing founding the Know Your IX campaign against college and K–12 campus sexual assault, young women are paving the way forward for nearly every social-justice movement you could name. This shouldn't be surprising: across all of our intersecting identities, young women are bound by the shared experience of being disproportionately harmed and oppressed by our status as women and girls.

Gun violence and mass shootings, for example, disproportionately harm women and girls, especially when domestic abusers have access to firearms. Climate change, which carries disproportionate consequences for the young people who will inhabit this planet for years to come, has always especially impacted young women and girls in the United States and around the world: Increased frequency of natural disasters can displace and further inconvenience and endanger women in rural parts of the country who must travel for reproductive health care. On the global level, women are the primary water-gatherers and agricultural workers; exposure to ecological hazards like pollution and lead poisoning can also lead to increased miscarriage and infant death rates. Additionally, although sexual abuse may impact one in six men, the power dynamics governing heterosexist societies have always made young women and girls most vulnerable to this violence.

When you exist as a member of any marginalized group, whether you're a person of color, or LGBTQ+, or low-income, and certainly when you're a young woman, anything you ask for from powerful people and institutions will always be too much, because your existence and questioning are inherently radical. To groups that have always been in power and maintained monopolies on credibility, authority, rights, and privilege, the premise of equality itself, let alone any measurable steps taken to achieve it, is perceived as a terrifying, radical threat.

For generations, marginalized people have been forced to celebrate compromises such as desegregation, legal abortion rights, and marriage equality as tremendous victories and triumphs, while our remaining, existential demands are regarded as "asking for too much." Queer people asking for legal rights against discrimination? Asking for too much. Black people asking to not be profiled and subjected to extrajudicial killings by law enforcement? Asking for too much. Women asking for taxpayer dollars to pay for abortion care? Way, *way* too much.

During a highly formative internship with the National Network of Abortion Funds in the summer of my college freshman year, a mentor and I discussed the alarming phenomenon of "pro-choice" Democratic Party leadership insisting that we support anti-abortion Democrats in their elections. She made a point that I've been thinking about ever since: Women's rights always seem to be the first to go.

Yet, rather than relegate women's most fundamental human rights to bargaining chips for the imagined electoral gains this would bring about, Democratic leadership could invest additional effort into mobilizing and getting out the votes of the countless disenfranchised marginalized people who remain either sidelined from elections or too disenchanted with politics to participate. And in either case, which purportedly key voting demographic anti-choice Democratic candidates would somehow, magically galvanize, party leadership has yet to identify. As New York Representative Alexandria Ocasio-Cortez said in 2018 ahead of her first general election, "Our swing voter is not red-to-blue. Our swing voter is the voter to the non-voter, the non-voter to the voter."

During the 2009 and 2010 writing of, and negotiations around, the Affordable Care Act, Democrats wound up scrapping key protections to reproductive health-care access and abortion coverage that had been demanded by female Democrats, due to skepticism by several male Democrats who—if you can believe—ultimately won the conflict. Of course, this wasn't some isolated episode or anomaly. Passive exclusion of women's rights and experiences and watered-down protections for women are codified into many male-led progressive movements and spaces, in order to make their demands more mainstream and digestible.

Progressive icon Senator Bernie Sanders's embrace of tuition-free public college would certainly disproportionately benefit young women, people of color, and marginalized people, in general. Yet, we should question why universal child care, or mass investment in testing rape kits, or similar measures that address traditionally feminine experiences are almost never discussed, or remain regarded as "fringe" within these same progressive spaces that so aggressively demand tuition-free public college.

In a patriarchal landscape in which institutions are fundamentally built to maintain an oppressive status quo, is it necessary to make some compromises, or temporarily leave some groups behind to make any progress at all? In progressive spaces, is it necessary to ask women and people of color and other nonmale, nonwhite people who will automatically be deemed more radical, to step back, and allow men and white people to be the faces of our movements?

Certainly, it depends on whom you ask and on the compromise or concession in question. But since the white-women-led suffrage movement of the nineteenth and early twentieth centuries, and its exclusion of and proactive attacks on black Americans' voting rights, whether to exclude and compromise to make incremental progress has been an ongoing tension in feminism throughout history.

The more time I've spent pondering this tension, the more I've considered the paramount importance of including and amplifying young women's voices in the debate. On several occasions, I've set out to engage young feminists across lines of race, geography, socioeconomic status, and identity in conversation, to hear about their work toward a more inclusive, intersectional feminism and the recurring conflicts and challenges they face as young women and women of color having a voice in this movement. The following were some of my conversations.

# GRACE WEBER

Grace Weber, nineteen, serves as the National Organization for Women's head of college students and traces her involvement in feminist activism to her mother's separation from her abusive father when she was fourteen. "I know I come from a place of privilege," she says, "I'm white, and my father is wealthy and corporate. But that experience of knowing what my mother went through showed me how much there is to be done."

Growing up, she and her mother would occasionally volunteer at shelters for survivors of domestic abuse, and around her freshman year of high school, Grace first began to engage in organizing work. "I started a feminist club, and we would have small meetings and do what felt like small fundraisers and bake sales for women's shelters," she recalls. "Not many people showed up, but it was so rewarding, and I built such strong relationships with the people who did. That was the best, most meaningful part."

Naturally, Grace's vocal feminist organizing and activism drew backlash and condescending attacks from her peers in high school "When are women and girls *not* attacked for 'caring too much?'" I ask. She says this "only riled [her] up."

"I was in debate, and I loved to have that chance to speak up and fight for and defend what I believed in," she says. But Grace understands it isn't like that for everyone; for some, especially young women who are marginalized across their intersecting identities, backlash and threats and attacks can be silencing and push them out of feminist activism entirely.

Where does Grace fall in that ongoing compromise-for-progress debate? "It's always going to be situational," she says, "but the thing that concerns me most isn't just that debate but all the people who still aren't part of it—all the people in places of privilege, who could safely get out there and do real activism, but think in this social-media age that liking and sharing things on is enough.

"One of my biggest fears is, performativity, that people from places of privilege who could be doing more, or doing anything, aren't," she continues. "How can we have more nuanced talks about compromise and progress when in a lot of cases, we're still not doing enough?"

Grace sees her place in the feminist movement and its future not necessarily in offering leadership, but "continuing the work" of all the radical feminists and thought leaders and activists who paved the way for the movement. "I see it as my place to follow their lead and know a lot of the conversations and fights aren't always very new or original and are happening now because of the women who fought before us," she says.

# SHIREEN SHAKOURI

Shireen Shakouri, twenty-seven, recalls growing up in a Catholic household with relatively conservative attitudes about sex. Going to college marked a distinct cultural shift as she discovered sex positivity and reproductive-justice activism.

"I got involved with Voices for Choices, and it started out silly and light-hearted, distributing condoms and raising awareness in the student quad," she recalls. Shireen was inspired to engage in activism and education work by her own experiences growing up and her desire to help younger people have more access to sexual-health resources and information than she had.

Today, Shireen works professionally as a campaign manager for an action-based organization that focuses on education and community engagement around reproductive justice. She also volunteers as an abortion doula, offering companionship, support, and conversation to people who seek abortion care, after previously volunteering as an abortion-clinic escort.

"Clinic escorts are warriors; what they do is so necessary. For me, being an escort just forced me to put what I felt was too much focus and emotional labor to the opposition, to anti-choice harassers outside clinics, when I wanted to give more of my focus and emotional labor to the actual people having abortions," she says. "Becoming a doula was transformative to helping me focus on relating to and supporting people having abortions."

In 2016, then-Democratic National Committee Chair Debbie Wasserman Schultz suggested that abortion rights had become more tenuous because young women had become more passive and complacent on the issue. Many young women pushed back on this comment by citing their own experiences of giving their time and even jeopardizing their safety to volunteer as escorts and doulas. Through this volunteer work, they have stood up for reproductive rights in the most personal and perhaps most powerful way possible.

Today, Shireen fears the "umbrella of stigma" around all things related to reproductive rights—including even stigma within the pro-choice movement itself—as one of the most important fights the feminist movement must take on. "It's so unfortunate that opposition has been setting the playing field, defining our movement, and choosing the language in such a harmful way, for decades," she says. "We're forced to be on the defense, letting them define us, celebrating compromises."

Shireen also thinks the movement is necessarily held back by how much emotional energy it requires just to be able to get involved at all. "The opposition is so strong, and the subject matter is so personal, the stigma is so prevalent, of course not everyone who wants to can be part of this," she says. "Our core base is also often mostly volunteers, so that can be a gatekeeper to people along socioeconomic lines who can't really volunteer their time. Yet, ironically, they're often disproportionately affected by this fight, and their experiences and voices need to be centered."

Shireen encounters criticisms of her reproductive-justice activism often, not just from conservatives but also from "pro-choice" people pushing back on her advocacy to stop incarcerated, pregnant women from being shackled during birth, and her advocacy to promote positivity around abortion.

"You'll have campaigns like Shout Your Abortion that don't fall in line with that traditional narrative of abortion as sad and shameful and always a difficult decision to make, when some people celebrate having an abortion and that experience of taking control of their bodies," she says. "People will say if you celebrate abortion you're not taking it seriously, because so many people either oppose abortion, or think it should exclusively be what they call 'safe, legal, and rare.'"

In terms of making concessions and compromises within the feminist movement to make any gains at all, Shireen acknowledges this tension is often complicated. "For reproductive rights, we've been losing ground and celebrating compromise for years, such that proactive work and fighting for more than what we have hasn't really been happening—we're forced to play defense, all the time," she says. "The notion that so long as we have *Roe v. Wade* we can be complacent has infected many people's mindsets for years, and that's part of why we are where we are today."

For some organizations and campaigns, discussion and inclusion of reproductive rights is often necessarily limited so they can appeal more broadly to donors and fundraising, which they rely on in order to perform any advocacy work at all. For example, according to Shireen, the work of groups that advocate for domestic-abuse survivors is necessarily entwined with abortion rights, because abortion and reproductive health care are often critical tools of survival for abuse victims to safely leave and become independent of their abusers. Yet, many groups for survivors avoid openly advocating for reproductive rights. "So often, it's a balancing act, when you have feminist groups who are trying to appeal to and have as many allies as possible, and it's not simple," she says.

Nonetheless, Shireen is hopeful about feminism's future and the inclusion of reproductive justice within that future. "We see abortion rights, today, as so vulnerable and closest on the horizon to fall, and that allows us to bring it closer to the forefront of the movement than ever before," she says.

"Young people today—and I don't mean to sound old, saying that—this is such a unique time because so much change has happened in such a short amount of time, recently. You could have people my age saying, 'When I was a teenager, this hadn't been done' or 'it wasn't like this,' about trans rights and so many other crucial identity-based issues," she says. "So we're fighting in a playing field that's become so much more open, and inclusive, and we're using that as much as we can to our advantage."

# HAYLEY FARLESS

Having grown up in a low-income community in Tennessee, Hayley Farless, twenty-four, holds an unshakable conviction that feminism must leave no one behind. And the way feminist issues so often are, this is personal to her.

Farless's high school was located right across the street from an anti-abortion "crisis pregnancy center," while the closest actual abortion clinic was several hours away. But she didn't even know this until she studied global health at Duke University and learned just how severely lacking in resources and sexual-health education her community had been.

Today, on top of working for a leading reproductive-rights advocacy organization and writing about reproductive justice for national publications and organizations, Hayley devotes some of her free time to volunteering as a clinic escort and supporting a range of reproductive-justice advocacy campaigns. One of her ultimate focuses is intersectionality and fighting for women of color, immigrant women, low-income women, and women with disabilities who face disparate, often unacknowledged barriers to access reproductive health care.

Suffice to say, she often encounters criticisms of her advocacy and demands as going "too far" and being "too radical," not just from opponents of reproductive rights but also from those within the movement. "It's frustrating that even within the movement if you fight for intersectionality, you'll hear criticisms that we're erasing the 'primary goal' by adding more things," she says. "But if we leave behind less privileged people in this fight, because it's easier that way, we're actively contributing to their oppression. In feminism, we can't work on sexism as if it's a vertical issue; we have to work horizontally, too, at all the intersections."

When Hayley considers the ongoing debate of compromise and exclusion of certain groups for incremental progress, she recalls the famous Audre Lorde quote, which she regards almost as a personal mantra: "I am not free while any woman is unfree, even when her shackles are very different from my own."

Hayley thinks a lot about the emerging narrative of "identity politics," or the increasingly popular liberal idea that broad inclusion of the most marginalized could somehow endanger the feminist movement and amount to asking too much of society. "The easiest course of progress and liberation is for those who are most privileged, so those who are less privileged—LGBTQ, people with disabilities, immigrants—are excluded," she says. "But we just can't leave anyone behind. I don't see it as progress if we're leaving people behind."

This reflection, in particular, feels especially worth pausing to fully consider: No one becomes a perfect feminist in one day, or perhaps ever. But everyone with a sincere desire to advance this movement's goals of justice and equity has a responsibility to continuously grow and hold themselves accountable, to question their own privilege and biases, and examine all the ways their feminism might be constrained by said privilege and biases. The solutions we fight for shouldn't exclusively benefit the least marginalized, those at the top for whom justice and equity are most easily salvageable. Our solutions must include and uplift everyone—or they aren't solutions at all.

But there's also a lot that Hayley *is* excited about: the relatively new development of the term "reproductive justice," which encompasses more than reproductive rights in theory to include access to the full range of resources that allow all people to make decisions about their bodies, lives, and families. And, certainly, she's excited about the growing potency of young women as a voting bloc: "Our political power is only growing, so if we vote and show up, we could be and arguably already are the most powerful demographic in politics," she says. "In that way, I'm optimistic about the feminist movement's future and my role as a young woman in leading it."

# JORDYN CLOSE

Jordyn Close, twenty-two, is a community organizer and educator for a DC-based reproductive-justice advocacy organization and member of the National Network of Abortion Funds' We Testify program to dismantle abortion stigma with storytelling. She has a brilliantly simple take on the feminist compromise/progress debate: "So, it's situational, first of all," she says. "We'll see maybe a twenty-four-week abortion ban, and 'pro-choice' people might say, 'Well, that's not that bad; let's compromise.' But it *is* bad, because any legal restriction is a restriction that shouldn't be there."

In other cases? "For me, I personally really embrace socialism and communism, but what I'll say is, we can't reject a good, progressive Democratic candidate because they're not a socialist. It's situational. And who suffers most when we have Trump and Republicans in office? The most vulnerable people," Jordyn says.

On top of her work as an educator and organizer, Jordyn views storytelling and speaking about her experience with having abortion as the most powerful work she does to promote reproductive justice and its inclusion in the feminist movement.

"It was 2015. I was living in Ohio, where recently, state lawmakers are introducing the craziest things," she says. Close says at eighteen she was relatively "fortunate" where others are not—she could afford the abortion with the help of her boyfriend, and anti-choice protest outside her clinic was minimal; she still had to wait the mandatory, "stupid" and unnecessary waiting period, but other than that, she says her abortion story is "what everyone's should be."

Today, Jordyn tells her abortion story with We Testify, a program that supports and trains people who have abortions and want to share their stories, and centers the voices and experiences of women of color like her. Jordyn views one of the ultimate challenges reproductive justice faces as misinformation, and so, on top of education and inclusive language, storytelling to dispel with cultural myths and stigma around abortion is arguably the most important activism she can provide.

"I'd like to say feminism is doing a good job including reproductive justice, and I'm optimistic about many things," she says. But in her experience, she sees the toxicity of the compromise/progress paradigm in common, everyday language and conversations around abortion. "You'll hear a lot of, 'I'm pro-choice but not pro-abortion,' when there's nothing wrong with that word, there's nothing wrong with supporting abortion. But people are afraid to go that 'far' out of fear of isolating or pushing people out—as if people who reject abortion rights have any business in feminism, anyway," she says. "I say, we don't want or need the people who would be 'pushed out' by including abortion."

Whatever the future holds for feminism, to Jordyn, young feminists like herself have to be a part of it. "Sometimes, you'll see infighting in the movement from feminists of older generations and younger people like me," she says, citing, in particular, her advocacy for organizations to use gender-neutral language in the dialogue around reproductive rights, because women aren't the only people who have abortions, or need birth control. "That infighting can be difficult. But it shows we're [young feminists] leading the way forward."

# STEPHANIE PINEIRO

Stephanie Pineiro, twenty-seven, is also a member of We Testify. On top of her work as a social worker and consultant to support reproductive-justice advocacy groups in crafting inclusive language and campaigns, she shares the stories of the two abortions she had when she was sixteen and seventeen, as a storyteller, and speaks about the unique stigmas and challenges she faced from her identity as a Latinx minor.

"Because of my Latinx identity, there was a lot of added shame and stigma associated with my abortions," she says, "and because I was a minor, and all of that shame and stigma, I needed to get a judge's approval for my second abortion, because I didn't want my parents to know I needed another abortion."

Today, Stephanie shares her story as a form of activism to ensure people like her are included in the conversations around reproductive justice. She embraces the "radicalness" of merely taking up space in these conversations and spaces as a Latinx woman who has had multiple abortions, and as a minor—experiences that remain widely stigmatized even within many "pro-choice," pro-reproductive-rights environments.

In her advocacy work, Stephanie focuses on speaking up for the reproductive rights of minors who face disparate challenges to access, like she did as a teenager in Florida. "Those challenges are certainly legal, but also very economic, because most minors don't have cars or money of their own," she says. That's why Stephanie feels so strongly about ending the Hyde Amendment, a federal law that prohibits federal taxpayer dollars from supporting elective abortion care. But she says even repealing Hyde isn't going far enough: "It's not just that Medicaid needs to cover abortion. It's thinking about all the undocumented women and girls without access to Medicaid who still need support, and it's about how Medicaid itself—as someone who grew up with it—is not the quality of health care we deserve. Nowhere near it."

When Stephanie thinks of feminism's future and how this future may be shaped by where we choose to make compromises, she ponders the generational disconnects within the movement. "In all movements, of course there's space for incremental progress," she says. "But a major question we should be asking is, who's making the decision of what we compromise on and what we fight for, who we include, and who we push out? Based on who in the movement is deciding those things, we'll see sometimes compromise is the only thing that's allowed for some people, and less privileged people not getting what they deserve because of that."

# VERONIKA GRANADO

Veronika Granado, nineteen, was seventeen when she sought and received judicial bypass to have an abortion in the state of Texas. "That was something my parents didn't support, so I had to go it alone," she says.

Since, Granado has joined Youth Testify, a program in conjunction with We Testify that highlights the disparate experiences of minors and young people seeking abortion care. She also works with Jane's Due Process, a reproductive health-care fund based in Texas, as a mentor to minors seeking abortion care and the judicial bypass this often requires.

Granado is concerned feminism sometimes fails to fully include reproductive justice and experiences like hers. "The ['pro-choice/pro-life' binary] can leave out a lot of that," she says. As for whether compromise is sometimes a necessary evil to achieve marginal progress, Granado is more concerned with "at least getting our foot in the door" to make greater demands and nuanced compromises possible in the first place.

"Abortion is health care," she says, "and I view one of my biggest goals as making sure others recognize that, within and outside the feminist movement. Talking about later abortion or minors having abortions can't even happen until we get *there* first."

It isn't missed on Granado that the inherently incremental, sometimes painfully slow nature of progress hits some groups harder, but she stays hopeful nonetheless. "I think change doesn't always happen quickly, and that's frustrating and especially hard for some people," she says. "But we're laying down the foundations for progress every day, even if it doesn't always feel like it."

------

There is no shortage whatsoever of young feminist activists who are pushing the movement's boundaries and paving the way forward and whom I would have loved to talk to—the young, college-age founders of Period.org, a national movement to fight menstruation stigma and support universal access to menstrual hygiene products; the young women partnering with organizations like EMILY's List, IGNITE, Emerge America, She Should Run, and other groups doing the backbreaking work to elect more pro-choice, pro-equality women to office; Alicia Garza, Patrisse Cullors, and Opal Tometi, the ceaselessly courageous founders of Black Lives Matter; the young people everywhere who are eagerly organizing and fighting for immigrant justice, criminal justice reform, affordable housing, food insecurity, gun control, tuition-free public education, and more.

I first began engaging feminist work through writing and journalism when I was sixteen, and I haven't stopped since. But as I've grown more confident and certainly more passionate about social justice, I've pushed myself to not just write about but also actively support the work of my favorite advocacy organizations and engage in community organizing and activist work.

My experiences working with organizations like the National Network of Abortion Funds, NARAL Pro-Choice America, NARAL Pro-Choice California, and *Ms.* Magazine, published by the Feminist Majority Foundation, in college were transformative and showed me that intersectional feminism could be infinitely more than a hobby, or a side-job, or ranting on social media; it could be a career, a lifestyle, and a family. And ahead of the 2018 midterm elections, I overcame my introverted nature and fell in love with canvassing, phone banking, and engaging with voters in the numerous swing districts an hour or two out from my South Los Angeles university.

Like the young feminists I spoke with, I know the skepticism my passion and activism and demands for justice and equity draw—from men, from institutions, perhaps even from feminists of older generations. I know many of the causes I hold closest to my heart—abortion access, an end to racist-state violence, justice and credibility for survivors—will always be seen as radical, often for no other reason than my identity as a young woman of color or the identities of the marginalized people who would disproportionately benefit from progress in these issues.

But I'm undeterred because I believe in the worthiness and humanity and moral necessity of the causes I fight for, because I believe in the women I fight alongside, and because I love this fight. More than almost anything in the world, I love this fight; for all the growth, passion, and humility it's brought to my life, I love and give it my everything each day. Rarely if ever do I think about

what I can't change, what I will or won't see in my lifetime; I think
only of what things I can and consequently must do every day to
advance social justice and give support where it is needed.

Where the ongoing compromise/progress tension is concerned,
I agree with many of the young women I spoke to—the decision
to make compromises, or concede this or that, is necessarily situational. For any given issue, there is so much at stake, so many grave,
disproportionate consequences for women, people of color, and all
other marginalized people, that unfortunately, we fight from a place
that requires us to be selective in choosing which hills to die on.

But in no shortage of cases, there are issues that are simply too
fundamental to compromise on; there is the universal, enduring
truth that human rights are never too much to ask for, nor will
there ever be justification for conceding them. Across all contexts
and situations, we must view women, people of color, immigrants,
people with disabilities, and LGBTQ folks as human beings, not
bargaining chips; any conversation we have about their rights and
existence requires their voices and presence.

I and nearly all of the young feminists I spoke with see ourselves as the leaders of something powerful and new; we see both
this moment and the future as ours to shape and grow through our
voices, demands, activism, and solidarity.

As young women and feminists, we stand on the shoulders of
giants who fought and died to make our activism possible. Merely
by existing, by experiencing and expressing human emotion within
a patriarchal society hellbent on our dehumanization, we are already
blazing our own trail forward.

Contrary to prevalent media narratives surrounding our movements, as young women, we and our activism are not the harbin-
gers of some hypothetical, incoming storm, something coming that
is greater than us. We *are* the storm. We are not waiting stagnant

for the last ball to drop, for a final line to be crossed; all the balls have dropped, all the lines have been crossed. We are here because we've *been* here, because it's been like this, and we've been fighting all along. And wherever we go next—as a movement, as a society, as a collective humanity—will be because of us and because of the work we've been putting in all our lives.

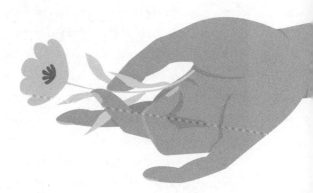

# 8

# On This "Scary Time" for Young Men

When the #MeToo movement caught fire in the fall of 2017, continuing to turn up episodic revelations well into 2019 and beyond, the chasm in gender-based experiences had never been laid more bare in modern history, with the everyday pains, frustrations, and dangers of being a woman in America—and everywhere, really—exposed for all to see. First launched by black-feminist activist Tarana Burke in 2006, #MeToo's entrance into mainstream consciousness eleven years later began with allegations against elite Hollywood executive Harvey Weinstein, accused of rape, harassment, and predation of women of all backgrounds and social statuses. Allegations against Weinstein comprised a tipping point that eventually led to countless powerful men exposed, in media, politics, academia, business, fashion, and, certainly, in everyday life. The breaking of silence was empowering; the stories of abuse, and the often diluted, minimal consequences they yielded, were horrifying.

But if women and survivors were looking for comfort and validation, we did not find it from the president, who had been accused of sexual misconduct, assault, and rape by more than twenty women. A few days after Dr. Christine Blasey Ford and then-Supreme Court nominee Brett Kavanaugh testified before the Senate about the allegations of assault she had brought against him, President Trump said to reporters, "It is a very scary time for young men in America, where you can be guilty of something you may not be guilty of. This is a very, very difficult time. What's happening here has much more to do than even the appointment of a Supreme Court justice."

Trump was right about one thing: Accusations against Kavanaugh, misogynist backlash against his accusers, and Kavanaugh's ultimate confirmation to the Supreme Court were, indeed, about something much bigger than the confirmation of one new justice. And, certainly, as he suggested, it was something much bigger not just for women but also for men. In the post-Kavanaugh era, American men are at a crossroads, as they must necessarily reflect upon their role in a society constructed by rape culture—a framework of misogyny and male privilege that systematically enables, encourages, and erases the sexual predation of women's bodies in patriarchal society.

The reality is that men—even nonviolent men—benefit from the institution of violence against women. They benefit from a society in which the threat of violence keeps women in a subservient state of perpetual fear. And they benefit from being allowed to perform the barest of minimums—not committing acts of violence against women—and still receive praise for acts of basic decency.

Certainly, none of this is to diminish the reality that men, too, are victimized by rape culture, and one in six men are survivors of some form of sexual abuse.[1] The same toxic masculinity responsible for trivializing or encouraging violence against women also accounts for the notion that men are biologically incapable of being sexually victimized, and reduces male survivors to objects of mockery.

But the disproportionate plunder of women and girls' bodies is an everyday, devastating consequence of life in a patriarchal society that accords white men an exclusive monopoly on credibility, which is subsequently weaponized to both erase and empower gendered, misogynist violence. An estimated one in five women are victims of rape; this statistic rises to one in four on college campuses, and also rises for women and girls of color. Yet, an estimated 65 to 85 percent of all sexual assaults are not reported,[2] and this number soars to 90 percent on college campuses.

Survivors often cite fear of victim-blaming, social ostracism (especially in the statistically likely event that their assailant was a friend or someone they knew), punishment, harassment, and, above all, disbelief as reasons they choose not to come forward. Through the legal system, the pursuit of justice for sexual violence can often amount to a second round of violation for survivors, from the invasive process of evidence collection, to drawn out, retraumatizing court trials, to stalking and harassment from law enforcement or those connected with their abusers. As the criminal-justice system currently treats survivors of abuse and their experiences, it is difficult to call the exchange of one's dignity and feelings of safety for the mere possibility of locking someone away for an amount of time justice.

In any case, survivors' fears are hardly unfounded, nor do they come out of nowhere. Whether it's experiences like my own with being blamed for the harassment I endured in high school because of my fashion choices, or the prevailing notion women can avoid being raped by not leaving the house at night, women and girls are told in so many ways that it's on us to safeguard ourselves from sexual violence. And if we fail to, what happens to us is either our fault or simply didn't happen. The majority of survivors—if you can believe it—were not equipped with body cameras, or ready with a collection of witnesses at the time of their assault, producing the only evidence most survivors can provide: their own testimony.

Rape kits are essentially only applicable evidence for sexual assaults that involve penetrative rape, while access to and processing of rape kits comprise a separate issue in itself. The process of collecting a rape kit can be not only costly based on insurance plans and state laws but also traumatic for some survivors. Hundreds of thousands of rape kits wind up being backlogged, filed away, and never even processed to be used as evidence at all. Using the sole evidence of testimony is an imposing challenge in a society where credibility is gendered to disfavor women and where the police officers who oversee many reports of sexual violence are—as credible research has repeatedly demonstrated—often perpetrators of sexual violence themselves. The starting point in nearly all cultural conversations about rape and sexual violence is that the woman or survivor must prove they are not a liar. It's always been this way, despite Department of Justice statistics that demonstrate over and over the virtual nonexistence of false reporting, and therefore, demonstrate that in the vast majority of cases, rapists and abusers are the liars, as they lie about not committing assaults.

So often survivors are blamed for the future rapes and violent acts committed by their abusers, which supposedly could have been stopped had the first survivor come forward. This notion, of course, is predicated on the fantasy that this first survivor would so easily be believed, their assailant neatly and tidily put away, even with the 3 percent of rapists who wind up convicted and incarcerated for their crimes.[3] But this only shifts blame away from the assailant to the victim: serial rapists (who comprise the majority of rapists) do not rape because the silence of their first or previous victims empowered them to do so—they rape because they choose to dehumanize and deny autonomy to another person; they rape because they choose to rape. Still, we absolve them of responsibility; still, society ensures survivors are more likely to be demonized for choosing to "ruin" a career or family by coming forward than abusers are for choosing to abuse.

In bemoaning the death of "due process" and "innocence until proven guilty" while offering no suggestions for sufficient evidence survivors could provide, rape apologists make it clear they do not aspire to fairness or justice, but to the oppression and demonization of women and survivors. Where evidence of sexual assaults is limited to a survivor's testimony, we encounter the perils of a society in which credibility is gendered male and women are often, at best, told their recollection of their own experience is inaccurate and, at worst, called liars.

The power dynamics that create and maintain a system of gendered credibility have always been enabled by institutions—from federal and local governments, to schools, to media and popular culture, to communities and households. These very dynamics often determine who is welcome in public life and, conversely, who at any moment could be pushed out by sexual and gender-based violence, and, by extension, who often suffers trauma in silence.

In the Trump era, the ongoing epidemic of sexual violence forcibly shifted to become a young women's issue. As previously noted, the Trump Education Department's proposed and implemented Title IX changes handling campus sexual assault purposefully stripped female students and survivors on college and K–12 campuses, alike, of credibility, resources, and protection and disproportionately empowered their male attackers.

The administration's Title IX agenda included increasing the standard of evidence for survivors who report their experiences and substantially narrowing the definition of sexual harassment from "unwelcome conduct of a sexual nature" to "unwelcome conduct on the basis of sex that is so severe, pervasive, and objectively offensive that it effectively denies a person equal access to the school's education program or activity." The first change could result in an increase in the already alarmingly high rates of unreported campus sexual assaults, while the latter could erase or dismiss many if not all of students' most traumatic experiences with harassment.

The agenda set forth by this administration clearly and decisively centered a highly infrequent male experience of being falsely accused. Yet, the intent couldn't even have been to protect men, who can hardly be protected from a problem that simply, provably doesn't exist. It seems more likely the administration meant to demonize disproportionately young, female victims. Such an agenda falls perfectly in line with a broader theme of this presidency: the codifying of cultural regression into policies as a means to satiate the president's base of resentful, white, male rape apologists. Young, college-age women are all but reduced to ritual sacrifices by President Trump's Title IX policies, which give a green light to mass violence on their bodies.

We encounter misogynist regression and the violence it inflicts upon women's bodies in the Trump administration's policy agenda. But on top of this, we see it in broad popular culture, more so in recent years than ever as a direct and explicit male-led reaction to bold developments in modern feminism. The glorification of rape culture and attitudes that lead to male-produced violence are a direct product of mounting anti-feminist backlash in recent years, contributing to mass shootings and killings by men and the nasty rhetoric and internet forum ideologies that paved the way for Trump's Title IX policies.

In recent years, the increasing popularity of modern feminism in mainstream spaces, and the rise of a new, energetic, and especially vocal, young women-led feminism for the internet age, appear to have led to a violent, reactionary male supremacist movement. Members of this movement have identified the survival of rape culture as central to their own survival in society, and in far too many documented cases, violence emerges as a real-world outcome of this ideology. Since 2014, the year Elliot Rodger created a launching point for the "incel" (involuntary celibate) movement by killing seven in a mass shooting at the University of California, Santa Barbara, and explicitly targeting young women as revenge for his feelings of rejection, there have been several mass killings and shootings in the United States led by men who identified their goal as exacting punishment on women. Nearly all mass killings have been led by men with established records of domestic violence.

At times, in the Trump era, it could feel needless, almost wasteful, to invest the exhaustive labor into explaining everything wrong with something said by President Trump. Yet, his statement that it is a "scary time" for young men in this country feels worth considering at length, because, unfortunately, this is not a radical, fringe viewpoint. Throughout the ongoing dialogue around endemic violence against women, the male experience has always been prioritized and centralized. This is meant to falsely equate the victim's trauma from experiencing sexual violence with the perpetrator's distress over justly facing accountability for hurting others.

In her 2018 essay "Whose Story (and Country) Is This?" author and feminist cultural critic Rebecca Solnit considers the phenomenon of media coverage of the women-led #MeToo movement focusing almost exclusively on male feelings, perspectives, and panic in response to the movement. #MeToo was launched to highlight the nearly universal experience of sexual abuse experienced by women and girls and produced well-documented socioeconomic progress for many women in the United States and around the world. Yet, as Solnit notes in her essay, you would hardly know this from consuming most media coverage of #MeToo:

> *We've heard from hundreds, perhaps thousands, of women about assaults, threats, harassment, humiliation, coercion, of campaigns that ended careers, pushed them to the brink of suicide. Many men's response to this is sympathy for men.... But the follow-up story to the #MeToo upheaval has too often been: how do the consequences of men hideously mistreating women affect men's comfort? Are men okay with what's happening? There have been too many stories about men feeling less comfortable, too few about how women might be feeling more secure in offices where harassing co-workers may have been removed or are at least a bit less sure about their right to grope and harass.*

A movement conceived to shine a light on women's experiences should not be usurped by male cynicism; male-centric cultural narratives around #MeToo are a shining example of the extent to which male identity and perspective are privileged with default status. According to many of these cultural narratives, including that which Trump gave voice to, a proven culture of misogynist violence and long-hidden, systemic abuse is somehow the same evil as—God forbid—accountability for abusive men; the same evil as men now being forced to—God forbid—consider how their actions could potentially cause women to feel.

Of course, long before the rise of #MeToo, we already knew the preservation of a man's reputation and feelings of safety from accountability would always take priority when women accuse men of assault. We certainly saw this in the 2016 case of Stanford rapist Brock Turner, when Santa Clara County Judge Aaron Persky's concern with the "severe impact" that years in prison could have on Turner led to a six-month county jail sentence (eventually reduced to three months) for Turner. Judge Persky, if you can believe it, had nothing to say about the "severe impact" Turner's actions had had on his female victim.

The case of Brock Turner is notable in the dialogue around rape culture from several vantage points. It forced us women and survivors to grapple with the reality that even if, by some miracle, we could provide all of the evidence that Emily Doe (Turner's victim has since come forward as Chanel Miller) had provided against Turner—forensic testing, witnesses, admission by Turner—our assailants would still likely evade any meaningful accountability, as Turner had. Rape and violence exacted upon women's bodies is often either erased altogether through denying women credibility, or in Emily Doe's case, trivialized as insignificant compared to the toll that facing consequences for their actions would have on young men.

But a particularly alarming component of the Turner case is the affirmation it gave to misguided notions of male victimhood. When we treat accused men as if they are being victimized by women who have the gall to challenge how men treated them, not only do we promote the aforementioned false equivalence between the victim and perpetrator's experiences, but we also send the misleading message that women would lie about assault with the sole intent of victimizing men.

Beyond internet forums and sexist social-media spaces, the appropriation of victimhood by men accused of sexual assault has dangerous, real-world implications for women and survivors who come forward.

During the first year following the advent of #MeToo, women were soon forced to grapple with the limits of the movement's power, in a society where anti-feminist men remain the pronounced majority of lawmakers, political leaders, and corporate executives. And #MeToo's powers to bring about long-term accountability will remain limited until such time as women are able to replace these men in spaces of power, despite the disadvantage and marginalization imposed upon them.

Certainly, the #MeToo movement has brought substantive, admirable reforms, all driven by female leadership and male allyship: Within two months of the first report about ousted Hollywood executive Harvey Weinstein, almost 90 percent of respondents to an NPR survey said they supported zero-tolerance policies for sexual harassment.[4] Some of the most prominent entertainers in Hollywood launched the Time's Up legal defense fund to support those who have experienced sexual harassment in the workplace, across all industries and walks of life. And in politics, female Congress members across party lines introduced and passed new policies addressing sexual harassment in Congress to better support victims in the reporting process, and also collaborated to hold several male politicians accused of sexual misconduct accountable.

Yet, for all the revelations and triumphs of #MeToo, we're often painfully confronted and constrained by the institutional power of backlash against our movement. We're reminded that men like comedian Louis CK, who admitted to harassing and nonconsensually masturbating in front of several women, can make easy, slick, and culturally sympathetic comebacks in their careers and be readily welcomed. We're reminded that companies will shun abusive men from their orbits only after these men are publicly exposed and shunning them becomes financially profitable.

And we're reminded that the Supreme Court confirmation of Brett Kavanaugh, facilitated by a predominantly male, Republican Senate and a president accused by more than twenty women of sexual abuse, happened not despite but because of the degrading message it sent to women and survivors. The whole affair empowered Republican leadership to showcase the structural limitations on #MeToo, to tell women and survivors that society has not yet changed so much, and men still rule. Certainly, when men in decision-making positions, from President Trump to Republican Senate Majority Leader Mitch McConnell, don't fear consequences and are quite literally incapable of feeling shame, #MeToo faces an unsettling impasse: the movement remains severely dependent on whether powerful men, who are often enablers or perpetrators of sexual abuse themselves, have consciences or some semblance of a moral backbone.

Due to the vast underrepresentation of women in leadership across all industries and certainly in politics, our movement necessarily relies on powerful, often corrupt or abusive men *choosing* to do the right thing. And because of this, there remains a distinct, overarching lack of legal consequences for the majority of famous accused men. For all men's claims that #MeToo has "ruined" their lives or forced them to live in fear, the movement's power has generally been limited to social repercussions.

Yet, the weaknesses of #MeToo lie not just in structural limitations on its power but also in its very first demand of us women. A culture in which women and survivors can safely, publicly speak about our experiences with sexual violence may be an ideal one, but it's simply not the culture we're living in. In other words, it simply can't be the job of survivors to humanize ourselves to people who are already determined not to see, respect, or accept us as human beings. It simply can't be our job to tell our stories and rehash our trauma in public spaces, to perform painstaking emotional energy, just to convince people who lack the fundamental empathy required to believe survivors that sexual assault is, in fact, real, and has impacted the ones they love. The pressure we face to sacrifice our comfort and our safety to be respected as human, as living, breathing people is a tremendous and unfair burden.

Credibility is gendered: whom our leaders and institutions are able to identify and sympathize with is gendered, and whose experience, comfort, and reputation are prioritized is gendered. The society we live in is not at all conducive to listening to and respecting survivors. That needs to change. But until it does, it's crucial we remember that survivors owe us nothing, that survivors who opt to keep their stories to themselves are just as brave as those who come forward, and just as deserving of respect and credibility.

And while the advent of #MeToo—the stories, the memories, all of the unresolved hurt—inflicted trauma and discomfort on many women, so, too, did its aftermath: the recurring headlines asserting the movement had gone too far, the irritated and defensive men all around us insisting that they felt unsafe, questioning the motives of survivors who had come forward. "Why did it take her so long to speak up? Why do these women seem bent on accusing powerful men and taking away their power? Why should we believe them?"

There isn't an adult woman in the world who hasn't faced these questions at some point since the emergence of #MeToo, as if it's squarely our job to make men see us, believe us, understand us, rather than their job to put in the work and educate themselves. And in a similar vein, there isn't a survivor in the world who hasn't been subjected to the quiet devastation of watching the male victim complex that's arisen in response to our movement be so widely validated—by media outlets, by men around us, by the institutions that govern our everyday lives. The complete erasure of our day-to-day trauma, of what it means to be a living, breathing woman as social revolution permeates every corner of our lives, happens not just at the top-level—in the White House, the upper-echelons of Hollywood, and beyond—but also in everyday life and in the everyday lives of all women, specifically.

The movement for women's and survivors' rights and safety can't fall solely on our shoulders; it's simply too much to ask of us, on top of the exhaustive day-to-day labor of survival and existence in the patriarchy. That said, perhaps the framing of men as central to #MeToo and the current dialogue around sexual assault—framing that Trump used in his aforementioned "scary time for young men" statement- -isn't always a bad thing: Men need to recognize that they do, indeed, play a central role in all of this. In the #MeToo era and beyond, they have a fundamental choice to make: actively support women and survivors, or be complicit.

Many men live in fear that if women gain the rights, respect, dignity, credibility, and autonomy we demand, men, in turn, will lose theirs. But it doesn't work like that. Equality is not a zero-sum game.

Rape culture is systemic, but the solution to it is personal and individual. Through actively choosing to believe women, to listen to women, to speak up for women—choices each of us across lines of gender can make every day—we can end rape culture. We are not helpless when we support each other. We are bigger than rape culture when we support each other. We have the power to create an equitable, safe society for all when we support each other.

No one can tell women and survivors what happened or did not happen to us. That is something we as a society, as a collective humanity, can no longer permit. The collapse of rape culture necessarily starts with all of us. And "us" certainly includes men.

The potency and clarity of the Kavanaugh episode almost seemed to frame it as an isolated episode showcasing the depths of Republican misogyny. But it was not isolated. Misogyny and abject cruelty are not glitches within the Republican Party or Trump presidency; they are deliberate and foundational to the politics of both.

Their policy agenda around issues of women's rights and gender violence can be interpreted as little more than a reminder to us women and survivors that this is not our country, that we do not matter. Following their agenda, affirming male hegemony, dismantling women's most fundamental freedoms, and assuring men it is their birthright to treat us however they want without consequence will always take higher priority than our rights, our dignity, and our existence as women. And, for all President Trump's feigned concerns over what a "scary time" it is for men, a country in which one of its two main political parties has embraced rape culture as the underlying apparatus of its platform is simply not a country that is safe for women.

Certainly, there is no shortage of Democratic men ousted as sexual abusers; however, in most cases, Democratic Party leadership takes swift action to demand their removal. There is hardly equivalence in how the two major political parties treat women: President Trump and nearly every leading Republican senator who facilitated Kavanaugh's confirmation owe their careers to patriarchal forces and crass, relentless misogyny, to political platforms that guaranteed the oppression, humiliation, and debasement of American women as a unit.

Republican Party unity and dedication to imposing Kavanaugh on American women and the nation at large was devastating, but it was not surprising. The epically long, notably all-white list of accused men who worked at some point for Trump's campaign or presidential administration includes former White House Staff Secretary Rob Porter, former speechwriter David Sorensen, former Chief Strategist Steve Bannon, former Labor Secretary nominee Andrew Puzder, and former Campaign Manager Corey Lewandowski. Throughout modern history, this has unapologetically been the party of rape culture.

Of course, it should speak volumes that Trump, the Republican Party's chosen president and standard-bearer, has been accused of sexual misconduct by more than twenty women himself. He has used his given platform to defend all of the aforementioned men in his administration, while advancing dangerous myths about sexual violence to cast doubt upon their female accusers and his own. And we can hardly ignore the racial subtext to his and the Republican Party's sympathy for the accused white male abusers in their ranks, all while centering their platform around racist lies and fearmongering about immigrant men and men of color as natural-born rapists and predators.

In 2016, when the *Washington Post* released the notorious, leaked *Access Hollywood* tapes in which Trump boasts about his predation of women, members of the Republican Party criticized or condemned Trump's sexist comments but ultimately continued to fundraise for, endorse, and support Trump. In the tapes, Trump can be heard joking and gloating about behaviors that literally equate to sexual assault: "You know I'm automatically attracted to beautiful—I just start kissing them.... I don't even wait," he said. "And when you're a star, they let you do it. You can do anything. Grab 'em by the pussy. You can do anything."

Just over a year later, when reporters asked Trump's Press Secretary Sarah Huckabee Sanders how the president could credibly criticize Democratic Senator Al Franken for allegations against him, Sanders retorted that allegations against Franken were valid, and those against Trump were not, because Franken had confessed. Yet the *Access Hollywood* tape directly contradicts this.

At roughly the same time in the fall of 2017, the Republican Party continued to endorse and fundraise for Alabama Senate candidate Roy Moore after Moore had been accused of sexually assaulting several teenage girls and minors years ago. Several news outlets revealed Moore had even had an established reputation as a sexual predator in his community. Moore, an anti-abortion hard-liner, deflected these allegations of child abuse by asserting that abortion rights, supported by his rival Democrat Doug Jones, were the "real child abuse." His rhetoric highlighted the deep divide between anti-abortion lawmakers' support for fetuses and their indifference to the actual living standards and treatment of born, living children, such that the sexual predation of young girls could be so easily dismissed to enable and empower anti-abortion law-makers like Moore.

Years before all of this, Clarence Thomas was nominated to the Supreme Court by President George H. W. Bush. And more recently, then-rising GOP star Todd Akin coined the term "legiti-mate rape" in his 2012 race for US Senate, arguing abortion should be banned without exception for rape, because women who are subjected to "legitimate" rape will naturally be unable to conceive. Akin is, of course, one man, and the majority of anti-choice politi-cians support rape exceptions in their oppressive anti-abortion bills with the self-serving goal of presenting as less extreme and inhu-mane. But Akin's disregard for the real, lived experiences of rape survivors is all but codified within the Republican Party platform.

In 2013, twenty-two Republican senators voted against the renewal of the Violence Against Women Act to protest its added protections for LGBTQ people and immigrants, in what Republi-can lawmakers perceived as a gross feminist attack on family values. VAWA, originally signed into law by President Bill Clinton in 1994, was and remains a landmark piece of legislation that has recognized sexual and domestic violence as urgent issues. In addition to fund-ing a wide range of resources for survivors and community sexual violence prevention, the law also fundamentally transformed the culture around how we think and talk about abuse in the 1990s.

VAWA requires law enforcement to respond to reports of domes-tic violence in a timely manner and creates funding for community violence-prevention programs and resources for survivors, including a national hotline, legal aid, and rape-kit funding. The law also establishes life-saving protections and services for victims who lose their homes due to incidents related to domestic violence, as well as women and survivors with disabilities. Access to the resources and full range of safety provisions mandated by the Violence Against Women Act can be the difference between life and death for women and survivors.

In 2015, Senate Republicans attempted to stall a $180 billion funding bill that would invest $41 million in helping states and local governments process rape kits, all just to protest the added protections for the environment established in the bill. As of this writing, hundreds of thousands of rape kits across the country have been collected and left untested, backlogged for years or forever. Notably, in states like Colorado and Wisconsin, which have invested extensively in testing rape kits and working to end the backlog, prosecutors almost immediately uncovered dozens of new leads on previously cold cases, yielding several convictions in rape cases spanning back decades.

In 2017, Republican senators also sought to deny rape and sexual-assault survivors access to health care through the proposed American Health Care Act. The AHCA would have allowed for sexual violence to be treated as a preexisting condition and empowered insurance providers to discriminate against survivors, charging them more or denying them care altogether.

Of course, health care is hardly the only policy area where the Republican Party takes stances detrimental to the lives and safety of women and survivors. Every month, fifty American women are killed by a domestic abuser with a gun; women in the United States are sixteen times more likely to be killed with a gun than women in any other industrialized country. When Republican lawmakers, their pockets filled with National Rifle Association contributions, reject common-sense gun control policies, including laws that would prohibit domestic abusers from legally purchasing firearms, their inaction enables and empowers mass violence of a distinctly gendered nature.

Additionally, the Republican Party leadership's unwavering support for alleged abusers and policies harmful to women and survivors has often served as a direct means to attack women's reproductive rights, as they stand by alleged abusers who have vowed to use their political power to further hurt and deny women bodily autonomy through opposing abortion and contraception access. This is no coincidence: reproductive coercion and sexual violence have always been two sides of the same coin, a coin that is, terrifyingly enough, foundational to American politics.

Men and boys are the perpetrators of nearly all assaults, rapes, domestic violence, murders, and mass killings. But as Jackson Katz's landmark 1999 documentary *Tough Guise*, and 2013 sequel documentary, *Tough Guise 2*, reveal, mass violence is seldom recognized as a crisis of masculinity or a gendered issue at all.

Mass shooters are often identified not as men, but as psychopaths, or mentally deranged, or as members of their respective racial group if they are men of color, while school shootings by young, male shooters are chalked up to "youth violence." In other words, mass shootings tend to be reduced to issues of mental health, despite how those with mental illnesses are more likely to be victims than perpetrators of violence. And despite how white men have led the majority of major mass shootings in US history, despite how often men of color are targeted or killed by police for legally carrying firearms, mass shootings are almost always understood as issues of race when the perpetrator is a minority—in typical fashion, in a country that treats every individual person of color as representative of all.

Each of these narratives roundly misses the mark: Plenty of women suffer from mental illness, plenty of young women and girls are bullied in schools, like their male peers. Yet statistically speaking, nearly all violence is committed by men.

Cultural narratives are so determined to separate violence from gender and masculinity that the term "violence against women" (who, exactly, is committing those acts of violence against women?) itself erases from the picture how 98 percent of all acts of violence against women are committed by men. The passivity of the phrase suggests the violence women face is just a naturally occurring experience, rather than acts actively performed by men.

Any rhetoric or dialogue that places emphasis on this reality and calls out toxic hypermasculinity is almost immediately subjected to backlash and sweepingly criticized for generalizing about "all men." This is because masculinity and male identity have always predicated upon one's ability—used or not—to dominate and hurt, such that criticisms of violent tendencies are widely regarded as criticisms of men as people.

In recent years, the rise of #MeToo and a more vocal, internet feminist movement have also been perceived as an attack on male identity and masculinity. In response to this perceived attack, far-right, male internet communities lash out by romanticizing ideologies of violent regression and the subjugation of women. Since the Isla Vista shooting by Elliot Rodger resulting in the deaths of seven in 2014, the rise of the incel movement has exposed the dangers of male entitlement to women's bodies, when paired with highly accessible firearms.

The incel, or involuntary celibate movement, first rose to mainstream visibility shortly after the shooting. Prior to the shooting,

Rodger shared a manifesto and a series of videos in which he revealed his motive to punish women for not having sex with him and punish the men that women chose to sleep with instead of him. His manifesto, on top of its violently misogynist language, is rife with racist language directing outrage at men of color women choose to be with over white men.

According to people who personally knew Rodger, who identified as a virgin prior to his death, he had never made any actual effort to connect with women, meaning he couldn't even have been rejected in the first place. In reality, he had never put any real effort into developing relationships with women but had simply felt entitled to their bodies nonetheless and sought to punish them for not giving him something he hadn't even asked for.

In the years prior to and following the Isla Vista shootings, nearly every perpetrator of a mass shooting has had a record of violence against women. At least two documented cases of mass shootings committed by men in the spring of 2018 had been associated with feelings of rejection from women, and one act of mass violence in Toronto was linked to a man who had shared incel content on his Facebook profile.

In 2018, the Parkland high school shooting that killed twenty-seven people had been carried out by a young man with an alleged record of domestic abuse and a reputation for being a social pariah. In the aftermath of the shooting, young people in Parkland and across the country emerged as part of the March for Our Lives movement demanding immediate gun-control reform. But a small number of parents and students coalesced to form the Walk Up, Not Out movement, which identified the solution to school shootings as kindness and anti-bullying policies, rather than gun control. (It should go without saying that kindness, anti-bullying, and gun-control legislation are hardly mutually exclusive.)

Walk Up, Not Out fails to acknowledge that school bullying mostly targets young people of color, LGBTQ youth, and girls, all of whom are statistically less likely than their straight, white-male peers to commit acts of violence. And while kindness is, generally speaking, a noble goal, it can't be stated enough that no woman has any obligation whatsoever to be kind or date, or offer sex, affection or emotional energy to any man she isn't interested in. The suggestion that women must necessarily give their time and attention to men who would otherwise go on to commit acts of mass violence is essentially a recipe for domestic abuse and violence and all but relegates women's bodies to human shields for the rest of society.

In recent years, feminist activists have shined a light on the problematic nature of narratives that suggest women are responsible for changing their male partners' harmful behaviors or investing the energy into changing bad men in general. We see it whenever women are shamed for ending relationships with men with mental illness and addiction problems or when women are extensively questioned and brought to task for allegations of sexual abuse against their male partners while their partners are subjected to hardly any scrutiny at all.

Women are understood as responsible for preventing mass violence by humoring men and conceding to violent male behaviors, staying with abusive partners, giving companionship and affection to suspect loners, and having sex with men they aren't attracted to, lest these men go on to embrace the incel movement and terrorize their communities. Yet, a persistent reality is that for women, conceding to men is often less about taking one for the team and protecting society from mass violence and more about survival—in far too many cases, women and girls are quite literally killed for telling men "no."

Never is the saying that "life imitates art" invoked more often than in discussions of what, exactly, inspires mass, male-led violence in society.

Jackson Katz's *Tough Guise* documentaries reveal a trend of increased gore and masculine violence in film and television in the last few decades. *Tough Guise* further offers insight into how feminism's perceived threats to masculinity have led men to demand and subsequently produce increased representations of violence and toxic masculinity in media, in response to these "threats." It sounds like the story arc of a blockbuster film: masculinity in crisis, as social progress and equal opportunity have threatened the very domination it has always subsisted on; masculinity in crisis, lashing out and embracing extremism and violent regression as a survival mechanism; masculinity in crisis, with the bodies of women and girls relegated to collateral damage.

Media has always been rife with damaging representations of sex, sexuality, and sexual violence and certainly plays a role in obfuscating cultural awareness of consent. Sexual-health education in public schools is often so lacking as to place young people— and disproportionately young women—in abject danger, as they grow up and explore their sexuality, by failing to teach what affirmative consent and healthy sex positivity look like. As a result, young people are often forced to rely on the media they consume to inform their understandings of sex and consent.

The mass production of male-led violence and masculinity in media necessitates criticism and conversation about how these representations influence male perceptions of masculinity and contribute to male violence in the real world. Yet, it's also worth considering how acts of violence against women's bodies in film and television are often intended as plot devices in a reductive, sexist attempt to make female characters' storylines more "interesting," rather than intended as meaningful commentary on rape culture and hypermasculinity.

In big-name productions ranging from HBO's *Game of Thrones* and the *Fifty Shades* film trilogy, to the Lifetime (and later Netflix) television series *You*, to earlier 2000s films like *The Duchess* and *Thirteen*, violence exacted upon women's bodies tends to be written to serve as shock factor or subversive, unexpected entertainment. Sometimes, even, it is a lazy approach to explaining why a female character is the way she is. But the message this ultimately sends is that violence against women is little more than fiction, fantasy, and media trope, rather than an everyday, devastatingly real part of life for countless women.

Watching the Season 1 finale of *You*, I experienced a visceral feeling of equal parts terror and frustration as the female lead, Beck, screamed and wept, trapped in a glass cage to be gazed upon, talked down to, and eventually killed by her male partner. The series *You* marketed itself as a subversive, edgy, and unique thriller series that would challenge the boundaries of audience expectations. But what is unexpected about a woman being stalked, terrorized, and killed by an abusive domestic partner, when this happens to real women every single day?

*Game of Thrones'* writers and producers often deflected criticisms of its frequent portrayals of violence against women by condescendingly citing the historical context of the fantasy series, inspired by the abrasive realities of medieval warfare—as if we women, survivors and allies, need it explained to us that sexual violence has always been a part of real life. But the dismissive use of women's naked bodies as props in contrast with fully clothed men and lack of consideration and sensitivity in portrayals of rape and its toll on women's bodies and minds imply a level of callousness that made it clear violence on the show was more about shock factor than historical accuracy.

Media reliance on violence against women as a narrative device central to storylines involving female characters sends the message that women and girls can only develop as characters and human beings through the abuse, violence, and rape that men subject them to. Violence against women impacts unsaid numbers of real, living women, and as it shapes the storylines of female television and film characters' lives, certainly, it shapes real women's lives. But ultimately, we, as women, as human beings, are so much more than what men subject us to. It's past time for media to reflect this and have a reckoning with its reliance on gender violence as a plot device.

Perhaps one starting point for media to feature healthier portrayals of sexuality and consent, and fewer portrayals—if any—of violence against women, could be creating more roles and opportunities for women directors, producers, and writers. #MeToo exposed dozens of abusers among top-ranking media men, and considering the extent to which identity and experience shape the art that one produces, what we see in media is hardly surprising.

"Men's rights" and conservative activists argue that artists and creators accused of abuse should not be denied platforms and opportunities, that male artists' private lives should stay private, that art is separate from abuse, and talent and merit should take precedence over allegations.

Of course, apart from being wholly void of compassion, none of this makes any logical sense. Abusive impulses shape art, and abusive behavior is necessarily more than just one's private life, insofar as it impacts the safety and opportunities of those around the abuser. Powerful men are the gatekeepers of their respective fields; a powerful man can end a woman's career on a whim, based on whether or not she concedes to him or is silent about his abusiveness. If we don't maintain moral standards for the people we accord power, we have nothing.

At any rate, it's difficult to believe that rape apologists are especially concerned with talent and good art when they complain about the exclusion of talented, abusive male artists and creators.

Talented people are excluded and denied opportunities from creative spaces every day, not due to their behavior and treatment of others but because of identity-based bias, discrimination, and lack of privilege and institutional connections.

Attitudes that defend abusive men's right to create over women's right to work in safe environments are just more of the same—more sexist prioritization of the male experience, more women as collateral damage.

———

More than 99 percent of American women have reported experiencing some form of street harassment, from catcalls and lewd gestures to stalking and, well, plain harassment.[5] Yet, meaningful reforms to address this nearly universal women's experience and promote women's safety in public spaces have been abysmal.

In no small part, this is due to the notion that street harassment is just flattery and flirtation, and if we women feel uncomfortable with this, then that's our problem for dressing a certain way or having the gall to leave our house and step out in public in the first place. After all, there's simply nothing women could wear that *doesn't* attract harassment; we attract harassment not for any particular fashion choice but for choosing to exist in public at all.

Positive or negative comments yelled at female passersby on the streets by men cannot be conflated with well-meaning compliments and flattery. Street harassment is a vile act of exploitation, and, specifically, exploitation of the power dynamics of public life. From a young age, we women and girls are socialized to recognize the implicit threat of violence that underlies nearly all interactions. In other words, if a man hollers at us, gives us attention, follows us, or anything like that, and we ignore, reject, or do anything that upsets him, he could kill us. He could hurt us. And what could we do after the fact?

The modern classic *The Power* is a 2016 science fiction novel by Naomi Alderman that considers a hypothetical world where women but not men possess a fatally strong, secret superpower that makes them the dominant gender. The whole moral of the book is that it's not about some good men, or whether men choose to rape and hurt and kill women; it's that many men have the ability to rape and hurt and kill women. And, regardless of whether they choose to use this ability, to have that option is social capital that most men but not most women have.

Still, street harassment remains normalized and shrugged off because young women are taught that we should view any and all male attention as flattering and somehow beneficial to us and, in turn, that we have an obligation to reward it. If we fail to reward it adequately, and thank or give attention to our harassers, then, as we encounter in everyday cases of street harassment, we run the risk of being called a "bitch" or even being subjected to violence.

Across many contexts, women and girls are blamed for the male violence enacted upon us, and we see this mirrored in the power dynamics governing street harassment. If women decline to return male attention, or fail to do so in a fully satisfactory manner, then responsibility for what our harassers do next is placed on our shoulders. We are obliged to enjoy, be grateful for, or at the very least, passively shoulder the harassment to which we're subjected, and all without complaint.

These power dynamics are present not just in street harassment but also in myriad gendered interactions. In the summer of 2018, then-Democratic Congressional candidate Alexandria Ocasio-Cortez compared right-wing writer and known misogynist Ben Shapiro's demand that she "debate" him to street harassment: "Just like catcalling, I don't owe a response to unsolicited requests from men with bad intentions. And also like catcalling, for some reason they feel entitled to one," she wrote in a tweet. Predictably enough, the tweet was panned by conservatives and trolls, who called her a "coward" or criticized her comparison of Shapiro's bad-faith debate challenge to street harassment a "reach."

But Ocasio-Cortez hit the nail on the head: In the same way Shapiro's intention was to humiliate and talk down to her rather than engage in good-faith intellectual discussion, street harassment is not about affirming and flattering and being kind to women. It is about objectification and entitlement—entitlement to women's time, entitlement to women's attention, entitlement to women's bodies to visually consume.

A preeminent rationale around street harassment is that if we women don't want male "flattery," the burden is on us, then, to dress differently, not go out at night, drive rather than walk, perhaps change our walking path altogether, or maybe shoulder the costs of a cab or an Uber. As long as we're in the sight line of men in public spaces, they can say and treat us as they please, regardless of our feelings of comfort and safety.

Street harassment relies on the expectation that women walk from one place to another solely for the entertainment and pleasure of men. As such, street harassment is fundamentally about ownership—specifically, male ownership of public spaces, male ownership of society; it is about who belongs here, in public, and who does not.

---

In October 2018, Hillary Clinton was asked in a televised interview whether she believed her husband, former President Bill Clinton, should have resigned over his affair with Monica Lewinsky.

"Absolutely not," Hillary responded, offering that her husband had not abused his power, because the relationship had been consensual and Lewinsky "was an adult."

Her suggestion that women who are legal adults can't be victimized or exploited by older, powerful men is simply wrong. And it was especially disappointing coming from a woman like Hillary, who had dedicated her career to women's rights, served as a role model to many young feminists for decades, and knew better. Whether or not a relationship between a male superior (and, frankly, what superior could be more imposing than the president of the United States?) and a female subordinate is consensual on the surface, nearly all such relationships involve some exploitation of inherent power dynamics.

Yet, multiple things can be true at once: there was no excuse for Clinton's comments, but it was simultaneously upsetting that she was asked the question at all. Women are still too often the ones forced to answer for men's abusive behaviors, and in the #MeToo era, with men's abusive behaviors drawing necessary media attention, questioning, and allocating responsibility to the women in an abuser's life, has only become more prevalent.

Such media narratives not only allow but also encourage men accused of abuse to use the women in their lives as human shields. Certainly, Hillary Clinton was reduced to a human shield when her husband's affair first became public in the 1990s, and however disappointing her more recent comments on the affair may be, we should neither forget nor minimize the pain and humiliation she was forced to suffer in the national spotlight, all because of her husband's transgressions.

Today, as one of the most influential and accomplished politicians of this generation in her own right, surely Hillary deserves some level of respect from media independent of her husband, and surely she deserves to be asked more questions about herself than about her husband.

#MeToo's central goal is to empower women to speak up about their experiences with sexual misconduct and about the prevalence of sexual misconduct, in general, on their own terms. This is not what we see when journalists ask women about the behaviors of allegedly abusive men in their lives. Often, the only people who are empowered by women being unwillingly brought to task over men's actions are the men who evade accountability for their own abuses of power as a result.

Women shouldering responsibility for abusive men has increasingly become a trend in American politics. In 2017, when former Senator Al Franken was accused of sexual misconduct by multiple women, female Democrats in the Senate were the ones who were forced to answer for his alleged inappropriate behavior, such that questions about his behavior were inescapable with every media appearance they offered.

Eventually, when women like Democratic Senator Kirsten Gillibrand took the lead on calling for Franken's resignation, they were met with immediate and intense backlash from male Democratic donors and leadership. Gillibrand was widely criticized across party lines for being the first senator to publicly call for Franken's resignation without an investigation, much to the chagrin of the usual, bipartisan "due process" police. Critics called Gillibrand "opportunistic" for purportedly seeking to eliminate a potential rival in the 2020 presidential race; of course, opportunism is a common, gendered criticism of female politicians, as if it is somehow inconceivable that Gillibrand could genuinely care about sexual violence or genuinely believe the seven women who had come forward with allegations against Franken.

Everyone across party lines has a responsibility to engage in conversations about systemic misogyny and sexual abuse, yet women are often the only ones this rule applies to. Why aren't Republican men in Congress who have yet to say a word about the more than twenty allegations of sexual abuse against President Trump incessantly confronted about their silence and inaction? If, as President Trump has said, it's such a "scary time for young men," why are women still the ones answering and shouldering responsibility for the actions of male abusers?

This is an issue that naturally transcends American politics. In 2018, actress Alison Brie was asked about allegations of sexual misconduct against her brother-in-law James Franco on the same night she received a Screen Actors Guild Award—a night that should have been about her and her accomplishments, rather than allegations against a man in her life. At the time, her husband, Dave Franco, had yet to publicly comment on or be asked about the allegations against his brother, himself.

Of course, taking women to task over allegations of abuse against the men in their lives isn't always exclusively about making women answer for abusive men. It's also often used to advance the harmful, deceptive idea that if a man did not abuse one woman in his life, then surely, he hasn't abused *any* woman.

Former CBS executive Les Moonves certainly relied on this strategy when he sent out his wife, journalist Julie Chen, to publicly deny allegations against her husband on any major platform that would have her. So too did Republican Party leadership when they swiftly shared a prepared, signed list of sixty-five women who knew Supreme Court Justice Brett Kavanaugh in high school and vouched for his respect for women.

For all the progress #MeToo has facilitated, and the solidarity it has instilled in many women and survivors, lines of questioning that require us women to answer for alleged male abusers serve another purpose: to stir up division among us despite our vast, shared experiences on the receiving end of gender violence. And when we continue to allow powerful accused men to hide behind women in their lives when they are faced with the prospect of accountability, we advance the false idea that systemic sexual abuse is necessarily a women's issue, and one that women alone must speak about and fix.

Female abusers exist—but women did not create the epidemic of systemic misogyny and sexual abuse that plagues every industry and walk of life in the United States and around the world. The overarching cultural narrative seems to be that it's women's responsibility to simultaneously change and accept responsibility for this epidemic—all while trying to survive it.

It's a scary time in America, and the world, for women and survivors. And for men, it's a time to finally step up, accept responsibility, and engage in meaningful allyship.

# 9

# Good News for Men Who Won't Date Feminists

The good news for men who won't date feminists is that feminists don't want to date them either.

In 2016, a man named Dave Hon published a delightful little op-ed titled, "Why I'll Never Date A Feminist" in *St. Joseph News-Press*. In the span of just under five-hundred words, the Missouri-based newspaper's digital editor denounced the gender wage gap and rape culture as myths, asserted the feminist movement itself was antithetical to women's happiness, and declared his feelings of repulsion toward any woman who espoused contrary views.

Promptly after launching into an admirably concise tirade about how feminists are wrong about, well, everything, Hon explains the ultimate reason for his active decision to avoid romantic relationships with feminist women: "People who are more loyal to their gender and not their significant other don't make good partners," he writes. "They will always look at you as inherently more fortunate than them. They've bought into the 'battle of the sexes' mentality and it often pervades their perceptions of romance. Romance turns into a power struggle rather than a partnership."

Internet feminists were quick to have fun with the op-ed, some starting with the especially ridiculous nature of a less-than-conventionally handsome man automatically assuming feminist women want to date him in the first place. All in all, Hon's essay was (rightfully) treated as so absurd and comedic as to not even merit serious criticism and response. I certainly thought little of it, at the time.

But as I've come to ponder the impact of self-identifying as a feminist as a young woman more and more often, the essay naturally came to mind. Perhaps one straight white man from Missouri is hardly representative of all men, but his essay made me think broadly about how men perceive women who identify as feminists, and the inherent assumptions—if any—that follow young, feminist women in the realm of dating.

Certainly, not all heterosexual men view feminist straight women through the same narrow, self-centered, self-victimizing lens that Hon does. Sometimes, the opposite extreme is true, to the extent that straight men will fetishize and pursue women they perceive as fiery and opinionated. These straight men may feel attracted to the airs of power and confidence that vocally feminist women exude, all while either doing little if anything to support their female partners' work and values, or engaging feminist activism that is so transparently performative that many feminist women have justifiably expressed concerns and anxieties about dating "feminist" men at all.

In a 2015 essay called, "Why I Won't Date Another 'Male Feminist,'" writer and cultural critic Kate Iselin laments the vast sense of entitlement men feel for doing or, really, performing the bare minimum. Her own experiences with male "feminists" have been wide-ranging far from ideal: "From the man who opened a text conversation with a photo of his naked chest and encouraged me to reciprocate in the name of the Free The Nipple movement, to the fellow who agonised over accepting a blowjob because, despite enjoying them, he found the act simply too degrading to let me perform; dating male feminists turned out to be one of the least empowering decisions I've ever made," Iselin wrote. "It's not that I don't want to be with a man who respects me, values consent, or is conscious of the various gender-based imbalances in the world today. These qualities are a bare minimum."

In other words, straight men's support for feminism shouldn't be an aspirational goal among straight women seeking romantic relationships, but a basic expectation.

Iselin concludes, "[M]en who use the term 'feminist' as either bait or an alter-ego, assuming that their opt-in respect for women will entitle them to legions of adoring lovers—really the most anti-feminist act of all."

Among the many men who maintain hesitations about feminist women similar to Hon's, women who self-identify as feminists are even more vulnerable to recurring tropes about the "crazy," "hysterical," "no-fun" girlfriend or ex-girlfriend that already exist for all women. The "no-fun" trope naturally follows feminist women around in dating and frankly everywhere, as if being entertained by racist, sexist, or otherwise problematic "jokes" is somehow requisite to being recognized as "fun." But the "crazy" and "hysterical" labels nearly all women will receive from male partners and their friends are part of a common, almost universal staple of heterosexual dating and relationships: gaslighting. Women are often gaslighted into believing basic respect or commitment or honesty are too much to ask for, that women who make such demands or are upset when disrespected or lied to are called hysterical. This gaslighting is necessarily inseparable from the politics of female existence in the patriarchy: Women are not credible witnesses to our own experiences, and women who ask for basic things that should be the bare minimum are "asking for too much."

Perhaps, for no shortage of reasons beyond Dave Hon's op-ed, not too many feminist women are especially interested in dating him anyway. But plenty of feminist women do fall into the trap of desiring and seeking to date actively misogynist or at the very least problematic men; like all human beings, we're hardly immune to cognitive dissonance.

That said, far be it from me, of all people, to tell others how to live their lives, or how to feel, or that being attracted to or dating men with subpar values must necessarily make women subpar, "bad" feminists. I spent the better part of my freshman year of college hopelessly latched to a straight, white man who never ceded an opportunity to explain to me how reproductive rights were a settled "nonissue" that "most Americans don't really care about," or how universal health care and taxation are "theft," or why Donald Trump's "Make America Great Again" slogan glorifying an America of segregation and forced birth isn't inherently racist and sexist, or what all the "gray areas" in rape culture are.

At the time, being with someone whose ideals and background contrasted so dramatically from my own felt special, even adventurous, and it required deep, lengthy self-reflection in the months and years after the relationship ended for me to become conscious of the privileges that allowed me to be with someone like that in the first place. Often, when I think about privilege and relationships, I think about it in terms of the ability to *not* talk about politics; yet, it wasn't as if my then-partner and I hadn't discussed politics. Politics was sometimes all we *did* discuss, in long, drawn-out, and emotionally laborious debates that consistently left me exhausted and mentally drained.

Over and over, it seemed no amount of statistics or moral arguments I offered could convince him that something Trump had said was offensive, or that reproductive rights and sexual violence comprised urgent, existential issues for many women—and, in light of my own experiences, certainly for me. But the bottom line is that his politics hadn't bothered me enough to leave; the eventual implosion of our relationship had come down to issues of commitment rather than our sharp ideological disagreements.

Despite how upsetting and even repulsive I found his views, and despite his unwaveringly rigid sense of self-righteousness, especially when it came to his "pro-life" views, from day one, I was often the one who fought harder for our relationship and wanted it more. From the get-go, after he had put me through what felt like hell and back at the time just to agree to an exclusive, monogamous relationship, all the way to the end, when the divides in our levels of commitment became decisively clear, I was the one who wanted to be with him.

Certainly, everyone has different boundaries and standards for what they seek in a partner, and by no means does feminism call for uniformity in what we as women seek in romantic relationships. Yet, for all the men who, like Hon, insist on their refusal to date feminists, I can't help but think that we, as feminists—now more than ever in a world where men like Donald Trump and Brett Kavanaugh rule—ought to have moral standards of our own for the people we date—that we, as feminists, have a moral obligation to refuse to entertain and socially reward and gratify men who do not respect our existence and human rights.

Sure, it would be nice to live in a world in which the personal were not so inextricably tied to the political. But the notion that dating is somehow separable from politics, that we can neatly compartmentalize our identities and lives and political experiences and relationships, comes from a place of privilege and complicity. Existence is political. The choice to reward and welcome certain attitudes and beliefs and behaviors into our life with our time and affection is necessarily political. The emotional energy we pour into people who are fundamentally lacking in empathy and respect for our human rights is better and more productively spent elsewhere.

Reflecting on my freshman-year relationship today, what comes to my mind first is how young I was—not necessarily in my physical age, but in the naive expectations I maintained for myself because I identified as a feminist. At eighteen years old, I'd held an unshakable belief that I had both the power and the obligation to fix and unconditionally support someone—despite the exhaustive cost to me personally, and despite the emotional energy nearly every conversation with him required of me.

Ultimately, I understand that relationships and human connections don't exist in a vacuum, that different people will find different interactions and conversations fulfilling and rewarding. Yet, in an age of migrant children in cages and abusers in the White House and Supreme Court, I don't hold it against anyone who would rather not be in a relationship with anyone else who needs it explained to them why children do not belong in cages, why abusers do not belong in power.

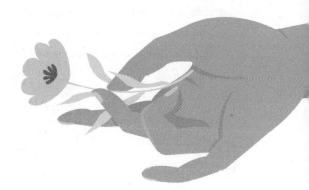

# 10

# Performative

The women's website Jezebel wrapped up 2018 with a "The Jezebel Thirsty 30" list recapping the thirty "thirstiest," or most attention-seeking, people in pop culture that year. Alongside the likes of teen heartthrob Noah Centineo, prominent YouTubers, and "comedian" Louis CK with his comeback tour, "male allies" were also included on the list. The online women's magazine offered some choice words to explain this editorial decision:

> *The worst thing I've ever seen in my whole life after The Family Stone happened as I was leaving the first Women's March in New York City last year. As the march dissipated ... and those who had assembled splintered off, I walked by a group of four young men, huddled in a circle, angrily shout-chanting, "HER BODY, HER CHOICE! HER BODY, HER CHOICE! HER BODY, HER CHOICE! HER BODY, HER CHOICE!" I always think*

*of this when I see self-identified male allies in action, the men who bum-rush the microphone to denounce sexism and misogyny without seeing all the women they shoved aside to do so. Do you want to be a good ally to women? Just listen to women.*

I've been writing and speaking about feminism and engaging feminist activism in a very public manner for years now. And for all the affirmation I receive from other women and my wonderful, supportive male friends, I can assure you, for young women, there is little to no personal benefit to embracing feminist and social-justice activism publicly. At best, you are derided for being a social-justice warrior, making up fake problems, or exaggerating injustices for attention and, again, some imagined individual benefit. At worst, you receive death and rape threats, stalking, harassment, or endless patronizing, condescending messages on social media, often from male strangers.

It's a little bit different for men. Standards for male behavior, decency, and maturity are so low in patriarchal society that acts as simple as listening to women speak, letting women speak, or offering up even one socially conscious insight tend to receive wide applause. The mere act of showing up to women-led rallies or investing even a fraction of the emotional energy countless women invest into social-justice issues on a daily basis often comes with tremendous benefits for men—and those who know this, like the aforementioned male Women's March attendees, take full advantage.

In my junior year of college, I spoke to one of my favorite race and gender professors about my uneasiness with white, self-identified progressive men's tendency to hyperscrutinize the politics and privileges of white women. Certainly, there are many white women who either embrace a problematic, exclusive brand of white feminism—albeit with good intentions—or decline to embrace feminism at all. History is rife with white women standing at the forefront of exclusionary efforts to gain the right to vote for white women and deny it to people of color,

of white women's pioneering efforts to promote birth-control access
for white women and forced sterilization for women of color, and,
today, of white, wealthy female CEOs celebrating women's empowerment, all while neglecting to pay working women of color a living
wage or support meaningful redistributive policy. Those white women
who gleefully, consciously engage in the oppression of others ought
to be called out by anybody and everybody. But I've often questioned
what gives straight, cisgender white men the right and moral authority
to be the ones to most vocally criticize white women's privilege.

That an estimated 53 percent of white women voted for Donald
Trump in the 2016 presidential election[1] has been a particular point
of criticism of white women as an electoral demographic since the
election. And it's a valid, deeply important criticism coming from
the women of color, LGBTQ people, and other marginalized groups
whose rights and safety were jeopardized by white women's role in
electing Trump. Yet, at times, when this criticism comes wholly
unqualified from white progressive men, I find myself taking a step
back and considering the power dynamics that enable this.

In her 2018 essay collection, *Call Them by Their True Names*,
feminist essayist Rebecca Solnit writes about the daunting cultural
realities and barriers to access feminism in many parts of the country.
Some of these barriers include domestic violence, religious funda-
mentalism, male authoritarian communities and households, and
the explicit demonization of feminism in these settings. These barriers do not necessarily excuse, but certainly explain, why so many
white women voted for Trump, and why so many white women continue to reject feminism in their politics:

> *[White women] were excoriated on the grounds that all women,
> but only women, should be feminists. That there are a lot of
> women who aren't feminists doesn't surprise me. To be a feminist,
> you have to believe in your equality and rights, which can make*

*your life unpleasant and dangerous if you live in a family, a com-*
*munity, a church, a state that does not agree with you about this.*
*For many women, it's safer not to have those beliefs in this coun-*
*try, where a woman is beaten every 11 seconds or so, and women's*
*partners are the leading cause of injury to women from their teens*
*through forties. And those beliefs are not universally available in*
*a country where feminism is forever being demonized and dis-*
*torted. It seems it's also worse to vote for a racist when you're a*
*woman, because while white women were excoriated, white men*
*were let off the hook.*

Of course, it's not just anti-feminist white women who are subjected to scrutiny—it's also white women who identify as feminists.
Criticism of a feminism that exclusively centers white women's
experiences is especially necessary when we consider how all women
are expected to be feminists yet all feminists are not expected to
support all women. For example, we expect black and Palestinian
women to be feminists, but we do not immediately expect feminists as a unit to support Black Lives Matter and Palestinian liberation. Many of the white women who attended Women's Marches
across the country were nowhere to be seen when black women
organized anti-police-brutality rallies and immigrant women organized immigrant-justice rallies in their communities. If all women
are necessarily expected to be feminists, then all feminists should be
expected to support all women.

These criticisms of white women and white-centric strains of
feminism are not just necessary but also vital to the survival and
success of the feminist movement. Yet, I question why those who
bemoan white women's privilege the most vocally tend to be self-
identified "progressive" white men—and often, as Jezebel put it,
the same "progressive" white men who "bum-rush the microphone
to denounce sexism and misogyny without seeing all the women

they shoved aside to do so." We feminist women of color are nothing if not wholly capable of calling out white feminists ourselves.

For all the privileges white women enjoy, and the oppression they are often either active or complicit in advancing, they simultaneously experience some gender-based oppression themselves—oppression their white, male "progressive" critics could never fully, comprehensively conceive of and will never personally experience.

My professor acknowledged the validity of my misgivings but built upon the conversation by offering consideration to a fundamental tension among those progressive white men who *are* well-meaning and genuinely seek to support progressive causes not just for their personal benefit.

Well-meaning white men who aspire to be real allies to women and marginalized people are, indeed, in a relatively challenging position—not more challenging than being a woman or person of color, sure, but challenging in a different way. They contemplate how to talk about and make use of their privilege without making feminist activism *their* show and without soaking up all the attention; they contemplate how to use their voices and platforms to uplift marginalized voices without inadvertently usurping the conversation to center themselves. "They struggle," she said, "and when I see them genuinely struggle, I trust them."

I know these men exist; I hope some of them are reading this. And I hope they know that so long as they are willing to listen, empathize, show up, and self-reflect, they can be wonderful allies.

Certainly, as a starting point, they could invest their advocacy and emotional energy into taking responsibility for their own kind. They could criticize and engage in meaningful conversation, not necessarily with staunch, anti-feminist, white-male Trump supporters, but with some of their fellow "progressive" white men—the ones they catch mansplaining to or talking over women, excluding women from conversations, and declining to pass the microphone to allow marginalized people to speak about their own experiences.

If performatively "progressive" men were willing to listen to women's and marginalized people's demands for our inclusion, we wouldn't encounter these everyday, aforementioned frustrations as often as we do. The problem lies with the fact that often they are *not* willing to listen us. And that's where we need real, nonperformative male feminists to step in.

———————

Throughout my years in college, I surrounded myself with a politically active circle of friends, most of whom were progressive-leaning to varying extents. But I often experienced tensions with one of them, in particular, who aggressively embraced communist politics; he perceived anyone who did not fully share his views as privileged, and he perceived it as his job as a straight, cisgender white man, to extensively judge and criticize their perceived privilege.

I can recognize a man who's desperate to explain and talk down to women pretty easily at this point. Writing about feminism on the internet as a young woman is a surefire way to draw men like that to you, because plenty of times, it's not just gross harassment and hatred that men send my way. Being a female writer also involves plenty of fending off or ignoring men who might agree or disagree with you but, either way, are certain they know more than you, certain they're qualified to explain to you, certain they're entitled to your time and attention in doing so. And men like this don't just live in your social-media mentions and inboxes. Once you express an opinion as a young woman within close proximity to any of them, you'll quickly find they exist all around you.

I've spent the better part of my time as a writer and activist focused on issues of reproductive justice, which is inherently an issue of racial and economic justice in light of the costly barriers to access reproductive health care and the broad racism that governs health-care access at large. But I've always tried to be forthcoming about my place of privilege as a cisgender, able-bodied woman from an upper-middle-class background and my lack of expertise in economic issues and class politics, such that these are issues I'm often unable to speak about at length. Suffice to say, my white-male communist friend did not always look kindly upon my activism, if he acknowledged it at all, and often regarded it with callous assumptions shaped by his own vastly limited experiences.

At different points, he would offer passive-aggressive commentary suggesting that most of the people I worked with at a leading national reproductive rights advocacy group were straight white women, which was plainly, objectively false. In other cases, he, as a person from a relatively affluent background himself, would criticize my authority to speak on social-justice and feminist issues at all due to my place of economic privilege.

Certainly, he is not the only straight, white, relatively affluent man I've received like criticisms from, and in many cases, I acknowledge criticisms I face as valid and do everything I can to adapt and expand the parameters of my activism. But of course, the criticisms and insights and conversations about feminism that I value most come from women of color and people with experiences of marginalization rather than those who understand marginalization from the abstract, bird's-eye view of their own privilege.

Men like my white-male communist friend are often critical of all politics and politicians within America's binary Democratic-Republican system, and many of their criticisms are deeply accurate and necessary. Capitalism is a critical actor of the white, cis-hetero patriarchy, and reining in purely capitalist systems is a necessary goal of feminism.

But often, it's the people who are safest and most privileged who are willing to call for dramatic, violent risks in an attempt to overhaul the existing system. It's easy to believe things can't get any worse and there's nothing to lose when you're white and male, when you're examining societal oppression from a distance as a matter of theory and can't see how much worse everything could still get for marginalized people, because of the blind spots produced by your own inexperience.

In November 2016, a staggering 12 percent of voters who had voted for Vermont Senator and democratic socialist Bernie Sanders over Hillary Clinton in the Democratic primary subsequently voted for Donald Trump in the general election.[2] I imagine many of these voters cast their ballots as a means to punish those stubborn, pro-Hillary women and people of color who foolishly could not see what was best for us—not the way that they, "progressive," intellectual white men could. Their votes were distinctly, decisively about precisely that—punishment, and reminding women like Clinton and her female supporters where political power truly resides: with men across ideological lines, as we've witnessed in every presidential election throughout US history.

But perhaps some Sanders-Trump voters also saw voting for Trump as strategic: The election and presidency of Donald Trump would push the existing, oppressive system of neoliberal austerity to its limits, and the chaos and devastation that ensued as a result would finally force consciousness among the proletariat, and give way to their coveted revolution. But the one component of this strategy they neglected to consider was who, exactly, would be disproportionately impacted by the aforementioned chaos and devastation of Trump's presidency.

Their gaze fell exclusively on the future, and they justified the immediate and deep present-day suffering yielded by the Trump presidency and the empowerment of the sexist, classist, racist Republican Party by citing the long-term, future utopia this suffering had the potential to yield. When I pointed out that present-day, "short-term" suffering is still suffering, my white-male communist friend retorted that marginalized people were suffering now, had suffered in the Obama era, and would necessarily suffer until the ultimate destruction of capitalism.

He wasn't wrong; suffering to varying extents is a natural consequence of capitalism and its inherent immorality. But suffice to say, the caging and separation of migrant babies were not incentivized in the Obama era at President Obama's explicit command, and likely wouldn't have been, either, under a hypothetical Clinton presidency. Anti-abortion Supreme Court justices bent on forcing American women to give birth wouldn't have been installed by President Hillary Clinton either.

The existing system is oppressive; capitalism is, again, inherently oppressive. But I'm necessarily critical of reducing marginalized people in the nontheoretical present to the collateral damage of attempts at inducing a communist revolution. The disproportionately affected women of color denied abortion access and either forced to give birth or placed in abject danger under anti-choice, Republican governments are not collateral damage; the migrant children purposefully, forcibly separated from their parents and locked in cages at the orders of President Trump are not collateral damage either.

In the 2016 Democratic primary, marginalized people who lacked the same access to the institutional resources that allowed white-male "progressives" to become aware of Bernie Sanders and understand the academic critiques of capitalism that are often inaccessible to lower-income, marginalized people were understandably wary of Sanders. They did not know him the way they knew Hillary Clinton, the way they saw her as powerful and established and as their best bet for survival. In contrast, however reasonable Sanders's economic policies actually are in practice, marginalized people were skeptical that a majority of American voters would accept these policies, and too much was at stake in the 2016 election for marginalized people to cast what they believed might be a risky vote.

None of this is to suggest that Clinton, Obama, or the Democratic Party at large have been Messiah-like saviors to marginalized people and working-class Americans. I would call on anyone to do their due diligence and research the oppressive or compromising policies espoused at different points by all of the aforementioned figures and party.

But certainly, in Clinton's case, and with all viable women presidential candidates we'll likely see for years to come, the hyperscrutiny to which women candidates' economic stances and progressive ideological purity will likely be subjected is gendered. Which candidates are forgiven for past, problematic stances and acts; who is given the clearance to learn, evolve, progress, and adopt new stances without being bogged down by gendered criticisms about "authenticity" and "pandering," tends to be rooted in identity, and certainly, in gender.

On the 2016 presidential campaign trail and throughout his career, Sanders has never faced the level of scrutiny progressive female politicians have for his previous support for an oppressive 1994 crime bill that Hillary Clinton was widely panned for supporting, herself, in the 2016 primary. He has faced little scrutiny for his record of relatively weak stances on gun control prior to the 2016 election, unlike New York Senator and 2020 Democratic presidential candidate Kirsten Gillibrand, who once shared these stances and has remained widely scrutinized for them.

However valid and important some criticisms of progressive-leaning female politicians may be, no matter what, the disproportionate scrutiny they shoulder often comes from a place of inherent, gendered distrust. Because female and diverse politicians don't look like the politicians we are accustomed to seeing, we subject them to rigid, unflinching, and often unproductive criticisms, and either passively or actively treat them as if they don't belong in politics at all.

Other less dogmatic, progressive white men may claim to fully embrace and support Democratic female candidates but equivocate about whether to actually vote for them because of purported concerns about their viability and electability. Yet, assertions about viability and electability coming from white-male progressives are especially condescending when directed at young women of color like me, who are perfectly aware that Senator Kamala Harris, as a black and South Asian woman, faced emphatic racism and sexism in response to her presidential campaign; that sexist backlash posed a significant challenge to Gillibrand, in response to her passionate work to support sexual assault survivors. And certainly, better than progressive white men do, we know from our own experiences exactly what is at stake in the 2020 election; we know better than anyone that Republican electoral victories are devastating for our safety and human rights.

It's important to understand words like "electability" and "viability" and "likability" in reference to women and minority candidates are microaggressions. They appeal to common, universal understandings of people in positions of power—people who are capable and worthy of acquiring power—as white and male.

Therefore, white-male political candidates are understood as inherently more electable and viable, safer bets than women and candidates of color, who are perceived as risky due to the attention drawn by their identities. Women and candidates of color don't fit the preconceived mold of what a successful politician looks like in a country where we've become accustomed to seeing white men in power. Many prospective voters might deny their choices have anything to do with personal preferences and prejudices regarding race and gender but, rather, with concerns about how their hypothetical, "less evolved" friends and neighbors might vote.

And where women candidates are concerned, "likability" is an especially strong factor, because often you'll find women who step out of the lanes assigned to them by the patriarchy and aspire to any sort of leadership position aren't exactly popular for it. A female politician might be well liked if she knows her place in a lower position than the presidency—but all that changes when she expresses that she wants more. Because of that wanting, because of that determination to not settle and step out of her lane as so many white men do all the time, her likability is immediately called into question.

Yet, those who support diversity in reality, and not just as an attractive, salient talking point, should be willing to fight for it. No longer can we sweepingly blame electoral losses on the failure of diverse identities, as a means to avoid investing the tremendous but ineffably valuable grunt work of fighting for real, meaningful diversity in our politics.

More than hard work and proactive effort to push back on identity-based challenges, support for diversity may at times require minor sacrifices and compromises in our politics: A progressive-leaning minority candidate may not reflect every single progressive policy point you support, and, certainly, there will always be issues too fundamental to compromise on.

Yet, we must be willing to place trust in the inherent value of lived experience, recognize the crucial ways identity can shape how one governs, and consider the unquantifiable symbolic power their election could have to galvanize marginalized communities and future generations to get involved in politics. If diverse candidates, who may naturally take precautions to avoid identity-based stereotyping of them as inherently radical and subversive, share your fundamental values and prove their determination to listen to, and fight for, you, they deserve your consideration as a voter, period.

***

It should go without saying that progressive economic policies are not the be-all and end-all cure for oppression and social injustice in this country, or the world. In my experience, I've encountered only a few progressive men who would refute this. My white-male communist friend, whom I'm sure you feel well-acquainted with at this point, recognized this—with the caveat that class is the most decisive factor in oppression.

Without a doubt, in a country that does not treat health care, food, and shelter as human rights, economic status is often a matter of life or death. And yet, police officers are hardly mindful of how wealthy a black man they perceive as threatening or dangerous may be before pulling the trigger. Across lines of class and economic status, black women remain significantly more likely than white women to die in childbirth or as a result of pregnancy complications, often as a consequence of health-care providers' implicit bias.

The belief that gender and race neutrality, if they go hand in-hand with a progressive economic platform, would be a one-size-fits-all solution for everyone isn't just misguided—it's also a form of gaslighting. It erases how economic struggles are disproportionately shouldered by people of color and women, and the reality that struggles of marginalized people often extend beyond the economic and take form in a wide range of potent, discriminatory forces that white men don't have to worry about. And it makes the vocal, feminist women who know these truths feel crazy, as we're forced to push back on these narratives espoused by male progressives, over and over.

Identity-neutral rhetoric even in the realm of progressive politics can be actively harmful if it hides or trivializes the salient economic power of social difference. Equality can't be achieved by pretending that all of our experiences are the same. Engaging in this charade will really only have the opposite impact by allowing existing inequality to persist and grow as a result of neglect.

Oppression and privilege are often simultaneous experiences across our intersecting, interacting, coexisting identities. Attempts to arbitrarily rank identities from most to least marginalized hurt all marginalized people, by suggesting we must necessarily pick and choose and oversimplify our range of identities to fit a false binary of privilege and oppression.

But such is often the lens through which performative, white-male "progressives" understand identity in America. Their view is that privilege and oppression are a binary, and if they support nonoppressive politics, these men cannot fathom how they could still be perceived as advancing oppression, no matter how many women and marginalized people they sideline and ignore. And when they view privilege and oppression as a binary, they view marginalized people who aren't 100 percent onboard with their oh-so-very nonoppressive politics as oppressors, themselves, despite how marginalized people experience daily oppression such progressives could never even begin to fathom.

Certainly, just as oppression and privilege are not a binary, nor are well-meaning intentions and performativity; aspiring male allies can be performative and have good intentions simultaneously. But when it comes down to it, it's just a matter of whether their intentions are good enough to yield meaningful self-reflection and listening, and real, respectful changes in how they engage in activism.

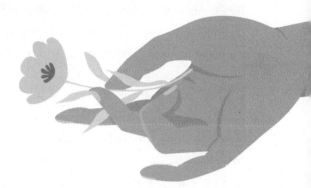

# 11

# Identity Politics? In This Economy?

Known for his candor and economic populism, Senator Bernie Sanders once said of a female, Latinx candidate who ran a progressive campaign for US Senate, "It is not good enough for somebody to say, 'I'm a woman, vote for me.' No. That is not good enough." Of course, she'd never said that. But nonetheless, Sanders's reductive translation revealed plenty about how men and male-dominated media hear and perceive female candidates and politicians.

Most women candidates and candidates of color are particularly cautious and ensure that they speak on a wide range of issues to avoid being so pigeonholed. But they are also more likely than white-male politicians to speak about these issues on an intersectional level. And because in appearance and background they differ so dramatically from our traditional constructions of power-ful people and political leaders, media and those complicit in the maintenance of existing systems of identity-based oppression fixate on these candidates' identity as a means to marginalize them and belittle their politics.

That is not to say that diversity in politicians should not be vocally and frequently celebrated, or receive attention. Objec-tively speaking, politicians who differ from the straight, white-male norm bring a litany of experiences and perspective that *do* make them special, more effective, and often better suited to represent the increasingly diverse electorate. The problem is not them, nor their invocations of their diverse experiences. It's men like Sanders, as well as mainstream media and people across the political spectrum, who weaponize diverse identity to suggest that it inherently, unfairly advantages candidates, granting them clear-ance to be weaker on the "real" issues—or, you know, issues that don't explicitly concern the rights and living standards of margin-alized people—and still be embraced.

Sanders added, "One of the struggles you're going to be seeing is whether the Democratic Party can go beyond identity politics." The term "identity politics," often used interchangeably with "social issues," involves recognition of identity-based differentials in people's rights and experiences in political contexts.

Identity politics pertains to such heavy issues as the maternal death crisis stemming from lacking access to abortion care, espe-cially among women of color, and the racist criminal-justice sys-tem's subjugation of black families and communities, who face disparate rates of poverty and police violence. Certainly, these issues are rooted in identity-based oppression, and could be regarded as "social issues" to the extent that they impact people's full ability to participate in public life.

Identity politics and social issues are not trivial by nature of the subject matter they entail but by the reductive intentions of most of the people and politicians who use these terms to marginalize and decentralize certain experiences from the mainstream. The underlying message of swiping marginalized people's experiences from beneath the umbrella of supposedly more serious and important economic issues is that the economy and identity are somehow inherently separate, that identity and economics comprise a zero-sum game rather than interact and feed each other.

In 2018, Sanders said at a summit hosted by the Sanders Institute, "Trump became president of the United States because there is a massive amount of pain in this country, which is not seen on television, which many of my Democratic colleagues do not know about ... and often that is taking place in rural areas." This message isn't inaccurate; poverty and suffering in rural parts of the country—ultimately due to policies enacted or supported by President Trump and the Republican Party—can't be ignored. But nor should we ignore that 53 percent of Americans earning less than $30,000 annually voted for Hillary Clinton, compared to 41 percent for Trump; the poorest demographic of Americans (black women) voted for Clinton at a rate of 94 percent; and 52 percent of voters who said the economy was their most important issue voted for Clinton, compared to 42 percent for Trump.[1] We can't rely on the economy to place very real and enduring white racism above criticism.

Donald Trump's 2016 presidential campaign relied on identity politics through catering to the rage and insecurities of rural white men. Certainly, he relied on identity politics substantially more than Clinton's campaign, which offered actual, in-depth economic proposals for affordable and accessible health care, housing, and job growth that would benefit wide swaths of the population. The relentless narrative that Clinton lost because she spoke exclusively about social issues in isolation of economic policies is baseless, and, frankly, sexist. For many pundits and voters, Clinton's gender clearly stoked so much discomfort that they literally could not hear what she was saying above the noise-canceling sound of her being female.

There is a distinct reason we call Trump's utilization of identity politics a "unifying message," while we reductively call addressing existential human-rights issues like criminal-justice reform, mass incarceration, immigration, and reproductive rights "identity politics." That is, white men remain prioritized and centralized as the default, standard identity in the United States—often, even by progressive leaders like Bernie Sanders.

This is a reality women like me and many feminist writers, activists and leaders have faced throughout our lives and careers—casual erasure and dismissal of the issues that matter to us, of the experiences that color our lives—not just by men but also in male-centric narratives in general. It's utterly exhausting to have to explain why our perspectives, our priorities, our uniqueness, our lives, matter in American politics, why broad strokes and identity-neutral policies and rhetoric erase and harm us, allowing the challenges we face to persist and grow by pretending they do not exist.

Many pundits who attribute Trump's victory to rural, white-male resentment and insecurity are onto something but always stop short of considering why rural white men are resentful and insecure in the first place. White-male identity is and always has been so utterly rooted in hegemony and domination, which are necessarily challenged when white men struggle while some women and people of color succeed. When we center white men's perspective, experience, and cultural narrative, all while we marginalize all others, we allow and empower their domination, even in a world that is naturally, steadily moving to leave it behind.

According to bipartisan media narratives rejecting "identity politics" as divisive and counterproductive, the suffering, needs, and struggles for survival of women, people of color, LGBTQ people, and all marginalized groups are merely a distraction. Yet, the fact remains that without sufficient attention from lawmakers, marginalized people will die—in far too many cases, exacerbated by the ongoing war on reproductive rights and institutionalized, racist state violence, they already are.

There's no question progressive economic policies like those espoused by Sanders will help to address some of the oppression marginalized people face. Sanders's policy proposals, including tuition-free public education, universal health care, and redistributive taxation—all ideals plenty of women of color before and since his presidential run have been fighting for—would disproportionately benefit women, people or color, and all marginalized people, because these groups are substantially more likely to live in poverty. But this does not magically negate the harmful nature of dismissive comments about identity politics and social issues in the political discourse.

The erasure of specific groups' unique, identity-based experiences is not progress, but its own form of regression. No matter what economic policies are enacted, the fact remains that much of the oppression in this country remains identity based, and as a result, identity-neutral rhetoric and policies of any kind simply aren't going to fix everything. Pretending or insinuating that they will is where problems arise.

The "massive amount of pain," as Sanders put it, among rural, white communities also exists in communities of color and certainly in urban and coastal areas that struggle with persistent homelessness, poverty, unemployment, and more, all exacerbated by racism, misogyny, and bigotry. The narrative of the out-of-touch, coastal, liberal elitist who ignores the pain of white, rural communities purposefully hides and dismisses those other experiences, just as it speaks volumes about whose experiences media outlets and politicians choose to sympathize with and prioritize over others.

Most human-rights issues that dictate not just people's economic opportunities but also ultimate survival are inextricably bound to identity: the plunder and incarceration of black and brown bodies within the current criminal-justice system; the death, trauma, and disenfranchisement faced by disproportionately women of color who are barred from accessing birth control and safe abortion care; the migrant families separated and ravaged by the Trump administration's immigration policies for trying to survive; the survivors of sexual violence systematically denied support, justice, and healing. All of these issues, on top of morally necessitating attention, are inextricably bound to economic justice and a thriving, healthy economy. As such, they deserve to be treated as urgent concerns the way explicitly economic issues are, not downgraded to the second-class status of the marginalized people disproportionately affected by these policies.

The chasm that separates how disenfranchised people and privileged people perceive and discuss these issues is clear as day in cable-news panels, in differences among legislators' work across gender and race, and, certainly, in everyday life. I've encountered this chasm on a personal level on many occasions, although one particular incident comes to mind. A white-male ex-boyfriend of mine once dismissed my concerns about Democratic Party conflict over the necessity of supporting pro-choice candidates as irrelevant to mainstream politics. As he so eloquently put it, "Most real people don't care about abortion."

Most "real people," to white men, *are* white men. That women comprise just over half the population, that the majority of Americans will soon be people of color who are disproportionately affected by issues of reproductive justice, and that most people *do* care about abortion and other identity-based issues, will never matter to them.

Thus, I write this with my fellow young women, who have increasingly become the trailblazing leaders of most movements for social justice, at the forefront of my mind. The issues we care about, the issues we are affected by, the issues we are fighting for, matter. Our work and our passion carry tremendous implications for many people's lives and certainly our own; it is not for others to tell us what matters and what does not. If we, guided by our experiences and compassion for others, care about something, then it matters, simple as that.

---

If ever there were an example of how identity is inextricably bound to economic outcomes and opportunity, it's the gender wage gap—the persistent phenomenon of women, and in particular, women of color, receiving less pay and fewer opportunities for raises and promotions than white men.

Of course, we must consider those who are excluded from the parameters of traditional, mainstream discourse around the gender wage gap, from LGBTQ people who are fired or unable to find work due to discrimination that is legal in most states, to undocumented people—and especially undocumented women—who could not even complain about their experiences with exploitation, sexual abuse, and general oppression without risking everything. But certainly, we can recognize the importance of advocating for fair pay, just as we can recognize the arbitrary limits of exclusively advocating for fair pay.

As of estimates from recent years, the gender wage gap for American women stands at about 78 cents for every dollar men make. This is, of course, an improvement from 59 percent in 1963, and our long national history of gender-segregated job postings—but gradual improvement is hardly an equivalent to cured sexism. Today's 78-cent statistic is the product of a range of factors, from blatant discrimination and biases about who is inherently more experienced and deserving of higher pay or promotions; to persistent discrimination around pregnancy and motherhood; to gender gaps in lucrative, higher-paying fields, caused by early enforcement of gender roles and disparities in role models and mentors available to boys and girls; to the broad devaluation of feminized lines of work. On top of the wage gap, and surely in part because of it, across the board, American women are 35 percent more likely than American men to live in poverty.[2]

In 2018, new findings by the Institute for Women's Policy Research revealed the 78-cent statistic's alarming underside. The IWPR examined how this statistic is derived from the salaries of men and women who work full time, and after comparing the wages of all adult men and all adult women, found that the gender wage gap is actually closer to 49 cents on the dollar.[3]

Why? Because women are substantially more likely to drop or be pushed out of the labor force by child-care needs and other domestic demands, in large part due to gender roles that demonize women but not men who fail to put their families first. The 49-cent statistic, which includes women who are unemployed or underemployed, offers critical insight into all the ways gendered, heteronormative social expectations impact economic opportunity, compensation, and constraints on who is able to fully, autonomously participate in society. It also highlights the vast, gendered disparities in uncompensated day-to-day labor and the general devaluation of traditionally female work and experiences, all of which are missing when we look at the 78-cent statistic in isolation.

That said, the isolated 78-cent statistic has always been white-washed and oversimplified. It has always marginalized black, Latinx, and Native American women, who make 61, 53, and 58 cents on the dollar, respectively, as of 2017. Twenty percent of LGBTQ people who live alone make less than $12,000 per year,[4] and the majority of states permit employers to legally fire them for being who they are.

Certainly, there are valid criticisms of the traditional gender-wage-gap statistic, and the marginalized groups it erases—just as there are many, many invalid criticisms. And one of the most common anti feminist criticisms of the wage gap is that it is self-induced because women actively choose to enter lower-paying fields.

Yet, this "decision" can only really be viewed as a decision in isolation of nearly all other factors. The wage gap has far less to do with poor decision-making from women than it does generational consequences of sexism: Young women and girls are substantially less likely than their male counterparts to have role models in STEM (science, technology, engineering, and mathematics) and other higher-paying, lucrative fields to encourage them to enter these fields. Spaces in these industries simply aren't created for women and girls the way they are for men and boys. Boys and girls are often socialized from a young age to engage in different subject matter, to view their value as intrinsically attached to different things, like appearances and likability for girls, and domination and authority for boys.

And in the same breath that women are steered away from lucrative, traditionally respected fields of work altogether from a young age, there is a long, persistent history of people in originally male-dominated industries receiving decreased compensation and respect as the industries gradually become female-dominated or even just allow women to enter at all. In other words, the notion that the wage gap is due to women proactively, independently choosing low-paying fields embodies something of a self-fulfilling prophecy. It's a lose-lose situation: enter a higher paying male-dominated field that may come to lose economic value as it becomes more feminized or stay in a lower paying female-dominated field.

That said, the wage gap can hardly be blamed on women failing to "take initiative"—especially in light of 2016 research that revealed male and female employees negotiate for higher pay at roughly equal rates, but women are about 25 percent less likely to successfully receive raises.[5] This research effectively subverts an age-old conspiracy theory among wage-gap deniers, that the gap is produced not by discrimination and misogyny but by a biological, predestined, sex-based disparity in initiative and ambition.

Speaking of initiative, women are increasingly becoming the primary earners in as many as 40 percent of heterosexual American households, as of the last decade.[6] The persistence of pay inequality reflects employers' failure to adapt with the times or perhaps even a proactive compulsion to punish the increasing numbers of women who decline to stay in their patriarchally assigned lane.

In light of the IWPR's 49-cent statistic, the wage gap seems a lot less about biology and biological disparities, and a lot more about sociology, and the enforcement of traditional gender-role expectations. In the context of public policy, research has shown paid maternal leave but not paid family leave tends to decrease the likelihood of women receiving pay increases or promotions in the future.[7] That's because employers continue to view child rearing as an inevitable fact of female employees' lives whether or not they are already mothers, and they understand child rearing itself as vastly affecting female employees' working capabilities, while having virtually no effect on male employees.

To that end, gendered, noninclusive expectations of how parenthood will affect women but not men have a very real but virtually unquantifiable impact on women's economic opportunities and living standards, as well as those of LGBTQ parents. Public and company-policy changes are a critical first step in addressing these disparities and raising awareness about how domestic and child-care responsibilities necessitate involvement from both parents. But full, equitable parenting, especially in male-female partnerships, necessitates cultural shifts too, starting with how we raise our children to view parenting as equitable and understand parenting responsibilities are not gendered.

In that vein, the traditional, 78-cent statistic is just one medium through which sexist gender roles and the devaluation of feminized labor operate. Following the IWRP's 49-cent statistic, we can also understand lack of fair compensation and broad erasure of feminized labor as a frontier of its own. In a 2017 debate about the Affordable Care Act, Republican Congress member John Shimkus asked Congress why male taxpayers should be required to help pay for prenatal and childbirth resources at all. By asking this question, Shimkus, who was notably birthed by a woman, offered a shining example of the extent to which traditionally feminized experiences and labor are trivialized and erased.

And it starts early: From childhood, research has shown girls do more chores for less compensation than boys. Similar research has shown that, upon reaching adulthood, men and women see a substantial gender gap in allocation of domestic responsibilities in heterosexual households. Women across the country living up to daily, gendered expectations imposed upon them perform household and parenting tasks with value amounting to a six-figure annual salary. Yet, this very labor is both widely dismissed and uncompensated when delivered by stay-at-home mothers or homemakers—hence, the 49-cent statistic unearthed by the IWPR.

I find myself considering the concept of victim-blaming whenever I hear predominantly male responses to both the 78- and 49-cent statistics: specifically, there is a deeply condescending sort of victim-blaming to the assertion that the gender wage gap is the product of women "choosing" lower-paying lines of work, or "choosing" to leave the workforce to meet the needs of their families. Men, children, and, broadly speaking, society, rely on women's labor, all while refusing to acknowledge, appreciate, and pay for it. Traditionally, feminized labor is the backbone of society—yet, it's also a decisive factor in why the controversial IWRP study has shown American women make less than half the earnings of American men.

Ultimately, both the 78- and 49-cent statistics are incomplete without necessary consideration of the phenomena of sexual abuse, exploitation, and complicity perpetuated by the powerful men who preside over the labor force, altogether. The economic effects of their abuses, from firing and denying opportunity to women who decline their sexual advances, to creating and maintaining hostile, male-dominant workplaces and industries, are unquantifiable.

Sexual violence, exploitation of workplace power dynamics, and intimidation tactics amount to more than the private, inconsequential affairs their perpetrators attempt to dismiss these acts as. Rather, such acts are inseparable from men's work and legacies, contrary to assertions from sympathizers of powerful abusive men, and contrary to the suggestions of many conservative thinkers. Those who perpetuate these behaviors affect the safety and careers of every single person around them—and comprise an unmistakable economic hazard to all women.

In the face of systemic disadvantage, opportunity gaps, and threats to women's safety, the existence of gender-segregated women's-empowerment scholarships, organizations, and other programs are not only sensible but frankly necessary for women's survival and inclusion in the workforce. The backlash these programs often draw in the form of everything from violent trolling to costly lawsuits filed by men's-rights activists highlight the perversion of context-neutral definitions of "equality." Such definitions are a driving force in the ongoing conflict between notions of equity and equality in movements for justice and carry the potential to undo generations of progress for the rights and opportunities of marginalized people.

The Equal Rights Amendment was first introduced in Congress in 1921, but it wasn't until 1972 that the proposed amendment to the US Constitution passed out of the House and Senate, moving to state legislatures to seek approval from at least thirty-eight of fifty (two-thirds) states for ratification. The proposed amendment would formally recognize American women's equal status, guarantee equal legal rights, and prohibit sex-based discrimination. The ERA appeared slated to pass during the same decade of a vast litany of landmark, pro-equality Supreme Court decisions and laws but ultimately received the support of only thirty-five of the required thirty-eight states prior to the 1979 deadline for state ratification. The deadline has since been extended, with Nevada, Illinois, and Virginia passing the ERA decades later, in 2017, 2018, and 2020, respectively. A legal battle over the deadline will likely ensue, thus putting ratification of the amendment on hold.[8]

It's worth considering why a proposed amendment to codify the simple premise that women are citizens with the full rights of citizens remains controversial. The ERA enjoyed expansive bipartisan support starting from the 1960s but has stalled since conservative leader Phyllis Schlafly led an aggressive and ultimately successful opposition movement in the 1970s. Schlafly asserted that the ERA would lead to women receiving sweepingly equal legal treatment with men, to women being drafted to wars, or losing protective legislation that granted women workers safer working conditions than men, for example. Yet the feminist movement has a long history of universally opposing the draft for men, women, and all people and supporting safe working conditions for people of all genders as well.

Schlafly's arguments and their legacy categorically misrepresent the goals of the feminist movement and also falsely, dangerously equate equal status with broad, rigidly equal treatment. Today, an oft-made mistake in the dialogue around how to best achieve equality across lines of gender, race, and all identities is the notion that equality necessitates ignoring and doing nothing about existing difference.

I often think of the near-legendary anecdote of the murder of Kitty Genovese outside an apartment building full of her neighbors, who heard her screams and bore witness to her rape, assault, and murder in 1964. It is cited as the most culturally well-known example of the bystander effect, of the dark, human inclination toward complicity. But more often than not, recollections of this event neutralize all roles identity played in the attack (an act of rape and gender violence) and the biases that brought about complicity (an absence of sympathy for women victims, and, surely, a tacit approval of domestic violence, as one witness said he thought Genovese was simply being beaten by her husband in a run-of-the-mill "lover's quarrel"). Bystander apathy and complicity are grave concerns—so, too, are their disparate impacts on women and survivors and minorities. Yet, these are impacts we are trained to ignore in a culture that so frequently prioritizes identity neutrality, the comfort of the powerful and privileged, over difficult, nuanced conversations about how identity-based differences shape every aspect of our lives.

Within progressive circles, words such as "equity" and "justice" have emerged as popular alternatives, meant to recognize the reality that sweepingly equal, identity-neutral treatment can be harmful and oppressive. Instead, our institutions must proactively act to combat existing disparities or accept responsibility for empowering said disparities to grow with each generation.

An example of proactive efforts to address persistent, identity-based inequalities is gender empowerment and professional mentorship groups that actively address the disadvantages and exclusion women and particularly women of color experience in workplaces; the aforementioned legal backlash such groups and programs have faced in recent years reflects everything that's wrong with staunch, uncompromising conceptions of equality.

The conflict between approaches of equity and hard-line equality similarly lies at the heart of ongoing debates about affirmative action and pro-diversity policies increasingly being practiced by companies. Equality hard-liners often purport that affirmative-action proponents are the racist ones for regarding black and brown people as inherently inferior and in need of more help. Yet, affirmative-action opponents are the ones who will never cede an opportunity to discredit black or brown people's achievements as the purported products of affirmative action.

Across decades of lawsuits initiated or bankrolled by rich, mediocre white men to challenge institutions' right to consider race as one of infinitely many factors in college admissions, the subtext of these lawsuits has always been racist gaslighting. The erasure of underprivileged minority groups' ongoing, challenging, and certainly unique experiences in this country is rooted in gaslighting, the pretense that systemic oppression we know and face every day has magically ceased to exist, that we've all had the same opportunities in life, and that none of us have faced jarring discrimination in a country built for and fundamentally centered around the experiences of white and wealthy people. Following the logic of these lawsuits, being a minority within the white, capitalist patriarchy is somehow socially, professionally, and politically advantageous.

In many nonwhite, low-income communities, college is not something many children and young people are even raised to consider as an option, as their families' financial situations can often require them to work full-time immediately after or before high school graduation. Access to college-preparatory resources dictates many students' access to college in today's competitive higher-education environment, and socioeconomic privilege often dictates access to these resources, which include standardized test-prep classes, subject tutors, college counselors, and application fees that can total in the tens of thousands of dollars.

And, make no mistake, access to socioeconomic privilege is often inextricably dictated by race and racism, cemented through a long, persistent, and still very-much-happening history of racist policies: Slavery and Jim Crow segregation laws were a few short generations ago, while race-based segregation through gentrification and zoning policies persists in many if not most communities. As a result of the racist War on Drugs, initiated by President Nixon and continued to an extent by every US president since, 80 percent of black people in federal prison and 60 percent of people in state prisons for drug offenses are black and Latinx, despite equal rates of drug use between communities of color and white communities.[9]

One in nine black children has an incarcerated parent, compared with one in fifty-seven white children.[10] "Family separation" exists not just in the Trump administration's cruel border policies but also on a systemic level within the criminal-justice system, disproportionately targeting black families.

Of course, ultimately, the War on Drugs is just one example of communities of color being disproportionately policed, often to costly, life-threatening, and, certainly, intergenerational consequences. Research has indisputably demonstrated how racism impacts black Americans' access to basic, everyday needs for survival, such as housing, employment, car insurance, health care, and education, and, certainly, what parents are able to provide for their families. White convicts are more likely than black people without criminal records to be hired for the same jobs.[11] Car-insurance companies charge higher rates to people from black communities than people from white communities, regardless of whether the black person's neighborhood is objectively safer than the white person's.[12]

In 2018, an extensive *New York Times* investigation that traced the lives of millions of children found black boys raised in America, even in the wealthiest families and neighborhoods, still earn less in adulthood than white boys with similar backgrounds.

For black and brown youth, double standards with the potential to impact the trajectory of their lives occur early. Young black men are between nine and sixteen times more likely than any other group to be killed by police officers,[13] and those who are killed are often fathers, sons, and providers to their families. Black students across the country consistently face more severe disciplinary actions for committing the same infractions as white students,[14] laying the foundations for the notorious school-to-prison pipeline. Today's black families are forced to exist in a country that remains ravaged by mass incarceration, racist policing, and continued hate crimes, with white-supremacist terror attacks underreported on and certainly insufficiently discussed in mainstream media.

"Equal treatment" will not magically bridge any of these disparities, which necessarily dictate the resources black and brown children, youths, and potential college applicants have access to. In far too many cases, institutionalized barriers disempower those who are most affected by racist laws and realities from fighting for meaningful change: one in thirteen black people of voting age are denied the right to vote as a result of transparently racist laws that disenfranchise people with felony convictions.[15]

Subjecting people with fundamentally different lived experiences to sweepingly equal treatment only widens existing inequalities. Turning a blind eye to existing inequality only exacerbates it and cruelly asserts that those who are disadvantaged are to blame for their own disadvantage. But one of the most damning components of opposition to affirmative action is that abolishment of the policy would necessarily, sweepingly harm all groups across lines of identity, because absolutely everyone benefits from cultural heterogeneity in their lives. Privileged opponents of affirmative action are deluding themselves if they think homogeneous campuses or workplaces would in any way benefit them, rather than deprive them of the expanded worldview that free-speech-loving, conservative thinkers pretend to advocate for. Universities are institutions of learning and necessitate meaningful cultural education that can only be achieved through admitting and supporting a student body of diverse backgrounds and lived experiences.

That said, amid new revelations into how segregated many neighborhoods and schools across the country remain, universities must take seriously their responsibility to treat diversity and affirmative action programs as more than numbers and proactively work to promote inclusivity and authentic cultural interaction on campuses. Anything less than a full commitment to diversity, not just in numbers, but in practice, would fall short of affirmative action's ultimate goals of cultural education in higher learning.

None of this is to say there are no valid, deeply important criticisms of affirmative action—specifically, for failing to do enough to address inequalities. Michelle Alexander, author of *The New Jim Crow*, has argued that affirmative action promotes an innocuous strain of respectability politics that uplifts the most "respectable" members of marginalized groups, while ignoring the existential, often life-threatening challenges faced by many other members of these groups. To name just a few examples, the school-to-prison pipeline, police violence,

substance abuse, and human trafficking pose tremendous, disproportionate challenges to young people in communities of color. And I
daresay all of these issues pose a more severe threat than not receiving
admission into an Ivy League or four-year university.

Perhaps there are valid criticisms of affirmative action, and its
arbitrary limits in promoting justice and equity for all members
of marginalized communities. But nothing could ever make holistic consideration of race in college admissions or hiring practices
harmful to anyone. Race, like gender, sexual orientation, and all
other identity-based facets, distinctly impacts our experiences and
often our ideas and outlook on the world around us. Diversity
offers irreplaceable benefits to all who engage with it.

This nation's history and foundations in violent, racist injustice and trauma have always necessitated a decades-long, ongoing
journey to correct these moral failures and their generational consequences. Yet, somewhere on this journey, many have come to internalize the idea that anything that does not appear to directly benefit
people born into privilege is inherently unfair and oppressive, that
loss of monopoly is somehow equivalent to loss of opportunity.

Recognizing the lingering, extensive residue of our country's
foundations is the only starting point there is: Equality can never be
achieved through passivity and playing dumb about what marginalized people and racial minorities continue to face in this country.
Equality and progress can only ever be achieved through consciousness and action and, certainly, discussion of identity politics.

---

I grew up in the sort of affluent, predominantly Asian-American
suburb that loathes affirmative action as much as nearly any wealthy
white community. My classmates and I were predominantly the

children of immigrants who came to this country with nothing (but often, did not come with intergenerational debt, incarcerated family, and stereotypes painting them as lazy, violent, and dangerous), and many of my peers invoked this traditional "rags to riches," model-minority narrative to justify their opposition to affirmative action.

It is never lost on me—especially while living under an unapologetically white-supremacist presidential administration that equates immigrants' refusal to assimilate with stupidity and inferiority—that my parents are immigrants who dedicated their lives to creating any opportunity for me that they could. They instilled in me a work ethic not unlike their own, insisting that I should never fear failure but laziness. My father has always been certain that there is no problem in the world that cannot be solved through hard work. "There are only two kinds of problems: those that can be solved, and those that can be worked around," he once told me.

This work ethic certainly worked for my parents in their experience as immigrants, convincing them that anyone willing to put in the work can be successful, that failure and poverty and suffering are choices—choices disproportionately made by black and brown people. I believe in hard work too; I believe many of my achievements I am most proud of are in no small part the products of hard work. But they are also indisputably the products of luck—that I was born into an upper-middle-class family and community with access to all the resources college attendance necessitates today, that I was born to relative safety in my body compared with the daily existential threats shouldered by black and brown bodies in highly policed communities.

Historically and today, Asian American immigrants face real struggles that should never be invalidated. For the better part of the twentieth century, racist immigration quotas barred nearly all non-western European people seeking refuge or new lives in the United States from entering. And in the modern era, Asian

American immigrants are more likely than any other immigrant group to receive permanent residence or citizenship through merit-based visas, indicating active recruitment of only "the best of the best"—per conventional, Western standards—from Asian countries. Crime and poverty remain persistent realities in Asian countries, which should dispel with the Western myth that "model minority" Asian Americans are somehow inherently better behaved or more successful and "civilized" than other minorities.

Asian American identity in the United States is far from the monolith portrayed by traditional Western cultural narratives. Many Asian American communities, and particularly Vietnamese and Indonesian American immigrant communities, continue to struggle with poverty, such that they are actually the least likely in the country to go to college. There are distinct differences between the lived experiences and access to traditional academic success of Asian immigrant communities, based on when and how they came to America. The oversimplification of our experience as a collective unit is an invention of whitewashed, decontextualized narratives meant to lump Asian communities with white communities when it is convenient, and when our nonuniversal successes can be misrepresented and weaponized to invalidate the struggles of other people of color.

Ever since I was a teenager, I have always been critical of the apathy I've perceived in wealthy, Asian American communities and circles, often stemming from the notion that the oppression and experiences of other people of color are not relevant to us because we've "made it." But when I look at the caution of my immigrant parents and the caution of many older immigrants, on some level, I understand. All that we as minorities have gained through years of struggle and solidarity we could easily and far more quickly lose. Such is the fact of being a person of color, whether Asian or black or Latinx—that any individual person of color, for better but more often for worse, represents the entirety of our race in everything we do in America.

Still, in many ways, some Asian American experiences are not comparable to those of people who historically did not come to this country by choice or came here fleeing death, violence, and communities ravaged by generations of Western imperialism and oppression. Discrimination and harmful Western narratives about Asian American identity persist, but the simple, objective truth is that many of us have not been disenfranchised by the criminal-justice system and dehumanizing, racist perceptions of us in the same way that black and Latinx communities have. Oppression and privilege are simultaneous experiences, and no experience is universal. As members of marginalized groups, the test of our solidarity and commitment to collective liberation in the white, American patriarchy is our ability to listen to, learn from, and support each other.

Race and gender are not the sole mediums through which identity-based oppression operates, nor are they the sole determinants of economic opportunity and participation in public life. As of 2019, thirty-one states in the United States permit legal discrimination against members of the LGBTQ community on the grounds of "religious freedom." Gay couples could get married one day and legally be fired, evicted, or denied service the next. Following the "logic" of right-wing politicians, religious freedom speaks exclusively to the experiences of people who adhere to traditional, puritanical societal norms—or, in America, straight, white Christian people. This narrow, oppressive conception of religious freedom is meant to uphold the dominance of people who have always maintained a monopoly on cultural and political power in the United

States and equates freedom with the punishment of anyone who deviates from Christian patriarchal norms.

The term "marriage equality" is a pointed example of this. Conservative rejection of marriage equality stems not only from homophobia and bigotry but also from the perceived erosion of traditional, obligatory gender roles within the institution of marriage itself. Marriage equality necessitates that dominance and heading a household are no longer traditionally male roles, that what we give and take within marriage and romantic relationships is no longer inherently gendered.

The legalization of marriage equality and increased media and political representation of LGBTQ people signal crucial progress, but contrary to popular belief (80 percent of self-identified LGBTQ allies incorrectly believe it's illegal to fire, deny service to, or evict people on the basis of orientation or gender identity),[16] these cultural shifts have hardly eradicated systemic oppression of LGBTQ people, with relatively minimal effects on high rates of anti-LGBTQ hate crimes and harassment, economic disenfranchisement, and living standards.

Over the course of 2017, more than 129 anti-LGBTQ bills were introduced in state legislatures across the country;[17] these bills included proposed bans to prohibit same-sex couples from adopting, and other protections for anti-LGBTQ discrimination. LGBTQ youth are 120 percent more likely than their straight peers to experience homelessness, and as many as 40 percent of all homeless young people are queer;[18] as noted earlier in this essay, 21 percent of LGBTQ people living alone in the United States make less than $12,000 per year.

Over the course of 2017, the first year of the Trump presidency, reported homicides of queer men increased by 400 percent.[19] Between 2016 and 2017, the FBI reported a 5 percent increase in hate crimes targeting LGBTQ people.[20] The year 2017 already marked the deadliest year in recent history for LGBTQ Americans, involving at least fifty-two people killed by anti-LGBTQ violence. Forty-one percent of trans adults report having attempted suicide at some point in their lives.[21]

LGBTQ people are also more likely to experience sexual violence and domestic abuse: According to the Human Rights Campaign in 2018, 44 percent of lesbian and 61 percent of bisexual women have experienced rape, physical violence, or domestic abuse, compared to 35 percent of heterosexual women. Twenty-six percent of gay and 37 percent of bisexual men have experienced the aforementioned forms of abuse, compared to 29 percent of heterosexual men. A 2015 survey revealed 47 percent of trans people are sexually assaulted at some point in their lifetime. And these rates of sexual violence are often even higher for queer people of color.[22]

The average life expectancy for American trans people as of 2018 is between thirty and thirty-two years,[23] and one in every five trans people living in the United States is homeless.[24] Ironically, considering the popularity of state and local-level bans on trans people using the restroom of their gender identity, trans people are far more likely to be assaulted than to commit assault in bathrooms. These discriminatory bans, justified by feigned concern that manly, hypermasculine transgender women will assault women and girls in restrooms, are often introduced and signed by the same lawmakers whose rhetoric and policies violate and harm the unsaid numbers of women who experience sexual violence from cisgender men.

Living conditions for LGBTQ Americans—and certainly, LGBTQ people abroad in the absence of American foreign policy advocating for their rights—have only worsened under the Trump administration, despite candidate Trump's assurances that he would support LGBTQ Americans. (Of course, these assurances were hardly credible in the first place once Trump selected noted anti-LGBTQ champion Mike Pence as his running mate in the summer of 2016.)

In 2017, just months into Trump's presidency, then-Attorney General Jeff Sessions reversed a policy that included protections for transgender people from discrimination in Title VII of the Civil Rights Act. Shortly after, President Trump announced an unconstitutional ban on trans people in the military, reductively referring to inclusion of trans people as "social experimentation," and punishing trans people for their perceived, inherently burdensome nature. (Trump, himself, had opted to dodge the draft by citing a minor foot injury in the 1960s.) The proposed ban had the potential to cost the US military $960 million, according to a study by the Palm Center and the Naval Postgraduate School, rendering Trump's claims that the policy was motivated by fiscal conservatism to avoid paying for trans people's health care costs almost laughable.[25]

And while the Trump administration's ongoing attacks on funding for Planned Parenthood and accurate, comprehensive sexual-health education are often exclusively categorized as part of the War on Women, these efforts also comprise a direct attack on the rights, health, and safety of queer people, placing them at increased risk of contracting sexually transmitted diseases or experiencing unsafe, violent sexual encounters without expansive sexual education. In 2015, when the state of Indiana defunded Planned Parenthood at the direction of then-Governor Mike Pence, a county that lost its only clinic experienced an HIV outbreak that involved an average of twenty new reported cases of HIV per week for ten consecutive weeks.

LGBTQ youth have been a particularly popular target of the Trump administration: In 2017, Education Secretary Betsy DeVos announced her department would no longer investigate complaints about transgender students being barred from bathrooms, arguing trans students' right to use the bathroom of their gender identity was not protected under Title IX. Throughout her confirmation hearings, DeVos repeatedly refused to promise her department would protect the rights of LGBTQ students against discrimination, but her 2018 proposal to grant $1 billion to private schools that notoriously discriminate on the basis of orientation and identity made her stance fairly clear.

Of course, DeVos hardly invented the persecution of LGBTQ youth in schools and society. LGBTQ students and trans students in particular disproportionately face school disciplinary action, such as suspension, expulsion, and dress-code violations for wearing clothing that does not align with the sex they were assigned at birth. The ostracism, bullying, and institutionalized punishment of LGBTQ young people in schools has consistently yielded disproportionately high dropout rates, as well as the jarringly high rates of homelessness, poverty, and suicide in this demographic. Between 5 and 10 percent of LGBTQ youth, depending on age and sex groups, have attempted suicide, a rate that is 1.5 to 3 times higher than heterosexual youth.[26]

Intolerance remains rampant in our institutions and among our elected leaders, to the continued disenfranchisement and endangerment of the LGBTQ community. In recent years, particularly since the *Obergefell v. Hodges* marriage-equality decision in 2015, the erasure of this intolerance from mainstream visibility has posed a threat almost as grave as the intolerance itself. There are no clear solutions to the deep, persistent disparities in LGBTQ people's rights and living standards, but there is one crucial starting point: listening, centering LGBTQ people's voices and experiences, and, certainly, protecting the place of identity in the political discourse.

In no uncertain terms, the modern Democratic Party relies on the votes and activism of diverse constituencies and marginalized people, who have historically paved the way forward for democracy for generations. After all, white men have left the Democratic Party in droves since the 1960s and the era of desegregation, and they also comprise a steadily shrinking voting bloc in an increasingly diverse America. In other words, it's far past time for unifying and empowering messages of diversity from the Democratic Party to become more than lip service: We marginalized people who have carried the party and its goals on our shoulders deserve to finally see ourselves represented by the leaders who serve us and represented by leaders who look like us, share our experiences, understand our lives. We deserve to be led and represented by women and women of color. We deserve to see our faces in the face of the president of the United States someday. And we deserve, at the very least, to have our demand for a government and society like this validated.

Amid a #MeToo era that has unearthed nearly unquantifiable, alarming episodes of abuses of power that target, disenfranchise, and marginalize women from nearly every place of decision-making power, embracing female leadership has never been more important or beneficial to the majority of society. Yet, as with former Democratic presidential nominee Hillary Clinton, we continue to hear the same excuses used to reject or discredit decorated, vastly qualified women presidential and political candidates, in general, for being "inauthentic," or not "electable" for any other reason. The notion that women are inherently weaker candidates can really only be attributed to misogyny and bipartisan yearning to maintain the gender status quo in politics: political-science research has demonstrated that when women are on the ballot, they win at equal rates with their male counterparts.[27] And let's not forget, too, that in 2016, then-Republican presidential candidate Donald Trump defeated some thirteen white men in the Republican

primary, effectively proving white men are hardly guaranteed to win ·
against candidates like Trump.

Perhaps some arguments are more valid than others, but all are
infected to varying extents with misogyny and gendered, self-fulfilling
prophecies. Drawing specifically from the Democratic presidential-
primary campaign trail in 2019, the first presidential race after
Clinton's 2016 loss, many of the less-than-progressive past stances
and actions of female candidates in the field were immediately and
aggressively put on full blast: Kamala Harris's record as a prosecutor,
Elizabeth Warren's invocations of race science to explain her claims to
Native American ancestry, Kirsten Gillibrand's past hard-line stances
on immigration and gun rights. No one should have called these candidates perfect, or utterly ignored harmful pieces of their records. But
who is forgiven for past, problematic stances and acts, who is given
the clearance to learn, evolve, and adopt new stances without being
harangued with gendered criticisms about authenticity and pandering is often plainly rooted in identity.

The disproportionate scrutiny female candidates and politicians
shoulder often comes from a place of distrust foremost because they
don't look like the politicians we are used to seeing. They don't look
like the people who belong in politics, and so we treat them like they
don't, with rigid, unflinching, and often unproductive criticism.

Following the 2016 election, identity politics emerged as the
popular, bipartisan explanation of Hillary Clinton's loss, despite
how Clinton won by a substantial margin among low-income
voters and voters who identified the economy as their top policy
priority. But in a political climate that remains insistent on recognizing white-male voters as the default, priority electorate (and on
white-male voters as the exclusive faces of the working class, despite
disparate numbers of impoverished women and people of color),
the reduction of Clinton's historic campaign to identity politics

should hardly be surprising. The term "identity politics" is inextricably bound to any and all actions of women politicians as a means to trivialize their work and power.

Contrary to narratives often heard from male political leaders across party lines after 2016, mass incarceration, criminal justice, reproductive rights, maternal death rates disproportionately affecting women of color, and an ongoing epidemic of sexual violence are existential issues of survival and human rights, and certainly economic opportunity. Who understands this better than female candidates and candidates of color?

Women and people of color know what's at stake if the wrong person is elected president, better than anyone—the last thing we need is white men explaining to us the importance of candidate viability and electability. Yet, if Democratic and progressive voters and leaders support diversity to the extent that they claim, they should be willing to fight for it. It's past time for us to stop blaming electoral losses on attention to and support for diversity, to stop parroting messages that equate losses by diverse candidates with the broad failure of diversity and identity, as if there is an inherent unworthiness to candidates who are not straight, white, and male.

Support for diversity may at times require sacrifices and compromise: a candidate who is a member of marginalized, politically underrepresented groups may not reflect every single progressive policy point you support, and there may be some issues that are too fundamental to compromise on and accept in a candidate. But the value of lived experience in shaping how a lawmaker legislates and treats constituents deserves to be considered and taken seriously too. Ultimately, if diverse candidates, who may naturally take precautions to avoid identity-based stereotyping of them as radical, share your fundamental values, they at least deserve your consideration.

Elections have always been a high-stakes affair for marginalized people in this country, considering how divided the two major parties are on key issues that disparately affect marginalized people. For all the leftist male griping about how the two parties are fundamentally the same, perhaps they are similar in some harmful ways that must be addressed—but on key issues of human rights and dignity for women, people of color, LGBTQ people, and minorities, there is simply no comparison.

For elections during and after the Trump era, frankly, the stakes have felt especially high. The moment he was elected, an intense urgency to remove him emerged, and in the years after his presidency, there will be an equally intense urgency to ensure we do not elect someone like him again. Yet, the reality is that actual support for diversity is not just words or salient talking points in politically convenient climates. More often than not, it is backbreaking, contentious work to overcome the disproportionate challenges and barriers that nonwhite, nonmale candidates face. But no one who is unwilling to put in the work to elect a president representative of all of us can claim to support diversity.

Many if not all men and male politicians still simply don't understand misogyny, and the full, exhaustive toll it has on every single woman in society, every single woman who has had to step aside in some way or another, in private or public life, so that the men around her could consolidate power. The fact that men do not fully understand misogyny isn't necessarily the problem—it's men and male politicians *pretending* that they do, erasing our voices, speaking for us, and pushing us aside to do so.

I think a lot about the gall of men to be offended when women insist that white-male politicians like Joe Biden, Bernie Sanders, or

Beto O'Rourke ought to take a step back and instead support and uplift women and minority presidential candidates, rather than try to represent us. I think about the outrage of these men in the face of unsaid numbers of women who have given up doing things we love, things that could change the world, because we can't afford child care, or because the misogyny and harassment and abuse we face in our industry is too much, because the men around us who do not harass and abuse look the other way for the men who do.

I think about the chiding from men like Sanders, the outrage from men across the country when Hillary Clinton dared to return to public life with statements and speeches following her 2016 loss to Donald Trump. Of course, prior to her loss, she had won the popular vote (and been the first woman to do so in US history); won the Democratic primary over Sanders, who faced no such similar demands for his silence despite having lost to her; and dedicated more than four decades of her life to public service and civil-rights advocacy. Still, she was asked to step aside for the next Democratic star, and in light of the ceaseless criticisms of the Democratic Party's reliance on identity politics for supporting her, a woman, needless to say, next "Democratic star" was code word for a charismatic white man.

The maintenance of male notions of stability, safety, and authority take precedence over everything we do as women, everything we want to do, anywhere and everywhere, and certainly in politics. And of course, this is not merely some abstract electoral concept; it's an everyday experience that every single American woman has shouldered at some point or another.

As women, we give up so much just by nature of living in the patriarchy; we ask powerful white men, at this fraught, most salient moment in American politics for marginalized people, to step back rather than seek even more power than what they already have. Yet, they remain insistent that they know best, that they are the best to speak for us, that this is their power to take. And in doing so, they ask us—as always—to step aside.

─────────

When we do elect women, one thing is clear: they govern differently from men, and for the better. Female lawmakers often pass and introduce almost double the number of bills their male counterparts do; annually, liberal female legislators on average cosponsor 10.6 bills concerning women's health compared with liberal male legislators' 5.3.[28] Districts represented by women in Congress have on average received $49 million more in federal funds annually, compared to male-represented districts.[29]

Women legislators necessarily tend to be more productive, effective, and ambitious and fight harder on behalf of their constituents because they are necessarily more weathered and seasoned from what they had to overcome just to be elected to office in the first place. They face substantially more hurdles due to sexism and other gendered disadvantages on the campaign trail and in life, and as a result, are often more skilled, qualified, and ambitious, all around, than their male counterparts, just to make it to Congress at all.

Female lawmakers also tend to focus more on key, oft-neglected domestic policy areas, such as health care, education, paid family leave, and the environment, than their male counterparts. They're more likely to engage in successful bipartisan efforts and substantially more likely to take issues of sexual harassment and assault seriously and pass meaningful reforms to address these inequalities.

In 2018, women across party lines in the House and the Senate introduced and passed reforms to support victims of harassment and misconduct in Congress. The reform bill in the Senate drew unanimous support across party lines from female Senators, but was stalled by both male Republican and Democratic leadership. But even on top of women lawmakers' initiative in demanding and passing these reforms, following the ousting of several male Congress members across party lines due to allegations of sexual harassment and assault, it also seems fair to say electing more female lawmakers could help create safer, more inclusive political spaces, in general.

Identity can often make a difference—and a positive one—in politics that remain governed by the necessarily limited experiences of older white men. Electing women has real, meaningful impact, from inspiring other young women and marginalized people to follow in their footsteps, to creating safer and less toxic work environments for all, to boosting legislative productivity, to bringing important, traditionally excluded policy areas to the forefront. In other words, identity politics benefits us all.

I take issue with the reductive contexts in which terms like "identity politics" and "social issues" are used, not the critical subject matter that each of these terms encompass. In young feminists' embrace of intersectionality, or the recognition that oppression is experienced across lines of gender, race and ethnicity, sexuality, ability, and class, it is necessarily our fight to destigmatize identity politics, to demand a political dialogue that respects marginalized people's disparate experiences as part of mainstream politics, and to end the cultural narrative that white men are the default, central electorate.

Identity politics is criminal justice, immigrant justice, reproductive justice, and survival; the choice to devalue or ignore it is rooted privilege, and the deep cruelty and ignorance that privilege far too often tends to yield. Young women know the challenges we face in engaging in this fight. We know our activism, advocacy, and voices are treated dismissively from the get-go because of who we are, before we even speak about these issues that are already treated dismissively enough, even without our voices. Still, we lead and participate in this fight not because it is easy, but because it is worth it, because it is necessary, because lives and progress and a just and equitable society rely on our participation.

# 12

# Cool Girls and the Burden

I spend a lot of time thinking about how young women view feminism in a country that accords us voting rights, (technically) anti-discrimination protections and labor rights, and (technically) autonomy over our bodies through *Roe v. Wade*. As often as I can, I engage girls and women, people of color, LGBTQ folks, and sometimes even straight men in conversation about feminism.

As I noted at the beginning of this book, plenty of the young women I've spoken with are actively skeptical of feminism or consciously choose not to engage in feminism and social-justice issues at all. In many cases, this relates to the reality that oppression and privilege are simultaneous experiences; gender and gendered experiences don't exist in a vacuum, and racial identity, socioeconomic

status, sexual orientation, and other facets of one's identity naturally may accord privilege that makes complacency an option for
some, where it isn't for others.

Often, I look to my own life as an example of this. My experiences
with misogyny and racism as the daughter of Asian immigrants have
always coexisted with crucial privileges: my family's upper middle-
class status, my upbringing in a diverse community with substantially watered-down racism, and my physical and mental health.

My two older sisters have rejected feminism and activism in their
lives, which, I suppose, is ultimately their decision to make. Certainly, plenty of men make this decision to none of the repercussions or chastising anti-feminist women sometimes face. After all,
the expectation that all women are feminists, but not that all women
must show up for and support all women—women of color, immigrant women, women with disabilities, low-income women—is one
of the more harmful and limiting stereotypes about who chooses to
engage in feminist work and what feminist work entails.

But as a girl and today as a young woman, I've often conducted
myself in different ways than my sisters and have often had very
different experiences from them as a result. The targeted abuse and
harassment I experienced through my early explorations of sex and
sexuality and the deeply personal, formative challenges I overcame
to access autonomy to my body all called me to action early in my
life. Reading feminist authors and following the news cycle certainly helped, but the self-reflection I've engaged in about my lived
experiences as a teenager and young woman has always been the
most influential informant of my feminism and my activism.

Lived experience steered me to devote myself to advocacy for
those who have similar experiences or identity-based challenges; that
experience first made these fights real to me. Without that, sometimes I fear I might have chosen complacency. Women and girls

universally share in the experience of otherization and oppression by way of the very-much-still-existent patriarchy, but many of us share very few experiences beyond this; these divides, as well as varying levels of empathy and compassion, can make all the difference in whether we self-identify as feminists or engage in activist work.

There is also, as I noted in the first essay of this book, the phenomenon of the "cool girl" and her unique, relatively pleasant role and experience in the patriarchy. Publicly and vocally embracing feminism often yields stiff social repercussions for young women, who may be perceived by others as "no-fun," prudish "social-justice warriors." But in contrast, there are often temporary and conditional benefits to patriarchal complicity among young women, to being "cool girls."

In the patriarchy, the singular function of the "cool girl" is to give men cover for their misogyny by being perpetually unoffended and, by merely being by their side, to validate and implicitly defend the men in their lives who are accused of sexism. So long as they remain unoffended and present, they enjoy the benefits of male approval. So long as they look the other way when their boyfriends or male friends casually throw around bigoted slurs, so long as they have nothing to say about remotely controversial identity-based issues, they are accepted by the patriarchy within a mutually beneficial relationship.

I've wanted to be a "cool girl" before, to date cool, funny, apathetic men, to avoid discussing meaningful issues, to silently reap the aforementioned rewards of this. I've spent a regrettable amount of time with uninteresting, disinterested men—too much time to judge any other woman for it, really—and I know it can be fun and feel good to be liked and seen as fun by other men. But it doesn't take long to realize the benefits are temporary and conditional. Because when you're a "cool girl," the moment you step out of line, that you experience or witness sexism and oppression to an extent that you can't ignore it, you'll recognize the toxicity of what you helped to build and maintain. And if you have any sense of decency, you'll get out of there quickly.

"Cool girls" exist everywhere, intentionally and unintentionally. But no amount of "cool girls" in a man's orbit will ever be enough to deflect valid criticisms and accusations of sexism. Core to feminism is the controversial assertion that women are human beings. As such, we are not tokens men can callously collect just to prove they don't hate us.

———

The "cool girl" paradigm is a staple of the male-led war on women's bodies and reproductive rights. I say "male-led" because research has shown time and again that the overwhelming majority of the lawmakers who introduce bills to restrict abortion and reproductive rights are white Republican men, and the majority of those who spread lies about abortion on cable news are men too.

Nonetheless, the expectation remains that we women who are governed by the vile misogyny and ignorance of these aforementioned men, ought to just compromise, coexist, or, as anti-choice Ohio Governor John Kasich once put it, "chill" about abortion rights. Yet, whether we agree or disagree, and whether we disagree peaceably or loudly, lawmakers will still have the power to make decisions about our bodies and rights, and anti-choice male commentators will still have the cultural power to write the narrative around this conflict.

In recent years, as the anti-choice movement has developed and rebranded; its leadership has realized the recurring narrative shortcomings and vulnerabilities the movement struggles with when it lacks female faces and speaks exclusively through male mouthpieces. To rectify this, the movement has proactively engaged in recruiting and delegating leadership roles to women. One 2017 study showed 71 percent of state lawmakers who introduced anti-choice bills were white, Republican men. But, notably, 25 percent were white, Republican women.[1]

In 2018, Iowa Gov. Kim Reynolds signed the radical, anti-choice, "fetal-heartbeat" abortion ban into law in 2018; in 2019, a pregnant Kentucky woman had her fetal heartbeat amplified on the state Senate floor to support a bill that would impose a similar abortion ban.

Within the Trump administration, its leading women have advanced gender equality insofar as they've used their power to oppress women on an equal or comparable level with their male peers: Press Secretary Sarah Huckabee Sanders used her post to explain to women why their fundamental right to access affordable contraception came second to the personal views of employers and insurers and reported that sexual assaults can't be taken seriously until the male perpetrator himself confesses.

Ivanka Trump, a self-identified advocate for women and families, once personally asked former Planned Parenthood President Cecile Richards to reduce the organization's abortion services to continue to receive funding, according to Richards. In 2017, Ivanka gave her stamp of approval to the reversal of an Obama-era policy to address the gender wage gap by requiring employers to report their employees' salaries to the federal government, and later stood by the administration through its policies of denying asylum to domestic-abuse survivors from Central America and separating migrant families. None of this is particularly surprising considering that prior to joining her father's administration, factories that produced Ivanka's clothing line allegedly exploited and abused unsaid numbers of women, mothers, and children, according to a number of reports and lawsuits she has yet to publicly address.

I don't relish the task of acknowledging the many, many women who support policies that are counterproductive to their health, who are happy to accept what measly rights male leaders see fit to hand them, who join sexist men in bemoaning feminists for exaggerating our struggles and oppression. It's exhausting to see women being weaponized against feminism and abortion rights, and it's exhausting to see powerful, sexist men repeatedly try to define feminism, as author Jessica Valenti has put it, as "anything women say or do," rather than a "defined set of principles for justice and human rights" that women, too, can violate. This "defined set of principles" can be advanced by men and women alike, just as it can be hurt by men and women alike.

Similarly, feminism is not about advancing any one, singular woman, or one, singular class of straight, cisgender, white, wealthy women. Feminism demands what would benefit all women and marginalized people most, and all women certainly do not benefit from more lawmakers voting against our rights and interests, regardless of the lawmaker's gender.

That some women oppose abortion rights doesn't change the indisputable reality that women die from unsafe abortions in the absence of safe, legal abortion; that the absence of safe, legal abortion means not only staggering numbers of maternal deaths but also many women being forced by the government to give birth, to give up on their goals, and effectively serve as state incubators. The complicity or active participation of some women in taking birth control and reproductive health care away from other women does not magically negate the impact that this has on women as a whole.

When Huckabee Sanders, Ivanka, or other prominent women in Trump's administration, from senior adviser Kellyanne Conway to Homeland Security Secretary Kirstjen Nielsen, are given key roles in the administration's work around women's and family issues, this isn't feminism, but gaslighting. It is women being used as the mouthpieces of a sexist president and administration in an attempt to make that sexism more digestible and tell American women that if we feel oppressed or attacked by the policies of the alleged abuser in the Oval Office, some women don't feel this way, so it is necessarily all in our heads.

Of course, the Trump administration's use of women to validate the president's misogyny is hardly out of the ordinary. In 2018, shortly after being confirmed to the Supreme Court, Brett Kavanaugh pledged to hire all-female clerks to his staff. Female approval is often especially important to alleged sexual abusers like Kavanaugh; in a society that inappropriately, selectively lumps all women and marginalized people's experiences as universal, men like Kavanaugh know that if they gather one or 100 women to say they *weren't* assaulted by or choose to work with him, it will automatically follow that he never abused any woman.

All the time, we hear adult men reference their wives and daughters and mothers and aunts and just about any women they've ever crossed paths with, as testaments to just how nonsexist they are. And all the time, we hear the underlying message of these long, preemptive lists of woman references: that men need familial female figures in their lives just to recognize that we are human beings, that women deserve men's respect and allyship only insofar as we have relationships with men.

Many leading anti-choice advocacy groups similarly rely on these tactics. Iowa's Governor Kim Reynolds and the female leaders of groups like Susan B. Anthony's List are women, but that does not reverse the patriarchal values inherent to the cause they fight for, a cause that says women who are pregnant and can't or do not want to be pregnant have no choice. The movement these women fight for has one overarching goal: forcing women to give birth by denying them any form of meaningful autonomy. And whether it's men or women on the front lines, theirs is a war on women nonetheless.

It seems worth reiterating that 25 percent of bills restricting abortion in 2017 were introduced by white Republican women, according to the aforementioned 2017 study. The experiences of wealthy, white, cisgender, heterosexual, able-bodied women are deeply, inextricably divided from those of women of color, low-income women, LGBTQ women and people, women with disabilities, and immigrant women. In the days preceding *Roe v. Wade* and, often enough, today, women of color, low-income women, immigrant women, and other women and marginalized people have been disproportionately prohibited from accessing life-saving care.

Black women in America are 243 percent more likely than white women to die of pregnancy or birth-related causes; Central American migrant women, 60 to 80 percent of whom experience sexual assault while crossing the border,[2] are being held hostage in detainment centers and banned from accessing abortion by conservative presidential administrations, or unable to access insurance coverage for abortion due to undocumented status. Stereotypes about Asian American women as being more likely to kill their babies on the basis of gender have led to anti-abortion policies that disproportionately impact women of color, and in several documented cases in recent history, Asian American women have been jailed for the outcomes of their pregnancy, falsely accused of feticide. When it comes to many issues—but especially abortion—white, wealthy Republican women can speak exclusively for white, wealthy Republican women.

None of this is to say that conservative women and "cool girls" can't be victims of sexism, themselves. In many, many cases, they are: crude comments about Ivanka Trump's body aired on Fox News, slut-shaming First Lady Melania Trump following allegations she once worked as an escort, and more. This happens because sexist men and patriarchal institutions fundamentally do not care about women's interests—and certainly, that includes the interests, even, of their women supporters.

They are happy to parade their female sympathizers without ever engaging meaningful advocacy work on their behalf, because keeping a coterie of reliable, token anti-choice women allows sexist men to market themselves or their blatantly harmful, misogynist policies as "women-approved." Their singular goal in the mutually beneficial relationships they contrive with these women is the humiliation and aggravation of feminist women.

At the end of 2018, Amnesty International released a report examining a global surge in women's leadership and activism on women's rights and social-justice issues that year.[3] According to the report, many international, women-led initiatives were responses to male, "'tough guy' world leaders pushing misogynistic, xenophobic, and homophobic policies." Some of these initiatives and policy victories included women in Ireland gaining the right to abortion, women in Saudi Arabia gaining the right to drive, and powerful women-led organizing to oppose Kavanaugh's nomination to the Supreme Court in the United States.

I know I felt empowered reading the report about the power and effectiveness of women's activism and leadership, but I also questioned why it so often seems women are the only ones willing to fight for women. The report read as a painful reminder of who is so often burdened with the backbreaking, sometimes dangerous work of facilitating social progress and liberation in any and all cultural contexts: women and marginalized people. On top of the labor of trying to survive the oppression we live in and certainly did not create, we are often the only ones willing to actively fight back against this oppression.

The opposite of the patriarchy-approved "cool girl" is necessarily the "social-justice warrior," who extensively speaks out and fights for feminist progress, in exchange for some imagined benefit of being "woke." As young people increasingly come to view society as post-gender and post-racial, despite all the challenges and barriers and inequities that persist, young women who engage in social-justice advocacy work are often told we exaggerate the injustices we are fighting, that we conjure up and imagine fake problems to be angry about, and many people believe this is true. That's why, so often, women and other marginalized people are the ones who singularly shoulder the burden of activism, and as time passes, this will only become truer.

Amnesty International's report didn't claim men were absent from women's-rights movements in 2018. But it did demonstrate that global victories for women's rights were attributed to an overall increase in activism among women rather than men—the group that arguably bears the greater moral obligation to actively fight for change. As inspiring as it is to celebrate victories against all odds by women-led movements, it can also be discouraging to see how comparably rare it is for men or individuals with substantial privilege to channel their respective social advantages into supporting movements for gender-based justice and progress.

On top of the prevalence of sexual violence and abuse, #MeToo also exposed the toxic, salient power of male complicity and silence in upholding misogynist power structures. As much as #MeToo was a call to action to women to support other women and survivors and share our stories, it should have also served as a call to action for men to get off the sidelines and get involved in actively supporting women's rights.

For men seeking to get involved, there is no shortage of areas in policy and culture that need more support. Again, according to the Amnesty International report, international women-led activism rose in response to a "growing body of policies and laws designed to subjugate and control women, especially around sexual and reproductive health."

Men and privileged people need to involve themselves in supporting women's rights and social-justice advocacy, not only because of the moral obligation they carry as human beings but also because they are in the best, most advantaged position to make change. When women lend our voices and advocacy to issues that affect us, the inherently gendered nature of credibility as well as biases in whose issues and perspectives and experiences are perceived as important often relegate our activism to tangential status or erase our work and perspectives from the mainstream altogether.

Women and marginalized people who engage in activism also face the realities of mental and physical exhaustion, as we shoulder the brunt of the work in fighting for our human rights and liberation. The energy that is naturally expended in living under patriarchy, let alone fighting to dismantle it, could be one explanation for the disproportionate prevalence of mood disorders like anxiety and depression among women around the world.

On the global level, women comprise a narrow but steadily growing majority of the population in many countries. It makes no sense that our experiences and oppression remain shrugged off as secondary, dismissible concerns, marginalized as "identity politics" in contrast with issues that are more directly associated with the default white-male experience. That women are leading the movements for our rights is empowering and important—but it's past time for us to demand that men step off the sidelines to give us their affirmation and proactive support. There's simply no good excuse for the fight for women's rights and freedoms, nor the rights and freedoms of any marginalized group, to fall exclusively on our shoulders anymore.

# 13

# One Size Does Not Fit All

Beloved Australian teen brand Brandy Melville has always been as controversial as it is popular among girls and young women. Its dainty pieces and overall aesthetic reflect the conventionally aspirational target demographic: white, skinny, long-haired, carefree, and beachy. And this is especially reinforced by the brand's notorious one-size approach, creating styles that are exclusively accessible to women and girls who fit its Eurocentric, "sizeist" beauty standards. Brandy Melville justifies its one-size model by asserting that one size truly does fit all; it's an efficient manufacturing approach, as this size is the most on-demand, meaning its clothing reaches most of its potential patrons anyway.

Of course, this simply doesn't make sense; 68 percent of American women wear a size 14 and above,[1] per a 2018 study, and any fashion brand that aims to be successful or "efficient" should fully embrace this diversity of size—if not for moral reasons, then, certainly, for economic reasons.

Regardless, Brandy is right about one thing: it *is* easier—and substantially so—to serve people at the top, to serve people with the most privilege, to serve those who are, simply put, the easiest and most convenient to serve. This is true not just in fashion but also, arguably, in feminist activism.

The history of mainstream incarnations of the movement is fraught with deliberate efforts to cut off those at the margins—women of color, poor women, women with disabilities, immigrant women, LGBTQ folks—and fight vigorously for the rights of those women who were easiest to serve, those whose rights were easiest to obtain. The Herculean quest for women's suffrage spanned generations before the passage of the Nineteenth Amendment in 1920. But at the very same moment (white) women and their (white) allies celebrated this achievement with parades and marching in the streets, in the South, black women and their communities faced lynching, violence, harassment, and other horrific intimidation tactics for asking for those same rights.

The suffrage movement in general has a twisty, mixed, and ultimately white-supremacist-tinged record that could be—and is—the subject of some other history book entirely. The point is, contrary to lazy, mainstream narratives that categorically lump all women together, assume all of our needs and struggles are the same, and exclude pretty much everyone who isn't a straight, cisgender, wealthy, white woman, one size does *not* fit all.

White leadership of the suffrage movement often attempted to negotiate with white men in power by highlighting their commonalities, which included agreement on the inferiority of people of color and agreement that the vote should be reserved for white people. Of course, some activists were more enthusiastic about this approach than others, who expressed reluctance to throw women of color—and people of color, in general—under the bus. But many of said reluctantly racist suffragists internally reconciled themselves with this cruelty because they understood the voting rights of white women were most attainable. Including women and people of color in the equation, they believed, would only further obfuscate and convolute the fight and make it less likely anyone at all would win voting rights.

The technical voting rights of women of color were hard fought for and won, eventually, and contrary to most history textbooks, certainly weren't won with the Nineteenth Amendment. The amendment ultimately helped women very little, if at all. Many white women, the majority of whom consistently vote for the Republican Party to this day, give their ballots to vote in line with their husbands, aiding and abetting their consistently racist, sexist politics. In either case, even in post-Voting Rights Act America, voting is still hardly a guarantee for communities of color. In southern states, many of which have disproportionately high populations of black voters, voter-ID laws, deliberate mismanagement of polling places, lack of multilingual ballots, and other more restrictive, targeted laws continue to ensure voting and democracy as guaranteed rights for white people, and white people alone.

The phenomenon of feminism made for those at the top, and noninclusive of those at the margins, persists to this day, despite critical and admirable progress on several key fronts. But the challenges the movement faces with inclusivity have become less black and white and are most visible through dissecting our conversations, the news we consume, the faces and the bodies that most immediately come to mind when we hear the word "women."

In our conversations about abortion rights, are we considering transgender and nonbinary folks and the added barriers they face to access reproductive health care in a health-care environment that is often vastly unequipped and unknowledgeable in how to support them? When pundits and newspapers reflect on the voting and electoral habits of women, are they talking about all women, or are they talking about white women? When we watch the news and see the faces of missing girls and women and their communities rallied around them, are they all notably white? Because you almost certainly haven't seen the faces of the thousands of missing Native American women and girls, whose disappearances and killings and rapes have all evaded coverage within a biased media environment, and attention from a government that frequently miscategorizes and mishandles reported Native disappearances.

Mainstream iterations of feminism, the activism and leadership that are centralized and accorded the most attention, esteem, and validation from society, remain whitewashed. They remain categorically focused on the needs and challenges of white women, following the assumption that these are the only needs and challenges of all women. But that is simply, provably not true, as I hope has been demonstrated over the course of this book.

Those of us in this fight for a feminist future have our work cut out for us to understand how the most visible, popular efforts of our movement fall woefully short in including all women and marginalized people, as feminism should. I wish I could list decisive, foolproof solutions beyond what you could already likely deduce on your own—more diverse feminist leadership, more diverse government representation, more listening to women of color, more awareness of oppression outside of our own.

But the simple truth is, as history has repeatedly demonstrated, things like this often take time and tough conversations, having the courage and moral fiber to be critical of even those we admire, those whose intentions we trust, those whom we know could do better. And, of course, the ability to have these conversations at all necessitates awareness and self-education of experiences that may diverge vastly from our own.

---

I became aware of the term "vote-shaming" in 2018, shortly before the pivotal midterm elections to be held that year. Vote-shaming is pretty much what it sounds like—shaming those who don't vote. But vote shamers promptly received some shaming of their own, as some activists asked them to consider the wide range of reasons people can't or don't vote. These reasons certainly include targeted, racist voter restriction laws but they also include justified feelings of hopelessness, exclusion, and distrust of a broken system that's failed them.

Let's be clear that voting is important, that voting can be transformative, that it's jarring and frustrating when people who lead comfortable, privileged lives choose not to be aware or educated, and choose not to vote. But their experience is considerably different from, for example, a low-income, single mother of color, working three jobs to stay afloat and feed her family. Is a white, upper-middle-class Get Out the Vote organizer really in a position to criticize her for failing to take time out of her exhausting life to learn about the upcoming election, for not believing her vote will actually change anything, for opting not to miss paid work to go out of her way to her polling place and put faith in a government that's failed her?

Among specific groups of women of color, there is a long history of distrust toward electoral processes. In their 2017 study, "For Love and Justice: The Mobilizing of Race, Gender, and Criminal

Justice Contact," Hannah Walker and Marcela Garcia-Castañon found that women of color affected by the criminal-justice system through partners or fathers who are incarcerated are more likely to engage in substantial political work, such as advocacy and community organizing efforts.[2] However, they are less likely to engage in electoral political activities such as voting and feel greater distrust of the government and government processes.

And far be it from white "feminist" women—or anyone, really—to be shocked or outraged at women of color who overcome exorbitant trauma and oppression and sit out elections. Far be it from white "feminist" women to be shocked or outraged when women of color distrust their feminism, in general. That white women as a voting bloc and political demographic have been either complicit or actively involved in the oppression of women of color is among the most well-documented, most infrequently discussed truths of feminist history.

Anyone who wasn't living under a rock following the 2016 presidential election would know an estimated 53 percent of white women voted for Trump,[3] and none of us should have been surprised: Through every presidential election in recent history, the majority of white women have voted for Republican presidential candidates. Why should we have expected 2016 to be any different?

But the oppression of women of color by white women has always been especially twisted and unique throughout history. In the years following *Brown v. Board of Education*, the landmark Supreme Court decision that technically rendered segregation illegal, angry white men became the faces of the militant segregationist movement. They were, after all, the Strom Thurmond-types who ran for office on segregation platforms, and in many alarming cases, won. But white women used the unique positioning accorded them by their gender to advance segregationist ideals in more long-term ways, with deeper, generational impact, as Elizabeth McRae asserts in her book, *Mothers of Massive Resistance: White Women and the Politics of White Supremacy.*

White women were the mothers who taught and reproduced segregationist values in their households. They were the PTA and school-board leaders who vehemently protested *Brown v. Board*, denying that they were racist, and asserting they were simply responsible, concerned mothers, worried about how going to school with children of color might affect their own children or affect housing value. They were the brains and organizers behind aggressive anti-busing protests. They were the social workers and secretaries who tagged and racially identified black newborn babies, who proactively discriminated against and dictated that black households be treated differently from white households.

Today, racism continues to sharply divide different women's experiences, and justified distrust—of white women, white people, men, and the government—remains prevalent in many women of color. But the impetus should not be on women of color to change this, to settle for the marginal gains we receive when mainstream iterations of feminism win grand victories for white women, to trust and believe that, against all awareness of history, white-centric versions of feminism and white American democracy will ever bring us the fundamental change we seek. Rather, the impetus lies on the shoulders of people with more privilege to fight for and win our trust—with listening, hard work, and inclusion of us in all the places where decisions are being made.

I often think the Walker and Garcia-Castañon study of women of color affected by the criminal justice system through incarcerated male family members is as thorough a reminder as any that caring, an often supposedly feminized trait and behavior, is an inherently political act. Women of color who lose male figures in their lives to incarceration or police violence rise to become leaders in their families, households, and communities at large, not because women are gentle, soft, innate caretakers but because they have to step up—for their survival, the survival of their families, and the survival of their communities.

Their caring is spurred by loss and tragedy, and it is as profoundly transformative as it is political. That's because—I can't stress this enough—caring is political work. Those with privilege can be indifferent without consequence. But for many of us, caring is tied to survival, empathy, and basic respect for the dignity of humanity. What feminism can achieve for years and generations to come will start and end with our ability as individuals to care about people who aren't us, who aren't at the top, who aren't just the easiest people to care about. Author bell hooks put it best in her book *Feminism Is for Everybody*, in its title alone.

Every young woman who identifies as a feminist necessarily faces recurring questions, because that's arguably the most quintessential part of identifying as a feminist: representing the movement, meeting the exhaustive demands for your emotional energy, from people with intentions good and bad. By and large, the most common question I received in the dark, often debilitating years of the Trump presidency was, "Do you have hope for the future?"

Growing up, certainly around the nascence of my feminism, I'd always been a bit of a pessimist where politics, culture, society, and human nature were concerned. I have had too many run-ins with bad, hurtful people, too many personal struggles within a broken, seemingly irreparable system. My general feelings of distrust and pessimism extended as a result of these experiences and had necessarily impacted my relationships, mental health, and general outlook on the world for years.

In the harsh social and political atmosphere of the late 2010s, my feelings about the future ebbed and flowed based on the news of the day. But in contrast with many of the young feminists I speak with on a regular basis, more recently, I've consistently felt deep and profound optimism for the future.

I think about all the problems that existed in history, which have certainly been exacerbated by the rise and consolidation of sexist, racist, uncaring men in power, and I consider how I once thought of these problems: frustrating, untouchable, ultimately out of my locus of control. I never bothered to dream up solutions, nor did I ever consider meaningful, actionable steps I could take as an individual to address these problems. That was wrong of me.

But in recent years, there has simply been no space for complacency and self-defeating feelings of helplessness in a world where the existential human rights of so many people every day hang by a thread. Around me, I've watched introverts and passive news media consumers and everyday people—myself included—embrace activism, attend rallies and marches, and canvass and phone-bank for progressive candidates for office. Leading up to the November 2018 midterm elections, an undeniable referendum on Trumpism, we worked arm-in-arm to flip the House of Representatives Democratic and elect more progressive women than ever before. All in the same breath, the Trump era both devastated and transformed so many of us for the better into proactive, caring people.

Nonetheless, we have to resist the temptation to accept the narrative that any of this started recently, or was singlehandedly created by Trump, or that all of it could end with his removal from cultural and political relevance. Years will pass, generations will pass; he and the men and women who created him, empowered him, enabled him at unspeakable human cost, will all be gone. What will remain is this fight for something much greater—greater than any one man, one woman, one person—for a society that is not "one-size-fits-all," a society that is safe, accessible, equitable, and just, for those not just at the top but also at the margins and at every intersection of oppression.

It's a fight that feminists will carry on our shoulders throughout our lives, a fight that will cut across generations, cultures, and continents, because there is always more work to be done. And it's simply not enough for life to get better for some women, for some people; as we strive to push back on a one-size-fits-all brand of feminism, this means leaving no one behind—today, tomorrow, and every tomorrow after.

When I think of the world we live in, I'm reminded constantly that the feminist movement has never hinged on one single outcome but persists through the everyday acts of love, sacrifice, and bravery that steadily bend the arc just a little bit closer to justice. We live in a changed world because of the testimonies of Anita Hill and Dr. Christine Blasey Ford, because of the bloodshed of unsaid numbers of women dead of coat-hanger abortions throughout our nation's history. Through every success and every loss and every draw, the work we put in each day to create change or lay down the foundation for future change will always matter. Whether I'm surrounded by sign-wielding mothers and daughters at a massive Women's March gathering, or sitting in a small circle of community members at the meeting of a local progressive group, I know this to be true.

Feminism is the fight of and for our lives, to live, to choose, to exist, to be; there is no ultimate end goal, no be-all and end-all solution to this struggle. For all I've seen and for all I've experienced, I am ultimately hopeful—cautiously, compassionately, steadfastly hopeful—because for all of the countless victories waiting to be fought for and won, there is only one way we can lose: by quitting.

# RESOURCES/ REFERENCES

In the process of writing this book, I drew on the ideas, perspectives, and original research of no shortage of brilliant authors, academics, filmmakers, and cultural critics. Their work has been invaluable to this project, and I have listed the most relevant titles below for additional reading:

Alexander, Michelle. *The New Jim Crow: Mass Incarceration in the Age of Colorblindness.* New York: The New Press, 2010.

Chemaly, Soraya. *Rage Becomes Her: The Power of Women's Anger.* New York: Simon and Schuster, 2018.

Davis, Angela. *Women, Race, & Class.* New York: Vintage Books, 1981.

Dusenbery, Maya. *Doing Harm: The Truth About How Bad Medicine and Lazy Science Leave Women Dismissed, Misdiagnosed, and Sick.* New York: Harper One, 2018.

Earp, Jeremy, dir. *Tough Guise 2: Violence, Manhood & American Culture.* 2013; Northampton, MA: Media Education Foundation.

Goldberg, Michelle. *The Means of Reproduction: Sex, Power, and the Future of the World.* New York: Penguin Press, 2009.

hooks, bell. *Feminism Is for Everybody: Passionate Politics.* Cambridge, MA: South End Press, 2000.

Jhally, Sut, dir. *Tough Guise: Violence, Media & the Crisis in Masculinity, with Jackson Katz.* 1999; Northampton, MA: Media Education Foundation.

McRae, Elizabeth. *Mothers of Massive Resistance: White Women and the Politics of White Supremacy.* New York: Oxford University Press, 2018.

Marcotte, Amanda. *Troll Nation: How the Right Became Trump-Worshipping Monsters Set on Rat-F*cking Liberals, America, and Truth Itself.* New York: Hot Books, 2018.

Marty, Robin, and Jessica Mason Pieklo. *Crow After Roe: How "Separate But Equal" Has Become the New Standard In Women's Health and How We Can Change That.* Brooklyn, NY: Ig Publishing, 2013.

Messner, Michael A., Max A. Greenberg, and Tal Perez. *Some Men: Feminist Allies and the Movement to End Violence against Women.* New York: Oxford University Press, 2015.

Solnit, Rebecca. *Call Them By Their True Names.* Chicago: Haymarket Books, 2018.

———. *Men Explain Things to Me.* Chicago: Haymarket Books, 2014.

Traister, Rebecca. *Good and Mad: The Revolutionary Power of Women's Anger.* New York: Simon and Schuster, 2018.

# NOTES

## CHAPTER 1

1   Rachel Jones and Jenna Jerman, "Abortion Incidence and Service Availability in the United States, 2014," *Perspectives on Sexual and Reproductive Health* 49, no. 1 (March 2017): 17–27, https://www.guttmacher.org/journals/psrh /2017/01/abortion-incidence-and-service-availability-united-states-2014.

2   Emily E. Petersen, et al., "Vital Signs: Pregnancy-Related Deaths, United States, 2011–2015, and Strategies for Prevention, 13 States, 2013–2017," *Morbidity and Mortality Weekly Report* 68, no. 18 (May 2019): 423–29, https://www.cdc.gov/mmwr/volumes/68/wr/mm6818e1.htm?s_cid =mm6818e1_w.

3   Roland G. Fryer, "Reconciling Results on Racial Differences in Police Shootings," (American Economic Review, Papers and Proceedings, 2018): https://scholar.harvard.edu/files/fryer/files/fryer_police_aer.pdf.

4   Sam Roberts, "Minorities in the US Set to Become Majority by 2042," *New York Times,* August 14, 2008, https://www.nytimes.com/2008/08/14 /world/americas/14iht-census.1.15284537.html.

5   Jasmine Tucker and Caitlyn Lowell, "National Snapshot: Poverty Among Women and Families, 2015," National Women's Law Center, September 2016, https://nwlc.org/wp-content/uploads/2016/09/Poverty-Snapshot -Factsheet-2016.pdf.

6   Elizabeth Nash, et al., "State Policy Trends 2018: With Roe v. Wade in Jeopardy, States Continued to Add New Abortion Restrictions," Guttmacher Institute, December 11, 2018, https://www.guttmacher.org /article/2018/12/state-policy-trends-2018-roe-v-wade-jeopardy-states continued-add-new-abortion.

7   Jones and Jerman, "Abortion Incidence," 17–27.

8   Nicholas J. Kassebaum, et al., "Global, Regional, and National Levels of Maternal Mortality, 1990–2015: A Systematic Analysis for the Global Burden of Disease Study 2015," *Lancet* 388, no. 10053 (October 8, 2016): 1775–1812, https://www.thelancet.com/pdfs/journals/lancet/PIIS0140 -6736(16)31470-2.pdf.

9   *Evaluating Priorities: Measuring Women's and Children's Health and Well-being against Abortion Restrictions in the States*, vol. 2 (New York: Center for Reproductive Rights and Ibis Reproductive Health, 2017), https://reproductiverights. org/EvaluatingPriorities?_ga=2.132761230.1645600396.1573162714 -810267609.1573162714.

10  "Pregnancy-Related Deaths," Centers for Disease Control and Prevention, https://www.cdc.gov/reproductivehealth/maternalinfanthealth/pregnancy -relatedmortality.htm.

11  "Reporting Sexual Assault: Why Survivors Often Don't," Maryland Coalition Against Sexual Assault, https://ocrsm.umd.edu/files/Why-Is -Sexual-Assault-Under-Reported.pdf.

12  Anna North, "#HimToo, the Online Movement Spreading Myths about False Rape Allegations, Explained," Vox website, October 10, 2018, https://www.vox.com/policy-and-politics/2018/10/10/17957126 /himtoo-movement-pieter-hanson-tweet-me-too.

13  *When Men Murder Women: An Analysis of 2015 Homicide Data* (Washington, DC: Violence Policy Center, 2017), http://www.vpc.org/studies /wmmw2017.pdf.

14  Jordan Misra, "Voter Turnout Rates Among All Voting Age and Major Racial and Ethnic Groups Were Higher than in 2014," US Census Bureau, April 23, 2019, https://www.census.gov/library/stories/2019/04 /behind-2018-united-states-midterm-election-turnout.html.

## CHAPTER 2

1   "Migraine Is a Women's Health Issue," Migraine Research Foundation, https:// migraineresearchfoundation.org/about-migraine/migraine-in-women/.

2   Tamara Mathias, "Women Diagnosed Years Later than Men for Same Diseases," Reuters, March 25, 2019, https://www.reuters.com/article/us-health -diagnoses-gender/women-diagnosed-years-later-than-men-for-same -diseases-idUSKCN1R62IJ.

3   "Women Drive Dems to 12-Pt. Lead in U.S. House Races, Quinnipiac University National Poll Finds; Voters Split On Confirming Kavanaugh," Quinnipiac University, July 25, 2018, https://poll.qu.edu/national/release -detail?ReleaseID=2558.

4   Amanda Barroso, "A Majority of Americans Think Abortion Will Still Be Legal in 30 Years, But with Some Restrictions," Pew Research Center, June 4, 2019, https://www.pewresearch.org/fact-tank/2019/06/04/a-majority-of-americans -think-abortion-will-still-be-legal-in-30-years-but-with-some-restrictions/.

5   Brian Levin, *Special Status Report: Hate Crime in the United States* (San Bernardino, CA: Center for the Study of Hate & Extremism, 2016), https://www.documentcloud.org/documents/3110202-SPECIAL -STATUS-REPORT-v5-9-16-16.html.

6   "Almost Half of Girls Aged 11–18 Have Experienced Harassment or Bullying Online," Plan International UK, August 14, 2017, https://plan-uk .org/media-centre/almost-half-of-girls-aged-11-18-have-experienced -harassment-or-bullying-online.

7   Michelle Ferrier, *Attacks and Harassment: The Impact on Female Journalists and Their Reporting* (Washington, DC: International Women's Media Foundation, 2018), https://www.iwmf.org/wp-content/uploads/2018/09 /Attacks-and-Harassment.pdf.

8   Shelby McNabb, *2016 National Clinic Violence Survey* (Arlington, VA: Feminist Majority Foundation, 2017), http://feminist.org/anti-abortion -violence/images/2016-national-clinic-violence-survey.pdf.

# CHAPTER 3

1   "Sexual Assault in the United States," National Sexual Violence Resource Center, https://www.nsvrc.org/node/4737.

2   "Sexual Assault in the United States."

3   Jon Huang, Samuel Jacoby, Michael Strickland, and K. K. Rebecca Lai, "Election 2016: Exit Polls," *New York Times,* November 8, 2016, https:// www.nytimes.com/interactive/2016/11/08/us/politics/election-exit -polls.html.

4   David Roberts, "The Most Common Words in Hillary Clinton's Speeches, in One Chart," Vox website, December 16, 2016, https://www.vox.com /policy-and-politics/2016/12/16/13972394/most-common-words-hillary -clinton-speech.

5   Dara Lind, "The Trump Administration's Separation of Families at the Border, Explained," Vox website, August 14, 2018, https://www.vox.com/2018 /6/11/17443198/children-immigrant-families-separated-parents.

6   Fryer, "Reconciling Results."

## CHAPTER 4

1   Christina Maxouris and Saeed Ahmed, "Only These 8 States Require Sex Education Classes to Mention Consent," CNN, September 29, 2018, https://www.cnn.com/2018/09/29/health/sex-education-consent-in -public-schools-trnd/index.html.

2   "Sexual Assault and the LGBTQ Community," Human Rights Campaign, https://www.hrc.org/resources/sexual-assault-and-the-lgbt-community.

3   "Survivor of Color Prevalence Rates," End Rape on Campus, https:// endrapeoncampus.org/new-page-3.

4   Mona Chalabi, "The Gender Orgasm Gap," FiveThirtyEight, August 20, 2015, https://fivethirtyeight.com/features/the-gender-orgasm-gap/.

5   Adam Thomas, "Policy Solutions for Preventing Unplanned Pregnancy," Brookings Institution, March 1, 2012, https://www.brookings.edu /research/policy-solutions-for-preventing-unplanned-pregnancy/.

6   David Lisak and Paul M. Miller, "Repeat Rape and Multiple Offending among Undetected Rapists," *Violence and Victims* 17, no. 1 (February 2002): 73–84, https://time.com/wp-content/uploads/2014/09/repeat _rape.pdf

7   *Global Study on Homicide: Gender-Related Killing of Women and Girls* (Vienna, Austria: United Nations Office on Drugs and Crime, 2018), https://www.unodc.org/documents/data-and-analysis/GSH2018 /GSH18_Gender-related_killing_of_women_and_girls.pdf.

8   Sarah Jane Glynn, "Breadwinning Mothers Continue to Be the U.S. Norm," Center for American Progress, May 28, 2019, https://www .americanprogress.org/issues/women/reports/2019/05/10/469739 /breadwinning-mothers-continue-u-s-norm/.

9   "State and Federal Prison Wage Policies and Sourcing Information," Prison Policy Initiative, https://www.prisonpolicy.org/reports/wage_policies.html.

10  Alex Ronan, "Menstruation Can Become Humiliation in Prisons," The Cut, *New York,* June 16, 2015, https://www.thecut.com/2015/06 /menstruation-can-become-humiliation-in-prisons.html.

# CHAPTER 5

1   "Sexual Assault in the United States."

2   Cecilia Mengo and Beverly M. Black, "Violence Victimization on a College Campus: Impact on GPA and School Dropout," *Journal of College Student Retention: Research, Theory & Practice* 18, no. 2 (2015): 234–48, https://journals.sagepub.com/doi/full/10.1177/1521025115584750.

3   "Overshadowed by the College Sexual Assault Debate, 154 Open Title IX Investigations at K–12 Schools," The 74 Million website, https://www.the74million.org/article/forgotten-in-the-devos-debate-over-campus-sex-assaults-the-154-pending-k-12-investigations/.

4   Sharita L. Forrest, "Sexual Harassment Common among Middle School Children, Study Finds," Illinois News Bureau, December 9, 2016, https://news.illinois.edu/view/6367/438783.

5   Adele Kimmel, "Title IX Litigation and Enforcement for K–12 Sexual Assault Survivors," Public Justice, 2016, http://www.publicjustice.net/wp-content/uploads/2016/05/Title-IX-and-K-12-Sexual-Assault.pdf.

6   Elizabeth Kennedy, "Victim Race and Rape: A Review of the Recent Research," Brandeis University, 2003, https://www.brandeis.edu/projects/fse/slavery/united-states/kennedy.html.

7   Heather Murphy, "What Experts Know About Men Who Rape," *New York Times,* October 30, 2017, https://www.nytimes.com/2017/10/30/health/men-rape-sexual-assault.html.

8   "Sexual Assault in the United States."

# CHAPTER 6

1   "Vasectomy Guideline," American Urological Association, 2015, https://www.auanet.org/guidelines/vasectomy-guideline.

2   Mathias, "Women Diagnosed Years Later."

3   Sharon Kann, "Study: How Cable News Keeps Getting It Wrong about Abortion and Reproductive Rights," Media Matters for America, April 18, 2017, https://www.mediamatters.org/sean-hannity/study-how-cable-news-keeps-getting-it-wrong-about-abortion-and-reproductive-rights.

4   "Induced Abortion in the United States," Guttmacher Institute, September 2019, https://www.guttmacher.org/fact-sheet/induced-abortion-united-states.

5   "Abortion Rates by Race and Ethnicity," Guttmacher Institute, October 19, 2017, https://www.guttmacher.org/infographic/2017/abortion-rates-race-and-ethnicity.

6   "United States Abortion Demographics," Guttmacher Institute, https://www.guttmacher.org/united-states/abortion/demographics.

7   Anna Bernstein and Kelly Jones, "The Economic Effects of Abortion Access: A Review of the Evidence," Institute for Women's Policy Research, July 18, 2019, https://iwpr.org/publications/economic-effects-abortion-access-report/.

8   Misra, "Voter Turnout Rates."

9   Mark Mather and Beth Jarosz, "Progress in Young Women's Well-Being Stalled in Recent Generations," Population Reference Bureau, November 9, 2017, https://www.prb.org/us-womens-well-being-stalled/.

10  Jones and Jerman, "Abortion Incidence."

11  Nash et al., "State Policy Trends 2018."

12  *Evaluating Priorities,* vol. 2.

13  "Abortion Rates by Race and Ethnicity."

14  Petersen et al., "Vital Signs."

15  NcNabb, *2016 National Clinic Violence Survey.*

16  "Parental Involvement in Minors' Abortions," Guttmacher Institute, last modified January 1, 2020, https://www.guttmacher.org/state-policy/explore/parental-involvement-minors-abortions.

17  "Hyde Amendment Fact Sheet," All* Above All website, January 25, 2019, https://allaboveall.org/resource/hyde-amendment-fact-sheet/.

18  "Novel Study Identifies 27 Large U.S. Cities as 'Abortion Deserts,'" Advancing New Standards in Reproductive Health, 2018, https://www.ansirh.org/news/novel-study-identifies-27-large-us-cities-%E2%80%9Cabortion-deserts%E2%80%9D.

19  Alexa Ura, Ryan Murphy, Annie Daniel, and Lindsay Carbonell, "Here Are the Texas Abortion Clinics That Have Closed Since 2013," *Texas Tribune,* June 28, 2016, https://www.texastribune.org/2016/06/28/texas-abortion-clinics-have-closed-hb2-passed-2013/.

20  "CDC's Abortion Surveillance System FAQs," Centers for Disease Control and Prevention, last modified November 25, 2019, https://www.cdc.gov/reproductivehealth/data_stats/abortion.htm.

21  "State Abortion Policy Landscape: From Hostile to Supportive," Guttmacher Institute, August 29, 2019, https://www.guttmacher.org/article/2019/08/state-abortion-policy-landscape-hostile-supportive.

22  M. M. Holmes, H. S. Resnick, D. G. Kilpatrick, and C. L. Best, "Rape-Related Pregnancy: Estimates and Descriptive Characteristics from a National

Sample of Women," *American Journal of Obstetrics and Gynecology* 175, no. 2 (August 1996): 324–25, https://www.ncbi.nlm.nih.gov/pubmed/8765248.

23 Michael Lipka and John Gramlich, "5 Facts about the Abortion Debate in America," Pew Research Center, August 30, 2019, https://www.pewresearch.org/fact-tank/2019/08/30/facts-about-abortion-debate-in-america/.

24 Rachel Benson Gold, "Lessons from Before Roe: Will Past Be Prologue?" *Guttmacher Policy Review* 6, no. 1 (March 1, 2003): 8–11, https://www.guttmacher.org/gpr/2003/03/lessons-roe-will-past-be-prologue.

25 Seth Stephens-Davidowitz, "The Return of the D. I. Y. Abortion," *New York Times,* March 5, 2016, https://www.nytimes.com/2016/03/06/opinion/sunday/the-return-of-the-diy-abortion.html.

26 D. Grossman et al., "Knowledge, Opinion and Experience Related to Abortion Self-Induction in Texas," (lecture, North American Forum on Family Planning, Chicago, IL, November 14, 2015), https://liberalarts.utexas.edu/txpep/_files/pdf/TxPEP-Research-Brief-KnowledgeOpinionExperience.pdf.

27 "Medication Abortion," Guttmacher Institute, last modified January 1, 2020, https://www.guttmacher.org/state-policy/explore/medication-abortion.

28 "About Half of U.S. Abortion Patients Report Using Contraception in the Month They Became Pregnant," Guttmacher Institute, January 11, 2018, https://www.guttmacher.org/news-release/2018/about-half-us-abortion-patients-report-using-contraception-month-they-became.

29 "Negative Impacts of Teen Childbearing," US Department of Health and Human Services, https://www.hhs.gov/ash/oah/adolescent-development/reproductive-health-and-teen-pregnancy/teen-pregnancy-and-childbearing/teen-childbearing/index.html.

30 Diana Greene Foster et al., "Socioeconomic Outcomes of Women Who Receive and Women Who Are Denied Wanted Abortions in the United States," *American Journal of Public Health* 108, no. 3 (March 2018): 407–13, https://www.ncbi.nlm.nih.gov/pmc/articles/PMC5803812/.

# CHAPTER 7

1 Advancing New Standards in Reproductive Health, "Assessing Barriers to Medication Abortion among California's Public University Students," issue brief no. 1, December 2017, https://www.ansirh.org/sites/default/files/publications/files/sb320barriers12-20-17.pdf.

2 "State Facts About Abortion: California," Guttmacher Institute, September 2019, https://www.guttmacher.org/fact-sheet/state-facts-about-abortion-california.

## CHAPTER 8

1   "Sexual Assault in the United States."
2   "Reporting Sexual Assault."
3   "Reporting Sexual Assault."
4   Danielle Kurtzleben, "Poll: Americans Overwhelmingly Support 'Zero Tolerance' on Sexual Harassment," *All Things Considered,* NPR, December 14, 2017, https://www.npr.org/2017/12/14/570601136/poll-sexual-harassment-ipsos.
5   "Statistics—Stop Street Harassment: Studies," Stop Street Harassment website, http://www.stopstreetharassment.org/resources/statistics/sshstudies/.


## CHAPTER 10

1   Huang et al., "Election 2016: Exit Polls."
2   Danielle Kurtzleban, "Here's How Many Bernie Sanders Supporters Ultimately Voted for Trump," NPR, August 24, 2017, https://www.npr.org/2017/08/24/545812242/1-in-10-sanders-primary-voters-ended-up-supporting-trump-survey-finds.


## CHAPTER 11

1   Huang et al., "Election 2016: Exit Polls."
2   Tucker and Lowell, "National Snapshot."
3   "Pay Equity & Discrimination," Institute for Women's Policy Research, 2018, https://iwpr.org/issue/employment-education-economic-change/pay-equity-discrimination/.
4   "Paying an Unfair Price: The Financial Penalty for Being LGBT in America," Center for American Progress and Movement Advancement Project, 2014, http://www.lgbtmap.org/file/paying-an-unfair-price-full-report.pdf.
5   Benjamin Artz, Amanda H. Goodall, and Andrew J. Oswald, "Do Women Ask?" Warwick Economics Research Paper, University of Warwick, Coventry, UK, July 2016, https://warwick.ac.uk/fac/soc/economics/research/workingpapers/2016/twerp_1127_oswald.pdf.
6   Glynn, "Breadwinning Mothers."
7   Claudia Olivetti and Barbara Petrongolo, "The Economic Consequences of Family Policies: Lessons from a Century of Legislation in High-Income

Countries," *Journal of Economic Perspectives* 31, no. 1 (Winter 2017): 205–30, https://www.aeaweb.org/articles?id=10.1257/jep.31.1.205.

8   Alison Thoet, "Virginia Votes to Ratify ERA, Putting Amendment One Step Closer to Constitution," PBS News Hour, January 15, 2020, https://www.pbs.org/newshour/politics/virginia-votes-to-ratify-era-putting-amendment-one-step-closer-to-constitution.

9   "The Drug War, Mass Incarceration and Race," Drug Policy Alliance, January 2018, http://www.drugpolicy.org/sites/default/files/drug-war-mass-incarceration-and-race_01_18_0.pdf.

10  "Children and Families of the Incarcerated Fact Sheet," National Resource Center on Children & Families of the Incarcerated, Rutgers University, 2014, https://nrccfi.camden.rutgers.edu/files/nrccfi-fact-sheet-2014.pdf.

11  Scott H. Decker, Cassia Spohn, and Natalie R. Ortiz, *Criminal Stigma, Race, Gender, and Employment: An Expanded Assessment of the Consequences of Imprisonment for Employment* (Phoenix: School of Criminology and Criminal Justice, Arizona State University, 2010), http://thecrimereport.s3.amazonaws.com/2/fb/e/2362/criminal_stigma_race_crime_and_unemployment.pdf.

12  Tom Feltner and Douglas Heller, "High Price of Mandatory Auto Insurance in Predominantly African American Communities," Consumer Federation of America, November 2015, https://consumerfed.org/wp-content/uploads/2015/11/151118_insuranceinpredominantlyafricanamericancommunities_CFA.pdf.

13  Fryer, "Reconciling Results."

14  Nora Gordon, "Disproportionality in Student Discipline: Connecting Policy to Research," Brookings Institution, January 18, 2018, https://www.brookings.edu/research/disproportionality-in-student-discipline-connecting-policy-to-research/.

15  Christopher Uggen, Ryan Larson, and Sarah Shannon, "6 Million Lost Voters: State-Level Estimates of Felony Disenfranchisement," Sentencing Project, October 6, 2016, https://www.sentencingproject.org/publications/6-million-lost-voters-state-level-estimates-felony-disenfranchisement-2016/.

16  Ad Council, "'Beyond I Do': Campaign Launches to Raise Awareness about the Prevalence of Discrimination against LGBT People in the United States," press release, April 18, 2018, https://www.adcouncil.org/News Events/Press-Releases/Beyond-I-Do-Campaign-Launches-to-Raise-Awareness-about-the-Prevalence-of-Discrimination-Against-LGBT-People-in-the-United-States.

17  "2018 State Equality Index," Human Rights Campaign, 2018, https://www.hrc.org/campaigns/state-equality-index.

18  C. Price et al., eds., *At the Intersections: A Collaborative Resource on LGBTQ Youth Homelessness*, 2nd ed. (New York: True Colors United, National LGBTQ Task Force, 2019), https://truecolorsunited.org/wp-content/uploads/2019/04/2019-At-the-Intersections-True-Colors-United.pdf.

19  "A Crisis of Hate," Anti-Violence Project, 2017, https://avp.org/a-crisis-of-hate-january/.

20  "Hate Crime Statistics," Federal Bureau of Investigation, 2017, https://ucr.fbi.gov/hate-crime/2017/hate-crime.

21  Ann P. Haas, Philip L. Rodgers, and Jody L. Herman, *Suicide Attempts among Transgender and Gender Non-Conforming Adults* (New York: American Foundation for Suicide Prevention and Williams Institute, January 2014), https://williamsinstitute.law.ucla.edu/wp-content/uploads/AFSP-Williams-Suicide-Report-Final.pdf.

22  "Sexual Assault and the LGBTQ Community."

23  Inter-American Commission on Human Rights, "An Overview of Violence Against LGBTI Persons," Annex press release 153/14, December 17, 2014, http://www.oas.org/en/iachr/lgtbi/docs/Annex-Registry-Violence-LGBTI.pdf.

24  "Housing and Homelessness," National Center for Transgender Equality, https://transequality.org/issues/housing-homelessness.

25  "Trump's Transgender Ban Would Cost $960 Million, Say Navy Professors in New Report," Palm Center, August 9, 2017, https://www.palmcenter.org/trumps-transgender-ban-cost-960-million-say-navy-professors-new-report/.

26  "Facts about Suicide," Trevor Project, https://www.thetrevorproject.org/resources/preventing-suicide/facts-about-suicide/.

27  Kelly Dittmar, "Candidates Matter: Gender Differences in Election 2016," Rutgers, Center for American Women and Progress, February 14, 2017, http://www.cawp.rutgers.edu/sites/default/files/resources/closer_look_candidates_matter_2.14.17.pdf.

28  Michele L. Swers, "Connecting Descriptive and Substantive Representation: An Analysis of Sex Differences in Cosponsorship Activity," *Legislative Studies Quarterly* 30, no. 3 (August 2005): 407–33, https://www.jstor.org/stable/3598642?seq=1#page_scan_tab_contents.

29  Sarah Kliff, "The Research Is Clear: Electing More Women Changes How Government Works," Vox website, March 8, 2017, https://www.vox.com/2016/7/27/12266378/electing-women-congress-hillary-clinton.

# CHAPTER 12

1 Teddy Wilson, "White GOP Lawmakers Behind Almost Every Anti-Choice Bill in 2017," Rewire.News, February 13, 2017, https://rewire.news/article/2017/02/13/white-gop-lawmakers-behind-almost-every-anti-choice-law-2017/.

2 Deborah Bonello and Erin Siegal McIntyre, "Is Rape the Price to Pay for Migrant Women Chasing the American Dream?" Splinter website, https://splinternews.com/is-rape-the-price-to-pay-for-migrant-women-chasing-the-1793842446.

3 Amnesty International UK, "Women Fight Back as Oppressive and Sexist Policies Dominate 2018: Amnesty Annual Review," press release, December 10, 2018, https://www.amnesty.org.uk/press-releases/women-fight-back-oppressive-and-sexist-policies-dominate-2018-amnesty-annual-review.

# CHAPTER 13

1 Hilary George-Parkin, "Size, By the Numbers," Racked website, June 5, 2018, https://www.racked.com/2018/6/5/17380662/size-numbers-average-woman-plus-market.

2 Hannah L. Walker and Marcela Garcia-Castañon, "For Love and Justice: The Mobilizing of Race, Gender, and Criminal Justice Contact," *Pollitics & Gender* 13, no. 4 (December 2017): 541–68, https://www.cambridge.org/core/journals/politics-and-gender/article/for-love-and-justice-the-mobilizing-of-race-gender-and-criminal-justice-contact/B929F7C5D847A7EA35ABBD96478DE39B.

3 Huang et al., "Election 2016: Exit Polls."

# INDEX

# ACKNOWLEDGMENTS

Contrary to Western capitalist narratives of rugged individualism, most things in life take a village, and this book was no exception. Foremost, I want to thank the brilliant, wonderful people at North Atlantic Books for their support for and dedication to this project. I especially want to thank my endlessly patient, endlessly positive editor, Shayna Keyles, for her help with revising this manuscript and creating the finished product I'd envisioned from the beginning.

I originally wrote this book in the span of a few weeks in my third year of college, and, if you can believe it, I relied on the emotional support of several wonderful people to make this possible. I want to thank my wonderful friends, Claire Zhang, Alec Vandenberg, Anya Kushwaha, Melina Mae Castorillo, Jennifer Huang, Nayanika Kapoor, and Catherine Yang, for blessing me with such a warm and reliable support system to nurture my writing and growth; my first mentors from my earliest days at university, Danni Wang and Sonali Seth, for giving me so clear a vision of the confident, vocal woman I aspired to be; Renee Bracey Sherman, Lindsay Rodriguez, and all the wonderful people at the National Network of Abortion Funds, whose passion and dedication showed me this was the fight I wanted to give my life to when I was still a freshman in college; and of course, my parents, Waichung and Janet Cheung, for the endless sacrifices they've made to give me a wonderful life.

In writing and publishing this book, I've challenged myself to be as vulnerable and honest about my experiences with sexual violence and reproductive health as I could be, where relevant. I know I'm not alone in what I've experienced and overcome throughout my life as a young woman. And so, last but not least, I'm thankful to all of the women and survivors who live in their truth each day. Your bravery inspires me to give my voice to the fight for gender and social justice and certainly inspired this book.

# ABOUT THE AUTHOR

KYLIE CHEUNG is the author of one other book of essays about feminism and politics, *The Gaslit Diaries*. She is a graduate of the University of Southern California, where she studied political science and gender studies, and has published writing about women's rights and reproductive justice in Salon.com, *Teen Vogue,* AlterNet, Bustle, Feministing, the Mary Sue, *Dame* magazine, PopSugar, Brit + Co, and others. She is a California native living in Washington, DC, where she writes about and advocates for reproductive justice.

# About North Atlantic Books

North Atlantic Books (NAB) is an independent, nonprofit publisher committed to a bold exploration of the relationships between mind, body, spirit, and nature. Founded in 1974, NAB aims to nurture a holistic view of the arts, sciences, humanities, and healing. To make a donation or to learn more about our books, authors, events, and newsletter, please visit www.northatlanticbooks.com.

North Atlantic Books is the publishing arm of the Society for the Study of Native Arts and Sciences, a 501(c)(3) nonprofit educational organization that promotes cross-cultural perspectives linking scientific, social, and artistic fields. To learn how you can support us, please visit our website.